Ferdinando Petruccelli della Gattina

Rome and the Papacy

A history of the men, manners, and temporal government of Rome in the nineteenth century, as administered by the priests. Including the life of Gian-Maria Mastai, now Pope Pius IX.

Ferdinando Petruccelli della Gattina

Rome and the Papacy

A history of the men, manners, and temporal government of Rome in the nineteenth century, as administered by the priests. Including the life of Gian-Maria Mastai, now Pope Pius IX.

ISBN/EAN: 9783337064174

Printed in Europe, USA, Canada, Australia, Japan

Cover: Foto ©ninafisch / pixelio.de

More available books at **www.hansebooks.com**

ROME AND THE PAPACY.

A HISTORY OF THE

MEN, MANNERS, AND TEMPORAL GOVERNMENT OF ROME
IN THE NINETEENTH CENTURY,

AS

ADMINISTERED BY THE PRIESTS.

INCLUDING THE

LIFE OF GIAN-MARIA MASTAI,

NOW

POPE PIUS IX.

BEING COMMENTARIES ON "THE ROMAN QUESTION" OF E. ABOUT.

By F. PETRUCCELLI DE LA GATTINA.

FATTO HA DEL CIMITERIO MIO CLOACA.—*Dante.*

TRANSLATED FROM THE FRENCH
BY ROBERT E. PETERSON, M.D.

PHILADELPHIA:
T. B. PETERSON & BROTHERS;
306 CHESTNUT STREET.

Entered, according to Act of Congress, in the year 1872, by
ROBERT E. PETERSON, M.D.,
In the Office of the Librarian of Congress, at Washington, D. C.

THE TRANSLATOR TO THE PUBLIC.

ON a visit to Rome a short time since, remarking the miserable condition of the people, I said to an Italian: "I do not care whether the Roman Catholic religion be true or not; if after ten centuries of almost exclusive influence it can show no better results than what is seen here to-day, for God's sake try something else, for it cannot be worse. Our people certainly do not know the condition of things at the present time in Rome. We hear a great deal about the oppression of Irish Catholics; but our people do not know that the people of Rome, Roman Catholic citizens, are kept in awe by the bayonets of foreign mercenaries. The Castle of San Angelo is fortified, with embrasures so arranged that cannon can be trained upon the city itself. I was informed by an intelligent Roman that the Pope was afraid to trust a Roman among his troops; he overawes the citizens by an army composed of Irishmen, Canadians, and other foreigners. The people are not their own masters, and the reign of the priest is death — death to labor, to enterprise, to progress."

When I reached London, this work was put into my hands. I thought that it would be well to translate it, which I have done as faithfully as possible, that the picture it presents might be laid before my countrymen — particularly at this time, when the institutions, which those brought up in the Roman Catholic faith have ejected and cast out of their own countries on account of their pernicious tendencies and influence, are finding a home in our own land.

The Church of Rome, and consequently the government of the Roman States, are at this time under the influence of the members of the Society of Jesus, known as Jesuits. This Society is probably the most powerful in the world: the most powerful, because at its head is found the greatest intelligence, while the doctrine of implicit obedience, which is the bond of the Society, conjoined with but one desire to promote its aggrandizement, renders it the most dangerous to civil and religious liberty of any society that ever existed. The Superior orders this or that to be done, it is done. The right or wrong of the action commanded cannot be and is not questioned. What does this

Society seek? It seeks universal power, authority, and dominion. It seeks to control you and me, to dictate to us what we shall do and what we shall not do. And, remember that the men who compose this Society are educated specially for these purposes; and are working and plotting by day and by night more assiduously, to attain their ends, than you or any of you do for the purpose of advancing your own private interest; that their code of morals is so lax, that what *you* would consider immoral and dishonorable, *they* would consider, if it conduced to their purpose, moral and honorable; that what I say is true, read "The Provincial Letters," by Blaise Pascal, not a Protestant, but a most pious Catholic — one of the brightest luminaries that France ever produced, who proves demonstrably from their own writings more than I have said. At one time or another this Society has been driven out of all the countries of Europe, and denounced by the Pope himself. To-day, in the Church its members again are in the ascendant; such is their vitality.

One evening, in Rome, an American friend came into my room, much surprised, and said to me: "I just now visited a book-store to purchase a Bible and a Common Prayer Book. The book-seller informed me that were he to sell them, his store would be shut up, and he himself probably thrown into prison." I do not want that condition of things *here*;—yet the institutions Catholic countries like Spain and Italy have cast out of their lands, as having been found enemies to humanity, are seeking and finding among ourselves a home. And those who have been fostered and warmed in our republican bosom, are already hissing forth, that they will soon have the control of this country, and that then they will not tolerate any other religion than their own.

It is said that the tiger, when once he has tasted human blood, disdains all other food; so, like him, Man, when once he has tasted power, rejects every thing else; and to obtain it will tyrannize and trample upon his fellows. It is not because the Roman Catholic clergy are worse than other sectaries that they do these things, but because in ages past they have tasted of power, and because they are men. Are they not already tampering with your legislatures, with your municipal authorities, with your public school systems, with your public charities? My countrymen, permit no sectarianism to enter into your civil governments; recognize no sect in your schools, in your charities, in your laws; recognize man only as man; legislate for man only as man. Be suspicious of your liberties. If you err at all, let it be on the side of excessive caution. Have no more faith in the Divine right of Priests than in the Divine right of Kings. Wherever such rights have been claimed and insisted upon, they have been founded on the tears, the blood, the wrongs, and degradation of the people. Believe and trust in yourselves only. If, however, you desire a priestly domination in civil affairs, read this book, and you will learn what you have chosen for yourselves and your posterity.

Philadelphia, *October*, 1872.

PREFACE.

THIS work, now presented to the public under the title of "Rome and the Papacy," was originally published in French under the name of "Preliminaries to the Roman Question of E. About." A change in the title was deemed necessary, as the greater number of readers would not otherwise be advised as to the character of the book now offered to them.

"The Roman Question," it has been alleged, was written at the request of the then Emperor of France, Louis Napoleon, and the first numbers appeared in the government organ, the *Moniteur*. Its publication gave such great offence to Pope Pius IX., that its appearance in the *Moniteur* ceased, and the book as it now stands was re-written and afterwards published at Brussels.

We have condensed from the work of Mr. About, a translation of which by Mrs. Wood was published at Boston, sufficient to give some idea of the character of the book. Mr. About is a Roman

Catholic, and neither his book nor the one now presented to the reader is an attack upon the Roman Catholic religion. The right of every man to his belief is nowhere denied or called in question. The right which is disputed, by the millions of Italian Roman Catholics, is that of the Pope and Clergy of their own Church to tyrannize over them in temporal matters, to the destruction not only of the proper end of government, which, according to the ancient Egyptians, is "to make life easy and the people happy," but of every principle of civil, moral, and religious liberty.

The Domains of the Pope.

The kingdom of the Pope extended over a surface of about 10,323,790 acres, according to the statistics published in 1857, by Monseigneur Milesi, now a Cardinal. It is traversed by the Apennines, which divide it into two nearly equal parts, one watered by the Po, descending in a gentle slope towards the Adriatic, the other watered by the Tiber, towards the Mediterranean. On each of these seas it possesses, on the East, Ancona, an excellent port; and Civita Vecchia on the West.

No country of Europe is more richly endowed, or better formed for agriculture, industry, and commerce.

The population of this kingdom amounts to 3,124,668 persons, which are divided by birth and fortune into four very distinct classes: clergy, nobles, citizens, and plebeians. The will of the Pope, which is the law of the States, consecrates this inequality, in contradiction to the Gospel. Benedict XIV. declared it honorable and salutary in his bull of the 4th of January, 1746; and Pius IX. expressed himself in the same terms at the beginning of his *Chirografo* of 2d of May, 1853.

The Pope.

The temporal power of the Pope is absolute. To-day, as in the most flourishing times of Pontifical despotism, the Pope is every thing; he has every thing; he can do every thing; he exercises perpetual, uncontrolled, and unbridled dictatorship.

There is no limit to the absolute authority of the Pope except the influence of his private virtues, should he possess them. Constitutions, when imposed upon him as in 1848, are eluded, trampled upon and evaded. The rights of the citizen are derided, and the affairs of the government placed almost exclusively in the hands of the Priests. The different powers of the government are confounded. There is no division into judicial, legislative, and executive. Governors of the cities,

Judge, and Bishops, administer government. The Pope exercises a controlling power, and in the exercise of his pleasure, limited only by his personal caprice, claims that he is infallible. Does a decree of a court of justice displease him, he reverses it. He appoints whom he pleases to office, and these for the most part priests or their minions. No law forbids him to despoil his subjects for the benefit of his family. Gregory XIII. gave to his nephew Ludovisi four millions of crowns. The Borghesi bought at one time ninety-five farms with the money of Paul V. In 1640, a commission under the presidency of R. P. Vitelleschi, General of the Jesuits, to put a stop to abuses, decided that the entail upon a Pope's favorite nephews should be limited to an annual entail of $80,000 conditionally, the dowry of each niece to $180,000.

The Cardinals.

It is nevertheless true that the Popes exercise this absolute power through the instrumentality of the Cardinals. If the *white* Pope, or he who is called the Holy Father, exercised himself the administration of affairs, we might hope that, being infallible, he would seldom err; for although he is very rarely capable or well informed, "we need no torch when we are lighted by Heaven."

Unfortunately, the functions of the *white Pope* are transmitted to a *red Pope*, to an irresponsible and all-powerful Cardinal, who is called the Secretary of State. The Cardinal exercising this function acts for the Pope without and within—speaks, acts, responds and commands for him. Not only does he express the wishes of the Pope, but frequently moulds and forms those wishes.

This Cardinal Secretary of State is more dictatorial than his Dictator. No restraint is placed upon his abuse of power, which he always uses to promote what he may consider his own private interests and those of his family. Once appointed Secretary of State, he never can become Pope, and therefore every inducement which a hope of succeeding his master might confer to cause him to act virtuously and honestly, and to assume the semblance of honesty or virtue, is lost. It is unheard of that a Secretary of State should be appointed by two Popes. Tradition absolutely requires that the favorite of the predecessor should be disgraced, and by conforming to tradition the new Pope renders himself popular.

Whenever, therefore, the Pope dies, the Secretary of State returns to the obscurity of the Sacred College; and as he is well aware that he will never be called to an account, he denies himself nothing while he has the power in his hands, and profits by all his opportunities.

Prelates and Ecclesiastics.

"All the ministers, all the prefects, all the ambassadors, and all the magistrates of the tribunals are ecclesiastics. The 'most' holy auditor, the secretary of the *Brevi* and *memoriali*, the presidents and vice-presidents of the Council of State and of finances, the director-general of the police, the director of public health and of prisons, the director of the archives, the attorney-general of the treasury, the president and secretary of the land-surveys, and the president of the board of agriculture, are all ecclesiastics. Public education is in the hands of the ecclesiastics, under the superintendence of thirteen Cardinals. All the benevolent institutions, all funds for the poor, are the patrimony of ecclesiastical directors. The assembly of Cardinals judge lawsuits in their leisure moments, and the Bishops of the kingdom are so many living tribunals."

The word *prelate* requires an explanation. In France it is a title tolerably well respected; it is not so much so at Rome. The Roman prelate is often a great boy, who emerges from the seminary with a tonsure for his only sacrament. He is a doctor of something, entitled to a small income, and enters the Church as an *amateur*, hoping to make his way there. He is permitted by the Pope to call himself Monsignor instead of Signor, and to wear violet hose. Thus clad, he aims at the Cardinal's hat. He passes through the tribunals, the administrative or domestic service of the Vatican; any road is good, provided he has zeal and a pious contempt for liberal ideas.

The prelate is sometimes the younger son of a great family. His house is one which has a right to a hat; he knows it. On the day when he puts on the violet hose, he may, in advance, command the red hose. Meanwhile, he endures his probation, takes his time, and sows his wild oats. The Cardinals shut their eyes, provided he professes sound ideas. Do whatever you please, son of a Prince, but let your heart be clerical.

Sometimes the prelate is an adventurer of fortune and of the Church, whom ambition of ecclesiastical greatness has allured from his country. The whole Catholic world furnishes its contingent to this corps of volunteers. To many of these the mother of a family would not trust the education of her sons. But however vicious a prelate may be, he never professes liberal ideas. To do so would involve him in ruin.

The Nobility.

The Roman nobility consists of thirty-one Princes or Dukes, Counts, Barons, and Knights; a multitude of noble families without titles, among whom Benedict XIV. inscribed sixty at the capital; a vast extent of seignorial domains; a thousand palaces; a hundred galleries, small and large; a valuable revenue; an incredible prodigality of horses, carriages, liveries, and armorial bearings; a few royal *fêtes* every winter; a remnant of feudal privileges, and the respect of the lower classes;— such are the most salient features which distinguish the Roman nobility and make it the admiration of all the idlers in the universe. Ignorance, idleness, vanity, servility, and especially insignificance, are the defects which place it below all the aristocracies of Europe.

The origin of the Roman nobility is very diverse. Some are descended from the heroes or brigands of the Middle Ages. Some are said to have descended from the ancient Roman nobility; but whether this be authentic or not, they are very ancient and of independent origin.

A second class is of Pontifical origin. The Popes have retained the habit of ennobling their relatives.

A third class includes the bankers, like the Torlonia and Ruspoli; monopolizers, like the Antonelli; millers, like the Macchi; bakers, like the Dukes Grazioli; tobacco merchants, like the Marquis Ferrainoli; and farmers, like the Marquis Calabrini.

To these may be added foreigners, noble or not, who buy a domain and hang on a title into the bargain. For they are all equal from the day when the Pope has signed their parchments; and whatever may be their origin, they walk off arm in arm without disputing for precedence. Why should they? Do they not all know that they are inferior to the most insignificant Cardinal? On the day when a monk receives the red hat, he requires the right to splash mud on them all.

Take a student from the Seminary of Saint Sulpizio, wash him clean, cause him to be dressed by Alfred or Poole, adorn him with a few jewels from Mortimer or Castellan, and teach him a little music and horsemanship — you will have a Roman Prince as good as any of them.

You suppose, perhaps, that the people educated at Rome, in the midst of *chefs d'œuvre*, interest themselves in the arts and know something about them: you are mistaken. One has never entered the Vatican but to make visits; another is acquainted with his own gallery, only through the reports of his steward; another never saw the Catacombs before he was elected Pope. They profess that elegant ignorance and good taste which will always be fashionable in Catholic countries.

The Roman nobility are mediocre in wealth as well as in everything else. Not only are they incapable of rivaling, or sustaining competition with the industrious citizens of London, Basle, or Amsterdam, but they are infinitely less wealthy than the nobility of Russia or England.

Pity them if you please, but do not cast stones at them. They are such as education has made them. Look at their children as they pass along the Corso between two Jesuits. These children of from six to ten years, pretty as cupids, notwithstanding their black dress and white cravats, uniformly grow up under the shadow of the broad-brimmed hat of their master. Their minds are already a well-raked garden, from which is carefully uprooted every vestige of an idea.

When they shall have passed through their final examinations, and obtained a diploma of ignorance, they will be dressed in the London fashions and let loose on the public promenades.

We must go far from Rome to find the true nobility. We may encounter here and there, in the province of the Mediterranean, a decayed family, who live with difficulty on the revenue of a small estate, and whom the wealthier neighbors treat with a certain respect. But, if you follow me beyond the Apennines into those glorious cities of the Romagna, I will show you more than one gentleman of noble name and ancient family, who cultivates his mind and his fields, who knows all we know, who believes all we believe and nothing more; who is actively interested in the misfortunes of Italy, and who, turning towards happy and free Europe, hopes, from the sympathy and justice of nations, the deliverance of his country. These genuine nobles are justly suspected by the reigning class, for they will share with the bourgeois the heritage of the Pope. I met, in certain palaces of Bologna, a brilliant writer, applauded in all the theatres of Italy; a learned economist, quoted with respect in all the principal reviews of Europe; a controversialist, dreaded by the priests; and all these men combined in the person of a marquis of thirty-four, who will, perhaps, play a principal part in the Italian revolution.

The Middle Class.

The middle class represents not only the wealth and independence, but the capacity and morality of a nation, and always constitutes the bulwark of a

State. Between the aristocracy which prides itself on doing nothing, and the common people who labor that they may not die from hunger, the middle class pursue their way toward a future of fortune and consideration. Sometimes the higher class is hostile to progress, because it is afraid of it; too often the inferior class is indifferent to it, through not understanding what is to be gained by it; the middle class, clearly perceiving its value, endeavors to attain it even at the peril of its dearest interests.

This honorable class should, therefore, be as numerous and strong as possible, for it is, on the one hand, the legitimate heir of the temporal power of the Pope, and, on the other, the natural adversary of the Mazzinist insurrection.

But the ecclesiastical caste, which prefers this fatal principle of temporal power to the most august interests of society, endeavors, by every means in its power, to keep down and ruin the middle class. It imposes upon it the heaviest burdens of the state, without admitting it to share in its benefits. It wrests from the petty proprietor not only all his revenue, but a part of his capital, while the plebeians and the Roman nobility enjoy all kinds of immunities. It offers the most insignificant offices at the price of the most humiliating concessions; neglects nothing to deprive the liberal professions of all the prestige with which they are elsewhere surrounded; keeps down science and arts to the point of suppression, degrades every thing, and then persuades itself that degradation is exaltation. Nothing can equal the contempt which prelates, princes, foreigners of condition, and even the lackeys of Rome manifest toward the middle class.

The Prelate has his reasons. If he is a minister, he sees in his bureaux a hundred *employés*, all belonging to the middle class. He knows that these active and intelligent, but poorly compensated men, are reduced, for the most part, to practise some humble position in society, — one keeps the accounts of a farmer, another balances the books of a Jew. Is Monseigneur the magistrate of a superior tribunal, — for example, the Sacred Rota, — he need not study law: a man of the middle class has taken the pains to study it for him. This secretary, this assistant of the Cabinet, is a jurisconsult of great talent, of which one needs much to find his way through the obscure labyrinths of Roman legislation. But Monseigneur, who uses him for his own profit, thinks he has a right to despise him because he earns a little, lives modestly, and has nothing to look forward to in the future.

The Roman Princes despise the middle class. The advocate who pleads their causes, and who generally gains them, belongs to the middle class. The physician who attends and cures them belongs to the middle class. When at Paris an advocate pleads the cause of a Prince, it is the Prince who is the client: at Rome, it is the advocate.

But those upon whom the Princes lavish the most violent contempt are the farmers and country merchants. The country merchant is a man of low birth, very honest, intelligent, very active, and very rich. He takes to farm some thousand acres, lying fallow, which the Prince would never cultivate himself, because he has never learned how, and has no money. On these lands the farmer places herds of oxen, cows, horses, and flocks of sheep. Sometimes, if his lease permits, he tills a square league and sows it with grain. He makes money, pays his rent promptly, sometimes in advance, and excites the envy of the Prince, who looks upon cultivation in the hands of these people as an attempt at ownership. This is not all. The country merchant, who never was Count, who is not a priest, who has a wife and children, wishes to meddle with the affairs of the country, under the pretext that he manages his own admirably. He points out abuses, he demands reforms. What audacity! He would be thrown aside, like a simple advocate, if his industry was not the most necessary of all, and if they did not fear to starve the country by turning this man out of doors.

If there were only two thousand of these country landholders or tenants, and the Government would allow them to act as they please, the Campagna of Rome, one of the most pestiferous regions of the earth, would soon assume another aspect, and the Roman fever would disappear.

In conclusion, I brought from Rome a poor idea of the middle class. A few distinguished artists, a few advocates of talent and courage, a few learned physicians, a few wealthy and intelligent farmers, do not suffice, in my opinion, to constitute a middle class; they only form an exception. Now, there is no nation without a middle class, and I tremble to recognize at last there is no Italian nation.

In the Mediterranean provinces, the middle class appears to me to be no more flourishing than at Rome. The people of this class, half citizens, half rustics, are plunged in a dense ignorance. They have almost enough to live upon without burning themselves in the sun; they therefore remain at home, in poorly furnished houses, where the very walls are redolent of *ennui*; the rumors from Europe which might awaken them are stopped on the frontiers. New ideas, which might fertilize their minds, are interrupted by the custom-house. If there are any who can read, the only book perused is the *Almanach*, or, perhaps, the *Journal of Rome*, which relates in a pompous style the promenades of the Pope.

Beyond the Apennines, the bourgeois does not sink to the level of the peasant, but the peasant rises to the level of the bourgeois. A persevering toil constantly improves the soil and the man. The smuggling of ideas, daily more active, defies all the custom-house laws. The presence of the Austrians provokes patriotism. The burden of the taxes exasperates common sense. All the divisions of the middle class — advocates, physicians, merchants, farmers, artists — boldly exchange their dissatisfactions and their enmities, their ideas and their hopes. This barrier of the Apennines, which separates them from the Pope, brings them nearer to Europe and liberty. I have never conversed with a bourgeois of the legations without saying, as I rubbed my hands, "*There is an Italian nation.*"

The Plebeians.

The plebeians of the Eternal City are overgrown children, badly brought up, whom education has variously perverted.

The Government, which fears them, treats them gently. It demands few taxes of them, gives them shoes and sometimes bread, the very recipe "*panem et circenses*" of the emperor in the decline of the Roman empire. It does not teach them to read; it does not forbid them to beg. It sends Capuchins to their dwellings; the Capuchin gives lottery-tickets to the wife, drinks with the husband, trains the children, and sometimes makes them. The common people of Rome are certain not to die of hunger. If they have no bread in the house, they can take it from the basket of a baker; the law permits it. All that is required of them is to be good Christians, to prostrate themselves before the priests, humble themselves before the great, bend before the rich, and engage in no revolution. They are severely punished when they refuse to commune at Easter, or speak disrespectfully of the saints. The ecclesiastical tribunal will hear no excuse on these matters; but the police are quite accommodating in every thing else. They pardon crime, encourage meanness;—the only thing which is never passed by is a claim for liberty, a revolt against abuse, the pride of being a man.

A government worthy of governing would first control and afterwards direct this ignorant force. Even on the Mediterranean slope the influence of the Vatican has not yet ruined every soul; the people are unhappy, ignorant, credulous, sometimes a little ferocious, but kind, hospitable, and generally honest. Cross the Apennines, and you will find in the towns and villages the materials of a magnificent nation. The ignorance is still great, the blood still warm, the hand always active; but here we find men reasoning. If the village workman is not happy, he understands why; he seeks a remedy, he foresees, he raves.

THE QUESTION.

If the Pope were simply the head of the Church — if, confining his labors to the interior of the temples, he would relinquish the government of temporal things, which he does not understand — his countrymen of Rome, Ancona, and Bologna would govern themselves as we do. The administration would then be all laic; the nation would provide for its own wants with its own revenues, according to the custom of all civilized countries.

The Italian people do not demand a Pope; the Cardinals nominate him, the diplomacy maintains, and the French army supports him. The Sovereign Pontiff and his staff constitute a foreign body introduced into Italy like a thorn into the foot of a wood-cutter.

The people therefore justly complain, when they find themselves crushed by taxes, which are disposed of to advance the interests of the clergy, and in which they do not participate; when they behold crimes committed with impunity, education neglected, and all the material interests of the State unprovided for.

Even Napoleon III., although he thought the restoration of the Pope to a throne necessary to the welfare of the Church, or if not to the Church, to himself, knowing that the restoration of the Pope would insure to his Imperial candidateship a million or two of Catholic votes, resolved to suppress the abuses, the injustices, and the oppressive traditions which urged the Italians to revolt. He thereupon wrote, on the 13th of August, 1849, a letter which was really a memorandum addressed to the Pope. *Amnesty, secularization, the Code Napoleon, a liberal government.* Pius IX. was offended at it; the Cardinals laughed.

In his *motu proprio* of Portici, the Pope promised the reform of some abuses. He returned to his capital to evade them at his ease. The nation — that is to say, the middle class — says that the good will of the French, which it does not doubt, is not of much use to it; that it would undertake of itself to obtain all its rights, to secularize the government, to proclaim an amnesty, to promulgate the Code Napoleon, and to establish liberal institutions, if we would only withdraw our soldiers.

The Roman Question then involves the welfare of the people or the despotism of the Pope. The sword alone has the privilege to strike out at one blow great difficulties. Diplomatists, who are the timid army of peace, only proceed by half measures. Mr. About proposes several measures, to which we refer our readers in his admirable book. The Italians asked but for one: "Withdraw your soldiers."

The Italians were right. France, obliged by her war with Prussia to recall her troops from Italy, the Italian army, on the 20th of September, 1870, entered into Rome, and proclaimed it the Capital of United Italy.

But the Roman Question still exists, but changed. The Pope, deprived of his temporal power, demands that the people shall be again enslaved, and his despotic power restored to him, asserting " that Rome claims to exhibit the perfect ideal of a Heavenly Kingdom — such, indeed, as the whole world should be." (*London Times*, April 12, 1871.) How should he be answered by every lover of civil, moral, and religious liberty?

When you have read this book you can intelligently reply.

9 WOBURN PLACE, RUSSELL SQUARE, LONDON,
April 14, 1860.

EDMOND ABOUT.

DEAR BROTHER:

When you wrote your learned and charming book upon the *Roman Question*, you were obliged to throw aside a considerable number of facts, as the condition of the press in your country did not permit you to publish them. Being in England, where one can speak and write freely his thoughts, I am, not about to complete your work — the subject is almost inexhaustible, — but to add a story to the magnificent edifice which you have commenced. Others will complete it for us. The aim of the work being the same, I ask your permission to entitle it: *Preliminaries to the Roman Question, by Mr. About*.

I seize, at the same time, this occasion to express to you how much my compatriots and myself are grateful to you for having raised one corner of the hideous picture of the Pontifical Government. You have written not only a sensible book, with the spirit and tact of a statesman, but you have done a good and noble action. Continue, sir, to apply your great and remarkable talents to the defence of great causes. You have the sympathies of the children of the country of Canaris and of Dante; will you add thereto, sir, my sincere admiration and my liveliest thanks.

Wishing you health, I am, Sir,

F. PETRUCCELLI DE LA GATTINA.

LA SCHLITTENBACH, PAR SAVERNE (BAS RHIN),
April 16, 1860.

F. PETRUCCELLI DE LA GATTINA.

SIR AND DEAR BROTHER:

I have this moment received, in my little village, the amiable letter which you have done me the honor to write to me. It has touched me to the bottom of my heart, in apprising me that I have one more friend. Use freely, I may say, all the rights which that title carries with it. Make of the book and of my name such use as shall appear to you most serviceable to our cause. We fight—you as an officer, I as a soldier—against the same enemies; it is right to place in common our munitions of war. I am well aware that I have not said the half which might have been said against the old enemy of Italy and humanity. My excuse lies a little in my ignorance and much more in the rigor of the French laws. I have, perhaps, used an excessive moderation; and yet, a harsh experience has demonstrated to me that I had not been moderate enough for my country. You, Sir, are in England; I have then room to hope that the first part of the *Roman Question* will not be seized like the second. I shall be much obliged to you if you will send me a copy of it.

Nihil Itali à me alienum puto.

I dare not add, *Italus sum;* and yet I have more than once had a mind to become a naturalized Italian, — especially the day after Villafranca.

After all, there is some resource. France hesitates greatly and often draws back; but when I measure the progress that we have made in advance in spite of our retrograde movements, I say to myself it will be good to live from 1860 to 1870.

Will you accept, with my sincere thanks, the expression of my most fraternal sentiments.

Edmond About.

TABLE OF CONTENTS.

CHAPTER I.

THE SACRED COLLEGE.

PAGE

The Unsettled Condition of Europe the 2d February, 1831. The Conclave elect a Monk. Spirit of the Roman Oligarchy: Egotism, Reciprocal Hatred, Indifference to the Future. The Secretary of State is the Actual Pope . 45

CHAPTER II.

ESSENCE OF THE PONTIFICAL GOVERNMENT.

Pope Gregory XVI. Cardinal Bernetti Secretary of State. Gaetanino, the Pope's Barber, appointed Chevalier, publishes an "Ecclesiastical Dictionary." A Concise Description of the Government and Administration of the Roman States 47

CHAPTER III.

CONCLAVE OF 1823.

Opinion of Cardinal Chiaromonte upon the Nature of Democratic Government. Opinion and Conduct of this same Cardinal, on becoming Pope Pius VII. Intrigues of Conclave of 1823. Attitude of the Diplomacy. Manœuvres of Mr. Italinski, Russian Minister. How the Cardinals were avoided. Portraits of the rejected Cardinals. Election of Leo XII. Watchword of the Roman People. His Irregular Life before being Pope. His Children by Madame Pfeiffer of Lucerne. Sportsman, even in his Bed 52

CONTENTS.

CHAPTER IV.
LEO XII.

Portrait of Leo XII. He sends the long Rapier and Chapeau to the Duke d'Angoulême. The Jubilee. Presents of the Popes to Sovereigns 57

CHAPTER V.
HOW LEO XII. ADMINISTERED JUSTICE.

His mode of rendering Justice. Terror of the Clergy. The Curate of St. Maria ai Monti. The Monopolists. History of a Violated Secret of the Confessional. Horrible History of the *Mazzolato*. History of Duke Ilario, Brother of the Pope, and of Monseigneur Nicolai . . 64

CHAPTER VI.
A GLASS OF LEMONADE.

Portrait of Cardinal Bernetti, appointed Secretary of State. History of Todini, Physician of Leo XII. Bernetti gets the Gout. Visit of the Pope. A Glass of Lemonade. End of Leo. Appreciation of his Reign. Cardinal Rivarola. Political Condemnations. Bernetti discharged by Leo XII. 79

CHAPTER VII.
PIUS VIII.

Pius VIII. His short Reign 89

CHAPTER VIII.
GREGORY AND HIS COURT.

Portrait of Gregory XVI. His Plebeian Amusements. He runs the risk of being killed by Cardinal Soglia in playing Blindman's-buff. His Buffoons. Monseigneur Arpi, Buffoon and Confessor to His Holiness. Sketch of Gaetanino. Shameful Behavior in the Vatican during the Night. Promiscuous Intercourse of its Inhabitants. Birth of the Barber Gaetanino's Son. The Pope and Court of Rome assist at the Baptism. Saying of the Roman People. The Pretty Nurse of Frascati and Gregory XVI. Scenes of Jealousy, etc. Picture of the Manners of the Roman Court. The Cardinals and their Public Mistresses. Monseigneur Marulli. Scene at the Austrian Ambassador's Ball between this Prelate and an English Lady. Monseigneur Ciacchi. Cardinal Ciali-Prela. Cardinal Piccolomini and Madame Restituta. Cardinal Zurlo surprised, by order of the Pope, in a House of Ill-fame. Monseigneur Dandolo-Foscolo in the Prison of Clichy, at Paris, on account of his Debts. Horrors and Scandals of Cardinal Grassellini, at Bologna, repressed by the Austrian General Degenfeld. Atrocious Act toward a Young Girl. Cardinal de Pietro: his Conduct at Lisbon. Challenged, he refuses to fight a Duel on account of a Woman. Other Cardinals and Prelates of Irregular Manners. Couplet upon Cardinal Cacciapiatti. Incredible Conduct of Cardinal Tosti. An Adventure of Antonelli. My Reserve upon Facts not so well known. The Revolution commences 90

CHAPTER IX.

THE DUKE OF MODENA.

Portrait of Francis IV., Duke of Modena. Intrigues of Prince de Metternich against Charles Albert. Sect of the Consistory. The Duke of Modena conspires with the Liberals; cheated by Louis Philippe. The Envoy of the Latter to Modena 104

CHAPTER X.

INSURRECTION IN CENTRAL ITALY.

Spirit of the Revolution in Italy. Revolution of Modena. History of Menotti. Cardinal Consalvi's Conduct at the Congress of Vienna. Intrigues of Austria. Mr. de Metternich's Secret Instructions to Mr. de Bombelles. Orioli addresses the Students at Bologna. The Révolution spreads. First Acts of the Provisional Government. Note of Cardinal Bernetti to Mr. de St. Aulaire. Proposition of Louis Napoleon to the Pope. Appeal of the Austrians. Protestation of France 111

CHAPTER XI.

DIPLOMATIC INTRIGUES.

The French Government proclaims the Principle of Non-Intervention. Mr. de Metternich's Despatch. Louis Philippe and Mr. de Metternich agree together. The Duke de Reichstadt pays for this Agreement. Conduct of the French People. The French Government retain the Italian Refugees in France. The Duke de Modena's Reaction: his Soldiers; his Executions. General Bentheim at Bologna. The Insurgents' want of Arms. Resistance of Rimini. Ancona capitulates with Cardinal Benvenuto. Gregory does not recognize the Capitulation of this Cardinal. Reaction 122

CHAPTER XII.

THE TWO SIDES OF POLITICS.

Bernetti's Note to justify the Austrian Occupation. Memorandum of the European Powers. Austria's Game upon this Occasion. Louis Philippe's Game. Game of Bernetti. Mr. de Metternich's Note concerted with France. The Austrians quit the Legation. Conduct of the Court of Rome. General Agitation among the People of the Roman States. The Pope's Resistance. Reactionary Edicts. Bernetti's Declaration to the Diplomatic Corps. Response of the Latter. Mr. de St. Aulaire's Note full of Zeal. Cardinal Albani marches with Armed Bands upon the Provinces. Rencontre at Césena. The Austrians return 130

CHAPTER XIII.

THE DUPERS DUPED.

Bernetti plots for the Occupation of Ancona by the French. Mr. de Rayneval treats upon this Affair with Prince de Metternich. Conditions laid down by the Latter. Casimir Perier hurries off the Expedition unknown to the King. The French at Ancona. Bernetti pretends Anger at Rome. Mr. de Metternich's Despatch. Note of Lord Seymour. Response of Mr. de Metternich 143

CHAPTER XIV.

DISMISSAL OF BERNETTI.

How Cardinal Bernetti is overthrown. Cardinal Lambruschini appointed Secretary of State 153

CHAPTER XV.

TRAVELS OF GREGORY XVI.

Portrait of this Cardinal. Fear which this Cardinal inspired in Gregory XVI. Weariness of the Pope. Journey to Ancona. Scenes upon the Journey. ǃ The Court which accompanied the Pope. They eat. The Pope's Fear at Jasi. History of the Vicar of Christ's Indigestion. What this Journey cost. Second Journey to Terracina. Reception of Baron Rothschild. Cardinal

Tosti at the Jew's Banquet. Third Journey to Civita-Vecchia. The Galley-slaves and the Holy Father. The Successor of St. Peter fishes for Red Mullet, and eats it. What these Pleasure-Journeys cost the Roman People. Political Persecutions 156

CHAPTER XVI.

FILLIPPO NARDONI.

History and Portrait of Nardoni, Chief of Police. On the Advent of Pius IX. he flies to Malta. Pleasant Adventure of Nardoni at Catania in 1848. He is shut up in a Chicken-cage and shown to the People. They do not examine his Trunks and Correspondence. He comes to reorganize the Reaction at Rome. Revolutions in the Roman States for Fifty Years. Czar Nicholas and Gregory XVI. 163

CHAPTER XVII.

POPE AGAINST POPE.

Affair of the Polish Catholics. Note of Prince Gagarin to Cardinal Bernetti. Encyclical of the Pope against the Polish Revolution. Rights of the Polish Catholics. Ukases. Complaints of the Nobility of Witepsk. Picture of the Persecution of the Catholics. The Court of Rome protests. Note of Count Gourieff. Gregory writes to Nicholas. Response of the Czar . . . 175

CHAPTER XVIII.

THE POPE AND THE CZAR.

The Meeting of the Pope and the Czar at the Vatican. Description of the Pope's Chamber. Attitude of the two Popes. Noble Words of Gregory XVI. He falls Sick 181

CHAPTER XIX.

THE END.

Sad Picture of his Agony. Universally abandoned by his Court. Gregory and his Cook. Manœuvres of Lambruschini and Cardinal Mattei. Gregory XVI. dies of Starvation. Autopsy of his Corpse. Character of his Pontificate 184

CHAPTER XX.

WANTED — A POPE.

What followed on the Death of the Pope. Importance in the Choice of a Pope at this Period, 1846. Speech of M. Guizot in the Chamber of Peers. Despatch of Lord Palmerston to Lord Ponsonby at Vienna. Despatch of Count de Nesselrode to Mr. de Brunow, at London. Despatch of Prince de Metternich. Saying of M. de Guizot in the Prince de Metternich's Salon. Curious Despatch of the Latter to Count d'Appony at Paris. Action of the Diplomacy and of the Roman People upon the Conclave. Mr. Rossi, French Ambassador at Rome, takes Action. Speech of Cardinal Micara. Inaction of the Austrian Ambassador. Cardinal Lambruschini's Faction 189

CHAPTER XXI.

THE CARDINALS BEFORE THE CONCLAVE.

Ceremony to verify the Death of the Pope. Portrait of Cardinal Micara; his terrible Speech to the People, who applaud him; his Conduct in the Preparatory Sittings of the Conclave; his Speeches. How the Cardinals were divided Outside. Three Parties and the Flying Squadron of Bernetti. Attitude of the People and Diplomacy. Cries of the People addressed to the Cardinals who entered into Conclave 196

CHAPTER XXII.

THE CONCLAVE.

Lambruschini believes his Election secured. Mr. Rossi's Speech to the Cardinals. Micara's Haughty Reply. How the Cardinals live in Conclave: their Dinner critically examined as it comes from without. Manœuvres of the Cardinals with their Friends outside. Letters received by Cardinals Bernetti and Lambruschini, and how. The Conclave is Opened. How the Cardinals are divided Inside. Composition of the Conclave. Chances for the Parties. Cardinal Gaysruck of Milan does not arrive in Time. Roman Caricature . . 201

CHAPTER XXIII.

HOW A POPE IS MADE.

First Scrutiny. Imprudence and Inexperience of Lambruschini's Partisans. What they should have done; what they did. How the First Votes were divided. The unsealed Ballot; what followed. The Second Scrutiny. Saying of Micara. Saying of Bernetti. Intrigues of the Cardinals on the following Night. Gizzi placed *hors de combat*. Possible Candidates. Counsels of Micara and Bernetti. Soglia, Amat, Falconieri, withdraw their Names as Candidates. Mastai Ferretti is agreed upon. Cardinal Fieschi's Activity during the Night. Attitude of Bernetti and the Flying Squadron. Agitation and Activity of the Lambruschini Party. Saying of Micara. Bernetti deceives the Friends of Lambruschini. The Day arrives 206

CHAPTER XXIV.

A QUARTER OF AN HOUR WITH THE HOLY GHOST.

Appearance of the Cardinals at the Second Session. Mr. Scarlett's Despatch to Count Aberdeen. Micara's

CONTENTS.

Speech. Counting the Votes. Mastai's Name commences to be heard. Attitude of the Latter. He becomes silent, agitated, faints upon the Tiara. Cardinal Gian-Maria Mastai-Ferretti elected Pope. Irresistible Joy of his Party. Saying of Cardinal Diario Sforza. Sayings of Micara and Bernetti. The Horrified Cardinals. Noble Conduct of Lambruschini after his Defeat. They hasten *the Adoration* of the Pope. He is announced to the People. Unusual Silence. Nobody knows Gian-Maria Mastai 213

CHAPTER XXV.

PIUS IX. BEFORE GRACE.

History of the Mastai Family. Albert Mastai, a Comb-Maker of Brescia, emigrates to Sinigaglia in the 16th Century. Activity and Intrigues of this Family. Fortune smiles upon it. In the 17th Century the Mastai slip in among the lesser Nobility of the Provinces. Marriage of a Mastai with a Ferretti of Ancona. From thence, the Nobility and Fortunes of this Family. The Father of Pius IX. Early Education of Gian-Maria (Pius IX.) Always subject to Epilepsy. Father Inghirami takes Interest in the Child. Gian-Maria leaves College on Account of his Ill-health. What he had become there. Sinigaglia at this Period. Napoleonic Spirit in the Country. Gian-Maria mad in Love with Bonaparte. He makes Verses; plays on the Flute. He fights. Life of the Young Man. His Amours with Lena; his Selfish Love for Elena, Daughter of Prince Albani. How he is checked by a Captain of Dragoons. Pleasant Incident on the Journey to Loretto between the Captain and Elena. Gian-Maria banished. He plunges into Pleasures. He gambles. Gian-Maria and the Princess Ghigi. Another Amour for Miss

Morandi, and how it ended. The Sisters of Gian-Maria a little light in their Behavior. Love of Gian-Maria for his Sister Isabella 219

CHAPTER XXVI.

ALL FOR THE BEST.

Gian-Maria goes to Rome. Small Annuity assigned to him by his Family. His Uncles. How he is Disappointed at Rome. How he lives there. Disgust for the Dinners and Person of his Uncle, Monseigneur Paolino. Gian-Maria becomes a fashionable Dandy. His Elegant Life in the Fashionable World. His Passion for the Countess Clara Colonna. He plays and cheats. He aspires to be a Noble Guard of Leo XII. What a Noble Guard is. Cardinal Consalvi learns that Mastai is epileptic and makes him resign his Commission. His Despair; he enters on the Career of the Prelacy. An Elegant Prelate. He studies the Ecclesiastical Sciences; his Uncle wishes to have him admitted as Coadjutor to a Canon of St. John de Lateran. Again Banished on account of his Malady. His Despair. He wishes to drown Himself. Mr. Cattabene meets him on the Road. Gian-Maria and his Confessor. He enters, as Superintendent, the Hospital of *Tata Giovanni*. His Severity. He becomes careless. He continues his Visits to his Little Jewess 227

CHAPTER XXVII.

PIUS IX. DURING GRACE.

Gian-Maria's Health becomes better. He believes in Miracles. He becomes a Priest. His First Mass. He begins to preach. He is noticed. A Troop of Missionaries. Gian-Maria Mastai engaged by the Enterprise of Odeschalchi and Company. Sent to Sinigaglia.

Great Success of his Sermons. Folly of the Women. Troubles; Intolerance. On his Return to Rome he goes to Naples to seek his Sister Isabella. Adventures of this Young Lady. Gian-Maria engages to go to Chili with the Missionaries. Cause of this Resolution. Sad Position. Voyage. Manœuvres of Mastai. Secularization of the Convent's Dog. Ridiculousness of Monseigneur Musio. The Mission Unsuccessful. Rage of Gian-Maria for Martyrdom. Return to Europe. Leo XII. wishes to make him a Prelate. Mastai refuses. He is appointed President of the Hospital of St. Michele at Ripa. His Excessive Severity . . . 232

CHAPTER XXVIII.

THE SEE-SAWS OF POLITICS.

He is appointed Archbishop of Spoleto. His Political Intolerance. He flies, and returns corrected. Alms and Avarice. His Brother among the politically Compromised. Gian-Maria suspected. He corrupts Sercognani who is marching upon Rome. Gian-Maria changes his Conduct and conceals the Liberals from Persecution. Gregory XVI. appoints him Cardinal. His Good Conduct at Imola. He resists the Dragonnades of Cardinal Albani. He persecutes Light Women. Amours of Mastai. Saying of Pius VII. The Abbess of Fognano. Quarrel with Monseigneur Folicardi. Dona Clara Colonna. The Chilian Paroquet. The Countess de Spaur. He comes to the Conclave . . 243

CHAPTER XXIX.

WHAT EUROPE DESIRED.

European Situation at the Period of the Advent of Pius IX. What Italy wished. Attitude of Foreign Powers toward the Despatch of Mr. de Kaunitz. Despatch of the Minister of Naples at St. Petersburg. Despatch of Lord Cowley to Lord Palmerston respecting the Politics of Mr. de Metternich; *the same* of Lord Ponsonby; *the same* of Prince de Metternich. Political Action of Lord Palmerston in Italy exaggerated 250

CHAPTER XXX.

WHAT FRANCE DESIRED.

Conduct of France in Italy. Politics of Mr. Guizot. Mission of Mr. Rossi. His Despatches to Mr. Guizot. Instructions of the Latter to Mr. Rossi. Duke de Broglie's Speech to Lord John Russell. Duke de Broglie's Despatch to Mr. Guizot upon Italian Affairs. Austria alone opposes Reforms. What the Pope did . . 261

CHAPTER XXXI.

PIUS IX. SUCH AS HE IS.

What kind of a Man was necessary. Portrait, Character, Conduct of Pius IX. I stop where Mr. About commences 272

CONCLUSION.

The Spiritual Papacy has no further Reason for existing, and it no longer exists. Actual Situation of the Papacy in Europe. The Papacy in Italy and England; the Papacy in France, Germany, Switzerland, Belgium, Spain. The Papacy in Italy, and in Face of the Church. Papacy and Civilization. Solution of the Roman Question 279

ROME AND THE PAPACY.

CHAPTER I.

THE SACRED COLLEGE.

ON the 2d of February, 1831, three millions of Italians had a new master, whose name was Gregory XVI.

Europe was on fire. The most eminent statesmen concentrated all the powers of their minds to search into the problem of the future. The peoples, like France, Poland, and Belgium, playing a chief part, selected the most experienced pilots to guide the helm in this terrible storm; and, strange to say, the Roman Conclave, with the revolution which muttered in the province, and the disturbance which knocked at its door, brought forth a Pope who was a monk! And what a monk! Gregory VII., Sixtus V., Paul III., Benoit XIV.,— they also had been in religious orders; but Mauro Capellari did not issue from the same mould. He had, when necessary, spoken like an angel upon the *real presence* and upon the *three hypostases;* but he absolutely understood nothing either of politics or of the world. Other states, other political bodies, the

Senate at Washington, the English Parliament, the Convention, on a similar occasion and in a similar place, would have chosen a man accustomed to business and conversant with the times and its requirements. Why did the Roman Senate choose a theologian?

The reason of this disastrous phenomenon is clear. The Court of Rome inherits a Past, such as it is, and enjoys, so far as it can, the usufruct of what it finds. It attaches itself to nothing, takes care of nothing, goes to the tomb without regret and without care, sure that its successor, like its predecessor, will do the best it can. Other oligarchies have a country, a party, even a family; they form a caste and a body. The Cardinals are isolated, without ancestors and without posterity; they belong to the world, enjoying a place and its benefits, which to-morrow another, unknown, a monad of the convent, or of the presbytery, will enjoy in his turn. The Cardinals hate each other. They mutually despise each other, and engage in competition with every species of arms. They have only one instinct: to preserve what exists, as far as they can, and to secure for themselves a master as little exacting as possible, under such conditions, that the oldest among them and the biggest fool need not despair of succeeding him. This is why, ordinarily, the Pope is either a lay-figure destitute of color, with whom every party has a chance of devouring the state, or, better, a sceptic: one who is complaisant and has signed a compromise to serve the interests of a faction. In one word, either a villain or an imbecile! The Secretary of State is the true Pope. He is the exponent of the faction that has decreed the tiara, of a political situation, or of the majority. He formulates or satisfies the necessities of the moment. A Secretary of State is never elected Pope because "one cannot be twice Pope!" He is the most abhorred of the cardinals.

CHAPTER II.

ESSENCE OF THE PONTIFICAL GOVERNMENT.

THE monk of the Camadules mounted upon the Holy Chair, with his heart filled with terror. He felt that the tiara was threatened upon every side; he wrestled with every kind of scarecrow created by his imagination, that he might fix it firmly upon his aged head. He threw himself into the arms of Cardinal Bernetti, who had been pointed out to him as a man of singular shrewdness, and exclaimed: Save me!

The Cardinal then banished him to the palace of the Vatican, which is a city, and consigned him to the care of his barber and his mistress. And the world knew, and the Roman States felt, that there was a new Pope called Gregory XVI., and that the true Pope was Cardinal Bernetti.

An indolent Pope was nothing new in the world. It was all the same to the people of the Pontifical States, that this Vicar of God was a drunkard, who passed his days between his breviary and his gossipings with Gaetanino, whom he had made a chevalier by his order; and above all, into the bargain, a savan. For Gaetano Morrone had just published, not only a volume of poetry, like the witty Burchiello, who reduced his precepts into couplets and sonnets, but an *Ecclesiastical Dictionary*, interlarded with Latin, Greek, and Hebrew. The Roman people suffered; and what this miserable people suffered, and what they still suffer, is incredible. See further.

Three millions of men are enfeoffed to some thousands of priests, or persons under the mask of ecclesiastical garments, who absorb, for themselves alone, more than fifty million of crowns ($55,000,000). All the honors, all the offices, the whole of the authority and nine-tenths of the property of the State, are in the hands of the clergy. The supporters of this caste were a band of assassins, called *sanfedistes;* six thousand Swiss, cared for like kept mistresses; a few regiments of national soldiers, despised, in rags, badly disciplined, and consequently always ready to turn their backs upon the priests. Besides this, no commerce; no industry. The smugglers organized like a regular government, with its bankers, its depots, its chiefs, its army, its correspondents, its docks, — stronger than the legal government, more beloved, always ready to give battle to the clerical agents, and feared by the latter when they were not accomplices. No agriculture; and neither statistics, nor regular and normal administration. Insupportable taxes, badly laid and distributed, charged almost entirely upon laymen, exciting everywhere, but principally in the Marches and in Ombria, a clamorous discontent. Innumerable obstacles were opposed to the development of the public wealth, particularly on account of the repulsion which the priests had for railroads, and on account of the preservation of the property in mortmain, and the conversion of large personal properties into real estate by a legal fiction.

There existed no codes, and no equality before the law. Privileges and immunities for the clergy in abundance. The administration of justice intricate, slow, ruinous, uncertain and complicated by wheel within wheel, by formulas and precedents without number, of which a few only have the key, and the priests are the supreme judges. A Legate makes an express law for a special case, according to his caprice. A public debt of eighty millions of crowns, of which Pope Gregory alone consumed twenty-seven millions for the purpose of repressing revolutions; Pius IX., forty millions to defray the Austrian occupation; both have wasted everything to chastise the rebels, pay the police, to pamper their parasites, to purchase fidelity, and to corrupt everybody and everything. A regular deficit of three millions every year. No control, nor account rendered of the administration of the public finances; no budget agreed upon; no court of accounts. The Cardinal-Minister of finance, with an authority more extended and more irresponsible than that of the Czar, or of the King of Naples, spends with confidence, under the gaze of God. And God never uses spectacles to superintend their Eminences.

Of public instruction there is nothing of account; and that which is tolerated, at the mercy of the Jesuits. The man who can read is a rebel in perspective. And if, perchance, there slips into the State a man like Orioli, Tommasini, Puccinotti, Silvani, Buffalini, Matteucci, Regnoli, Malaguti, Salvolini, Minghetti, he is hurried quickly into exile. They are chased abroad under any pretext whatever. A learned man is an enemy, because he observes and reasons. Every career then is closed to youth. The career of arms, because it is disgraced, sullied by foreign mercenaries, who change it into the trade of policemen; the career of diplomacy, reserved to the clergy; that of medicine, poor. Politics, administration, the magistracy, are limited, because ecclesiastics alone can occupy the prominent places. A triple censorship upon everything which issues from the press: the censorship of the government, of the police, and of the holy office, — a censorship minute, absurd, and ridiculous.

The citizens, penned up by thousands under the supervision of the high police, and consequently banished from public offices; the eye of the inquisitor prying everywhere, open upon all the world. Two-thirds of the families of the State, harassed on account of their liberal principles; more than ten thousand condemned for State crimes. Every species of complaint against the bad or arbitrary administration of its administrators is a state crime. Extra-judicial commissions always exist. Everything which breathes of progress, civilization, or science, neglected, shackled, or punished. The nobility of Rome — a nobility of the holy-water sprinkler, or of the petticoat — attached to the Pope; that of the provinces opposed to him. A part of the citizens and a part of the common people of Rome, half partisans of the priests, because interested; the people and citizens of the provinces opposed to them. The low clergy, bad enough; the high clergy, horrible and corrupt. Public morality is everywhere outraged by the priests. The sacred honor of the domestic fireside, everywhere in danger. The priest is inviolable, irresponsible, and all-powerful. A Monseigneur Grossi, judge of a supreme tribunal, falsified a decree of the tribunal; he was dismissed with a pension of fifty crowns per month. A Cardinal De la

Genga defiled every convent of nuns in his diocese of Ferrara; he was given two provinces, Urbino and Pesaro, to govern! One Diomella is condemned to twenty years forced labor for having stolen some objects from the Museum; he is sent an exile to Paris, with a pension! The Foundling Hospitals, those asylums for infancy, prohibited! Minister of war, a Cardinal! Prefect of police, a Monseigneur. Inspector of houses of ill-fame, a Bishop! In a word, the entire State — an ecclesiastical benefice made the most of *pro tempore*, an ecclesiastical property, the tenants of which succeed each other.

CHAPTER III.

CONCLAVE OF 1823.

FOR fifteen years this infernal rule had been submitted to. Pius VII., whom Napoleon called a *fanatic*, being Bishop of Imola, in 1797, had written: "The democratic form of government is not in opposition to the Evangile, but on the contrary it demands the sublimest virtues, which can only be acquired in the school of Christ." Pius VII., Pope, excommunicated the liberals; restored the Jesuits; brought back to life the bull *In cœnâ Domini;* re-established the Inquisition and the torture, which was immediately applied to the Carbonari; set again afloat the Jubilee, (a general indulgence granted by the Pope,) pilgrimages to miraculous sanctuaries, the exposition of relics, the images which amused themselves by performing miracles; prohibited the reading of the Bible under pain, sometimes, of forced labor; created the political inquisition; pursued those who were suspected of inclining toward a democratic rule; and, in opposition to all that the Congress of Vienna had counselled him, on giving him back his seat, he forgot every species of moderation, and sent back that same Cardinal Consalvi, who, sly fox! had governed until then by tacking between all parties and opinions. Finally, after having blessed and supported the Holy Alliance, which was just born under the auspices of sovereigns who were little or no Catholics, he fell upon the marble floor of his chamber, broke his legs, and died at the age of eighty-three.

Pius VII. died the 20th August, 1823.

The Conclave that followed was filled with Cardinals created by Consalvi — two only excepted, La Sommaglia and that famous Cardinal Ruffo, who had commanded the bands of the *Santa Fede* at Naples. The latter said to those who cared to listen :

"If Jesus Christ wishes me for his Vicar, he must commence by teaching me to read. I am an ass!"

The forty-nine Cardinals who entered into Conclave were all old men; the younger part were composed of Cardinals from fifty to fifty-nine years of age!

The Ambassadors of the diplomatic body, who had a veto, were Mr. de Vargas, who gave himself but little concern about the Conclave; the Duke de Montmorency Laval, so great a Jesuit and devotee that he would have considered it a sin and doing violence to the Holy Ghost, to force it to elect a Cardinal, a partisan of France; the Count d'Appony, who knew how to intrigue, but who had not a sufficiently brilliant intellect to conceal from others his inspirations; and a Russian, Mr. Italinski, who guided his bark according to his humor.

Among the Cardinal candidates there were the Cardinal Rodolphe, Archbishop of Olmütz, brother of the Emperor of Austria, thirty-five years old, and Cardinal de Gregorio, natural son of King Charles III. of Naples, and VI. of Spain. But neither of them could bring to their support sufficient strength to vanquish the repugnance of the Cardinals against a prince of the royal blood.

They commenced then by turning their regards toward Cardinal Cavalchini. The latter had the reputation of an energetic man, having caused many brigands to be hung, and threatening the revolutionists with the same fate. But the Conclave knew that France was about to make war against the Spanish liberals. Then it was said:

CONCLAVE OF 1823.

"Let us not choose a sanguinary Pope. He will, it is true, disembarrass us of the brigands and the liberals, but we will have to settle with him also. Austria and France will take care of our revolutionists."

Cardinal Dandini was then thought of.

This Cardinal had perjured himself in a celebrated lawsuit, and all Europe had heard of the anecdote. Choose a perjured Pope? that appeared to be going too far.

They consequently cast their eyes upon Cardinal Naro. But this wretched Cardinal had one day swallowed, in the presence of many persons, a cup of chocolate before mass.

"An incredulous Pope? impossible," exclaimed the Sacred College for the time. "Let us try Sommaglia."

This Cardinal, an octogenarian, had lived when young a debauchee, and now when old he was a bigot. This was promising.

They asked him who would be his Secretary of State if he were elected.

He answered, "Cardinal Albani."

"An Austrian! an assassin! a relation of the Duke of Modena! a dissolute, violent, atrocious man! Never! As soon would they have chosen him themselves," said the Sacred College.

Then they thought of Cardinal Severoli. Cardinal Albani opposed the *veto* of Austria. His Apostolic Majesty remembered that this Cardinal had stigmatized the marriage of an Austrian archduchess with Napoleon by the words *profanation of a sacrament*, and by *concubinage*.

Severoli died from chagrin a few days afterwards.

The indecision continued for three weeks. Finally, on the 29th September, 1823, the wall of the balcony of the Vatican fell, and Cardinal Ruffo presenting himself before the people, covered his head with his red cap, and with a loud voice cried out: *Annuntio vobis gaudium magnum : papam habemus!*

It was Cardinal de la Genga, who was called Leo XII.!

"The devil! a lion!" exclaimed the people in their turn; "*abbiamo dunque un papa bestia!*" (We have then for a Pope, a beast!)

Cardinal de la Genga had been a very pretty boy, so much so that frequently, in the scholars' processions, they had made him act the part of the Madonna. Afterwards, he had been a handsome man, and had made use of his prerogatives, leaving in his diplomatic career at Paris, Munich, and elsewhere, many traces of his industry. At Rome he had many children by Madame Pfeiffer of Lucerne, wife of a colonel of the Swiss Guards. He was, besides, so great a sportsman, that even when a Pope, and sick, he directed his bed to be moved to the window, and shot swallows on the wing. Elected Pope in his sixty-third year, he felt worn-out and sick. But they had elected him precisely because, upon entering the Conclave, he had shown his swollen limbs and had said:

"Don't think of me; you would only elect a corpse!"

Nevertheless, being elected, Leo got back his strength, cured his legs, and showed himself such as he was, throwing away a mask no longer of any use.

CHAPTER IV.

LEO XII.

CARDINAL de la Genga had, as we have said, followed the career of diplomacy, and had had a hand in all the intrigues which the courts of Europe had in secret plotted against Napoleon. He had acquired a knowledge of men in the boudoirs of women.

In the boudoir, much more than at the confessional, there are no heroes, nor great men, nor diplomatists, nor men of genius. There you are simply ingenuous, if the divinity who presides there is beloved; or else you are still worse, you are a brute, if this divinity is only ardently longed after. Besides, every prestige, trickery, ability, sagacity, the understanding of men halt at the door of these perfidious temples,— when they do not remain in the ante-chamber, under the charge of the domestics, and you do not take them away again with your cane and overcoat. You do not argue in a lady's boudoir, — you feel or you love.

Cardinal de la Genga, who loved to talk and who knew how to talk, made his mistresses converse. He then saw the whole heaven of the imperial epochs in France and Germany through a fan, and he saw it plainly and well. If he permitted anything to be gleaned from his cards, it was relatively of very small importance, for from 1789 to 1815 the Papacy only played a very secondary part, when it was not a tinsel in the Emperor's display. Cardinal de la Genga returned to Rome in 1816, at the age of fifty-six years, and received the red hat. He felt exhausted in body; but he had Europe at his finger's end.

Forced, by his past excesses, to live more abstemiously, he observed, during the five years that he was Vicar of Rome, the manners of his brethren and the clergy. He exacted from them a reformation; and he showed himself so rigid that they often said of him, "He is angry from spite; he can do nothing more himself, and he is not willing that others should do anything."

Cardinal de la Genga, by frequenting the courts and salons of Europe, had acquired aristocratic and elegant tastes and enlarged views in matters of social life. But, at the same time, he had acquired the habit of feigning, dissembling, and of mistrusting. He despised the people and the ideas which obtained in the world from 1789.

Crafty, knowing, concentrated, having the greatest control over his words, his movements, and his thoughts, understanding how to will, and how to execute his will and make it respected, he believed in religion as an instrument for power, as Napoleon believed in the charge of his imperial guard. Knowing how to observe, to understand, and to despise both men and their passions, anticipating everything, henceforth insensible to the electric shocks of women, jealous of his power, of its execution, certain of his superiority, understanding the force of the ideas which were advancing and obliging the old world to fall back, he resolved to resist and to wrestle with them. His speech was elegant, easy, flowing, but brief; his manners polished but stiff; and his person exceedingly dignified. He showed great facility of understanding in proving a paradox, laying a snare, escaping from a difficulty, and giving to a pretext the value of an argument. He had at all times more wit than benevolence, little patience, and no heart. Notwithstanding the charm of his manners, persons trembled on approaching him, and felt relieved when they had left him.

Leo XII. would have been an excellent Pope for the Middle Ages, if he could have concentrated in his hands the moral forces of the Popes of this period. He could have passed for one of the best princes of his time, if he had not been Pope, and if, being Pope, he had found men of his own size to comprehend and to aid him. But being Pope, and, in his quality of Pope and of Prince, hating liberty, science, and progress, he renewed the bulls against the Freemasons and the Carbonari; he persecuted the liberals in every way, sparing nothing for their discovery, neither the secrets of the confessional, the corruption of the conjugal alcove, the prattling of children at school, nor anything. He inundated the Roman States and Italy with monks, and set the Holy Office to work with great activity. Leo XII. published the Jubilee, shut up the Jews in the *Ghetto* as if they were plague-stricken; made war against the prerogatives of the Gallican Church; repulsed the demand of a great number of priests from certain parts of Germany who desired the abolition of celibacy; and neglected nothing that might revive the most absurd privileges of the Church. These things caused him foreign and internal embarrassments; but Leo XII. was frightened at nothing, and followed his own way.

He well knew, besides, how to administer the wealth of the State, not tolerating the rapine or wasting of the public functionaries and Cardinals, so that he greatly diminished the public debt, reduced the land-tax twenty-four per cent., and left, at his decease, five millions of crowns in the public treasury.

We now shall see in what manner he administered justice.

One of the first acts of his reign was to sanction, in his own way, the Spanish expedition which the Congress of Vienna had permitted to the very Christian king, in spite of England.

In the wardrobe of honorary distinctions of the Holy Chair there are: the *Golden Rose*, which the Holy Father sends to the women; the ribbon of St Gregory, which can be bought for twenty-five francs, or can be merited by becoming a spy; the title of Count of the Holy Empire, which can be procured by the aid of two hundred francs, or by getting a pretty woman to ask for it; the decoration of St. Sylvestro, which is worth as much as that of St. Gregory; and indulgences, *Agnus Dei*, the blessed scapularies and chaplets, the medals of the immaculate conception — and I know not what else. But, besides all this, there is the distinction of the *rapier* and the *chapeau*, blessed on Christmas night, which the sovereign Pontiff caused to be presented to the great warriors of the faith. Pius V. — that horrible man whose memory will be cursed forever, and of whom the Church has made a saint of paradise — Pius V. sent the rapier and the chapeau to the Duke of Alba for having exterminated the heretics of the Low Countries. Clement XI. sent them to Prince Eugene of Savoy in 1716, after the battle of Peterwardein, where the Turks were annihilated. The Spanish liberals appeared to Leo XII. to be of the same family as the Turks and the Protestants; he hastened then to send the rapier and **the chapeau to the Duke d'Angoulême.**

The chapeau was a hat with large rim and cupola, a species of barber's bowl, of crimson velvet, ornamented with pearls, precious stones, little images — a magnificent object for a masked ball at court. The rapier was an immense rapier, heavy, twice as long as a dragoon's sabre, but richly worked, and chiselled by the Mazzochi brothers, who superintended the manufacture of arms at the Vatican. The bigoted court of Charles X. impatiently awaited these presents, which should make miracles rain upon them like the louis-d'ors of Jupiter in the apron of Danaæ. They tattled about it greatly, both before and after receiving it. And as the Duchess de Berri then enjoyed all the favors of the court, Leo XII. paid her the delicate attention of not neglecting her. He consequently sent to her, in particular, a morsel of the wood of the manger of Bethlehem — authentic, on our word of honor; and the silver hammer with which His Holiness had opened the holy gate of the Jubilee at St. Peter's, or at St. John Lateran, I do not well recollect which. If the frivolous Duchess was charmed with it, I leave you to guess. The hammer above all things ravished her.

As to the Jubilee, Leo XII. got ahead of Austria, who did not desire this movement of travellers through Italy. Prince Metternich exclaimed:

"The Holy Father then has lost his senses! He does not then dream that some thousands of curious people come, see, carry in ideas, bring away sympathies, in one word, that there will be a reduplication of life in the midst of the Italian people? But a people does not awaken, does not even stir with impunity. This Jubilee is impossible!"

The Jubilee nevertheless took place. It cost the State a good deal of money; but a dozen of Jews were converted, a dozen of Protestants abjured their religion; Rome was amused, the clergy and the courtiers were enriched. St. Peter not having published the statistics of Paradise, we do not know whether the importation of souls was augmented this year.

In exchange for the hat and the sword, the Duke d'Angoulême sent to the Pope some Gobelin tapestries, and some Sevres porcelain. Leo XII. presented the tapestries to the Apostolic Palace, and the porcelain to the library of the Vatican. Leo XII. not being avaricious, bequeathed these things to the State. Gregory XVI., on the contrary, having given, at the expense of the State, to the Czar Nicholas, two magnificent collections of engravings of the Calcographic Camerale, two complete cabinets of medals — one in silver, the other in bronze, as well as a head of St. Peter, and a large Mosaic table, appropriated to himself the present received in exchange, — a superb snuff-box, with the Emperor's portrait surrounded by large diamonds; and sent to the library of the Vatican a great cup of malachite, too heavy for him to drink champagne out of.

The least generous of the three was Pius IX., who took for himself a bridle and saddle embroidered in gold, twenty-four pieces of Persian carpet, and twenty-four pieces of damask, sent by the actual Sultan, and sold the four Arab horses, which formed part of the present, and pocketed the price.

Leo XII. likewise sent rich gifts to the Emperor of Austria; but his Apostolic Majesty received them as the homage of his vassal, and gave nothing in return.

CHAPTER V.

HOW LEO XII. ADMINISTERED JUSTICE.

LEO XII. loved justice, administered however after a certain fashion, and did not tolerate the great scandal arising from the manners of the clergy. But as he knew that his orders would be powerfully resisted by those whose duty it was to execute them, he organized a special police for himself, a corps of private spies, of personal emissaries, who could obtain entrance into his chamber by a concealed staircase; and the commandant of the carbineers, Mr. Caldarari, his confidant, now in exile, fulfilled his orders. It was curious to see this private pack of bloodhounds give chase at night to the priests who frequented the theatres, the brothels, the gambling-houses, and the taverns.

The police of His Holiness seized them by the collar and led them to prison. They gave chase likewise to the clergy, who disdained to wear the ecclesiastical habit, in order to be more free. The play-houses, certain houses, and equivocal places were strangely surprised at seeing a descent upon them of carbineers and police, who rudely seized a gentleman and carried him off with them. These scenes took place, likewise, during the day in the sacristies, where the agents of the Holy Father went to hunt out the *dandy* priests.

The Roman women cried out as much as the priests. Pasquin promised to publish the statistics of the diminution of the population of the holy city at the end of the year; the nuns in the convents were demented; but, notwithstanding, even the Cardinal-Vicar Zurla, Leo XII., pursued his own gait. He made no person an exception: prelates, bishops, cardinals, monks — all game was good, — and Leo rarely made a mistake. He had a sure scent, from his old experience.

One day some one told him that the curate of S. Maria ai Monti pushed his zeal against young men, who had love-affairs, to intolerance, that this ecclesiastic was an exemplary man.

"Hum! hum!" exclaimed Leo, "how old is he?"

"Forty," said Cardinal Zurla.

"Very good," replied Leo XII.

The evening came; he called Caldarari and said to him:

"This night, at one o'clock in the morning, make an irruption upon the curate of S. Maria ai Monti, and see what is going on at his house."

"A domiciliary visit then, Holy Father," answers Caldarari.

"Imbecile," cried the Pope, in order to give him the hint.

"Very good, Very Holy Father!" added the gendarme.

At midnight a company of carbineers, commanded by the quarter-master Biaggio Ricci, accompanied by two robbers, presented themselves at the door of the curate, without making the least noise. The door is opened by the counsel and exquisite experience of the robbers, and M. Ricci and his amiable companions enter. The curate slept like a saint. He was lying between his two charming young nieces, both of them enceinte, who were lying close to his sides like the topical remedies of King David in his old age. This charitable man, thus disarranged, was placed by order of Leo XII. at the mercy of the Holy Office!

Three powerful personages, whose duty it was to superintend the supplying the markets of Rome, had made a pact with famine and monopolized provisions. They became rich; the people died from starvation, because nothing arrived in market except at a price fixed by Monseigneur Cicalotti, Count Cicalotti, and Mr. Mazio, brother of the cardinal of that name. Leo XII. made himself well assured of the fact; afterwards, one evening, he called Mr. Caldarari, commandant, as we have said, of the carbineers of the Sacred Apostolic Palace, and gave him orders to arrest the guilty. Monseigneur Cicalotti is seized, in fact, within the palace of the Vatican, erased from the album of prelates, and exiled the same night; Count Cicalotti condemned to twenty years, and Mr. Mazio to ten years forced labor. Cardinal Mazio succeeded afterward in having his brother shut up in the Convent of the Capucins at Viterbo.

Mr. About has admirably related what Cardinal Antonelli and his brothers do to-day. Pius IX. has made counts of the younger Antonelli, and has given to the Cardinal the administration of the minister of war, besides his other functions.

It has been often said that the secret of the confessional was violated, but the Catholic priests have always maintained that it was inviolable. Listen to this.

A certain Pontini, enrolled among the Carbonari, had incurred the suspicion of his brethren of having violated the secret of his sect, and of having informed against some persons. They continued, notwithstanding, to smile upon him very pleasantly; and not only did they not reproach him, but they flattered and caressed him, and invited him to parties of pleasure. Pontini grew fat; he dined with the police, and often at the lodges of the sect. A little incident happened, which troubled this happy existence.

One evening, after a very gay reunion, when they had read a letter from the Duke of Modena, and a little note from the Duke of Orleans, afterwards Louis Philippe I. by the grace of God, these heroic patriots separated, and each one took his own way. Pontini immediately took the street which led most directly to Monseigneur, the prefect of police. He went on his way singing, thinking upon what? who knows? Some project about the crowns he was about to handle. But on turning the corner of a lane, he found himself between two masked gentlemen who politely saluted him. Pontini stood seized. The two gentlemen embraced him fraternally; afterwards they plunged two poniards into his chest. Pontini fell, exclaiming, "Jesus and Mary!"

Pontini, notwithstanding, was only dying. In this very inconvenient position, a very officious priest presented himself at his pillow, with the doctor; and while the latter dressed the wounds, the former, who is no less than Monseigneur Piatti, commences to explore his conscience. This Monseigneur, a very smart man, who wished to advance himself, immediately understood the cause of the assassination. He took then fresh interest for the body and soul of the dying, that he might draw from him his secret. Pontini, so providentially escaped from the friendly advice of not speaking upon the affairs of the Carbonari, would have liked to have held his tongue, in order to save his friends the replication of correction. But how could he resist the affectionate attention of Monseigneur Piatti? He then avowed everything, under the secret of confession, and denounced a certain Tarchini, son of the cook of Pius VII., who had accompanied His Holiness to Paris, who was already under the surveillance of the police; and a certain Montanari, a doctor of Rocca del Papa.

Brought before the court, Montanari proved an *alibi*. There was nothing to establish the guilt of Tarchini. The tribunal appealed about it to the Pope, by informing him that it was about to acquit the prisoners.

Leo XII., who had already seen Monseigneur Piatti, sent one of his secret agents to Rocca del Papa, and this agent reported that Montanari was absent from that place on the night of the murder. The same inspiration, perhaps, equally revealed to Leo XII. that Tarchini was one of the murderers. The fact is that these two men, accused of crime at the particular request of His Holiness, were condemned to death. A movement was made by many persons, among others by Mr. de Chateaubriand, then French ambassador to Rome, to procure a pardon for the condemned from Leo XII. He was inexorable, and the two condemned men perished upon the scaffold. But, as after all they called themselves the victims of a secret revealed at confession, they sent priests, confessors, brotherhoods, to all the devils, and marched upon the gallows, singing an air of Rossini. The citizens applauded, the populace heaped upon them imprecations and revilings.

But this same populace did not act in the same manner in another case. I must relate it.

Monseigneur Traietto, of a patrician family of Naples, a prelate of infamous character, was found murdered one morning in his bed, by the blows of a hammer, like the celebrated Pope — a Pope Jean, of the 10th century — thus knocked on the head by the lover of his mistress. At this outrage on the life of a prelate, Leo XII. bounded with rage. He, as Vicar of God, was perfectly privileged to do as he pleased with his tonsured cattle; but the laics? Stop there! The example might be carried too far, God knows where! It might even become epidemic.

Therefore, Leo XII. gave formidable orders that at every risk the guilty should be discovered. Behold, then, the police and gendarmes in the field, confessors, nuns, and inquisitive saints on the lookout. There was but one index to the murder, too infamous for one to speak about.

Monseigneur Traietto, besides, had a young servant, a handsome boy, married to a pretty Transteverine with children. This valet-de-chambre, after having performed his services at Monseigneur's, returned home and slept there. The police made a descent upon Ludovico — he was thus called — at his house, and found upon him the watch of his master. Interrogated why he had this article with him, Ludovico replied:

"Monseigneur gave it to me, to carry to the watchmaker's, the evening of his death."

Nothing else had been touched at the prelate's house, neither silver, nor jewels, nor linen, nor clothes, nor papers,—absolutely nothing. Nothing else attested the guilt of Ludovico. Between him and his master there had been no discord, no anger, no ill-will, no visible reason for vengeance. The Tribunal, although composed of ecclesiastics anxious to avenge the murder of an ecclesiastic, could not decide upon his condemnation, not finding anything culpable.

Leo XII., to whom the crime was clear, being complete and consummated, exclaimed furiously:

"We must have an example! we must have a terrible expiation!"

The Tribunal condemned Ludovico. But Leo could not prevent it from adding to the sentence that the vice-god imposed it on it, *audito sanctissimo* —an old formula of the *Curia Romana*, which signifies: The votes being divided, the Holy Father decides it by his casting vote.

Leo XII. voted for his death.

The young wife and the children of Ludovico flew for succor to the Vicar of Christ, that they might obtain a pardon, since the sovereign had yielded to the demands of justice and voted for capital punishment. Leo XII. sent money to the wife, as if to purchase the life of her husband, and repulsed her demand for pardon. And as he desired that the punishment should be exemplary, he exhumed a mode of punishment of the Middle Ages.

They erected in the middle of the Piazza del Populo a very high scaffold, robed in black. The troops of the line surrounded it. Strong patrols of carbineers, of police and of dragoons, patrolled the streets adjacent to the place, and circulated slowly among the people who filled this fatal circus.

It was a beautiful day in April, the first feast of Easter, at nine o'clock in the morning.

Monks, peasants, young girls, priests, mendicants, canons, old procuresses, prelates, nobles and citizens, clerks and gentlemen,— a gay, variegated, extravagant, mixed and hideous multitude, jostled, crowded, and squeezed each other on this place,— some simpering, some telling jokes, and some praying, making assignations or cheapening a favor; all Rome was there. Strangers had not on that account left the Eternal City. Ladies in full dress — yes, ladies! Russian princesses, ladies of Great Britain, French countesses, disputed among themselves for a corner of the street, that they might see! And if those who were impatient at the delay, whispered, or perhaps hissed at the hangman and the laws, they were almost afraid lest a pardon should arrive, and the fête be disarranged. What an amiable creature is man! Finally, the condemned appeared.

Standing upon a cart drawn by oxen, the cart covered with red, was a man clothed in a black sack, his eyes covered with a bandage, having on his right a priest and on his left the executioner. Ludovico passed slowly through the crowd, always exclaiming, in a voice which God should hear and set down in his book of mercy, " I am innocent! I am innocent!" Assisted, I ought to say dragged, by the priest and by the hangman, Ludovico mounted the steps of the scaffold. He was made to kneel, that is to say, the hangman placed his hand upon Ludovico's shoulders and forced him to bend his knees. Ludovico obeyed, not weeping, calling in a stifled voice for his wife and his children, hardly praying at all. The priest, at the same time jabbering Latin to a man who scarcely understood the Roman patois, moved off a little. The executioner, Mastro Titta, stood up alongside of the condemned.

The crowd hardly breathed; men could have heard the beating of the hearts of the young women their neighbors.

Mastro Titta drew from under his red surtout a large leaded club, and examined it with care. He afterwards played with this cudgel like a drum-major with his long cane with a silver apple on the head of it, or like a mountebank with his juggler's wands. At last he grasped it firmly, waved it two or three times around his head, and struck the condemned upon the left temple.

A cry of horror rose from the crowd. The

victim fell like an ox, and his body began to be convulsed in agony.

But the justice of the Vicar of Christ was not yet satisfied, the punishment was not yet finished.

Mastro Titta threw his cudgel far from him into the midst of the crowd; he fell again upon his victim, drew from his side a long butcher's knife, and cut his throat. Afterward, with the same knife, he made a deep circle around the neck, as if to draw a line, and immediately cut off the head, which he showed to the people. The blood from the head reddened the executioner, while two jets of blood spirted from the cut neck and daubed the robe of the priest. You think it is at an end? No, Mastro Titta cuts off the two arms at the shoulder-blade, the two legs at the knee, and collecting together feet, hands, arms, legs, head, and trunk, he throws them all into a box at the bottom of the scaffold; draws from his pocket his handkerchief and blows his nose.

I shall say nothing of the horror of the populace at the sight of this frightful execution. A cry of malediction, unanimous and irresistible, escaped from the lungs of all these people, who, one quarter of an hour before, were so joyful, notwithstanding the soldiers, gendarmes, and the police.

The priest upon the scaffold tranquilly took snuff.

Leo XII. was not moved. He believed he had done his duty.

The year afterward a young man of good family

died in the Hospital of the Holy Ghost; he avowed that it was he who had killed Monseigneur Traietto to revenge an infamous outrage which this prelate had made upon his honor.

He boasted of it, the heretic! Is it not so, Mr. De Montalembert, Mr. Falloux, Mr. Bowyer, Mr. Hennessy, is it not so? — the Popes are infallible.

Leo XII. nevertheless committed these atrocities as a convinced man. He was ferocious; but he thought himself just because he spared nobody, and because those whom he struck appeared to be infamous.

I will relate one more fact, and then will stop. I could multiply them at pleasure.

Leo XII. had the most profound contempt for the clergy, high and low, Bishops, Cardinals, Canons, Abbes. In his disdain, I might almost say in his horror, he confounded them all. He at all times excepted from this general disgust Monseigneur Nicolai, whom he had nominated, in turn, President of the rivers and forests, then *Auditor* of the Apostolic Chamber. Leo loved this prelate on account of the zeal which he took in the execution of his duties, and on account of a certain conformity of character with his own, he being equally despotic and abrupt.

Besides all this, Monseigneur Nicolai lived with a mistress whom he had, according to the custom of the Roman Monseigneurs, made marry his valet-de-chambre upon those conditions which you are able to guess; and he kept this woman and her son, to whom he had given a good education, at his own dwelling. Leo XII. knew all this, and closed his eyes to it. He even shut them so tightly that he thought of appointing Monseigneur Nicolai Cardinal. In fact, as a very special distinction, Leo XII. one day announced to him, personally, the favor which he destined for him, in order that the candidate might first of all think of furnishing his court, composed of many servants — three of whom were priests, the trainbearer, secretary, and steward, — purchase his equipages — three at the least, — and obtain for himself the sacred habit and the red robes. Monseigneur Nicolai was very full of vanity; in less than eight days all his preparations were completed, and in order not to let his purple keep holiday, he dressed himself like a Cardinal, took his mistress by the hand, and went strutting before a Psyche, awaiting with impatience the receipt of the letter containing his appointment.

But Leo XII. did not hurry himself. For two months he had made no further mention of it; he had changed his mind.

They tattled a great deal at Rome about this affair, and attributed this pacing about of the Pontiff to the morals of the prelate, to his mistress, to his son, to this and to that. Here is the true reason.

A certain Vitelli, a breaker of stones upon the

public roads, had made the acquaintance of the famous Tommasino, valet-de-chambre of Cardinal Consalvi. The servants play a grand part at Rome; at first they assist in bringing their masters into the world, afterwards they marry their mistresses, sell them and scoff at them. From a breaker of stones then, Vitelli, becoming acquainted with Tommasino, the Frontin of the Cardinal Secretary of State of two or three Popes, had become a contractor on the public works. And he had made so much, and had stolen so much, that on dying he possessed a fortune of 200,000 crowns — or a million of francs, ($200,000.)

At Rome, whoever wishes to get clear of the expenses attending a will, nominates a fiduciary heir, who is obliged, in the shortest possible time, to carry out the last wishes of the testator. Vitelli, at his death, left a daughter of age, but not yet married, and two children of his son who had died before him. He had nominated Monseigneur Nicolai his confidential heir. Many months elapsed, and Monseigneur, notwithstanding the solicitations of the lawful heirs, did not hurry himself to make known the dispositions of the deceased Vitelli. At last Miss Vitelli appealed about it to the tribunal of A. C. (the Apostolic Chamber), of which Monseigneur Nicolai was himself chief.

Monseigneur Nicolai then spoke. He said that Vitelli had bequeathed his entire heritage to Mr. Louis, the son of him, Monseigneur Nicolai.

The indignation at Rome was universal, the outcry unanimous: everybody called Monseigneur Nicolai a robber. But the law is the law, and Monseigneur Nicolai was the prophet of the law, and he was right. Miss Vitelli appealed to Leo XII., who had already nominated this honest man Cardinal *in petto*, and had announced it to him. Leo partook of the indignation and general disapprobation. He broke the fiduciary testament, handed over the property to the legitimate heirs, disgraced Nicolai, and deprived him of his office. A short time afterwards this honest man died — of shame? I beg pardon — of chagrin? No! no! of an indigestion from *gnocchi* (a Roman dish).

Leo XII. did not even spare his brother Don Ilario della Genga, who played the Cæsar Borgia in a small way at Pierosara. Leo caused the arrest of his nephew, the son of Don Ilario, with seventeen other persons; he ordered the village to be disarmed, and gave directions to Caldarari to say to his brother to keep quiet, if he did not wish to partake of the fate of his sons. Afterwards, he dismissed Monseigneur Fieschi, the delegate of the province, who had closed his eyes upon the conduct of the Pope's relatives, and recalled him to Rome.

As customary, Gregory XII. appointed this prelate, recalled on account of his bad behavior, at first his chamberlain, afterwards Cardinal.

CHAPTER VI.

A GLASS OF LEMONADE.

I DO not write the history of this period. I draw, here and there, profiles with a pen, in order the better to photograph the men, the manners, and the government of Rome, and finally to notice some characteristics of him who calls himself the Vicar of God, and personify the whole of these men, these manners, these institutions, and this government. I add one more stroke of the pencil.

On coming to the throne, Leo XII. had taken Cardinal de la Sommaglia for his Secretary of State. As Leo did everything himself and wished to do it, this position, which ordinarily is the Papacy itself, became a *sinecure*. La Sommaglia suffered from it more or less, and in the end died from the sins of his youth, *delicta juventutis meæ*, as he said. Leo, after groping about for some weeks, chose as his successor the Cardinal-deacon Tommaso Bernetti de Fermo.

Bernetti descended from a plebeian family. His grandfather had been a town sergeant — that is to say, a policeman, *bargello*. Having entered the career of the prelacy, Bernetti passed successively from *chierico di Camera* to Minister of War, and finally to Governor of Rome. In this office he displeased Leo XII., because he did not participate in the *reveries* of the Pope concerning the reformation of the ecclesiastical morals. But at Rome there are four places of the prelacy, which are called cardinal—*cariche cardinalizie,* and also *cariche a fiocchetto,* because those who occupy them, on quitting them, are inevitably nominated Cardinals, even if they had been dismissed for outraging their mother,—and because during the exercise of these functions they can, like the Cardinals, decorate the heads of their carriage-horses with silk tufts, not red, like the Cardinals, but crimson. These places are: that of the *Auditor* of the Apostolic Chamber, that of Majordomo, that of Treasurer-General, and that of Governor of Rome. Leo XII. dismissed Bernetti from his office of Governor of Rome, by sending him as Apostolic Nuncio to Russia, to assist at the coronation of the Czar Nicholas at Moscow. On his return to Rome in 1826, he received the red hat which came to him of right; and he so well knew how to cajole the Pontiff, that Leo, notwithstanding his cunning, was duped by a man more adroit than himself. He made Bernetti Secretary of State.

But he was not very long in repenting of it.

Cardinal Bernetti refreshed himself, after the solemnity of church affairs, with a young and noble widow, the Princess Doria. This pretty woman was all at once seized with an immoderate taste for the theological sciences; and his Eminence complacently explained to her that mystery of the incarnation which had terrified Saint Augustine.

In a strict sense, the sweetness of this instruction ought to have been sufficient to distract the Cardinal Secretary of State. The Duchess was apt at the science. But, whether it was that Cardinal Bernetti had in his veins too much of the blood of the old bargello, or that he passionately loved the fine arts, or that he wished to make sport of the august figure of the Vicar of Jesus Christ for the painted faces of the daughters of Satan, he passed a great part of his nights in the midst of the female dancers and singers of the Argentino Theatre, and royally loaded them with favors. The contractors for these revels were Mr. Mariani, a gentleman of the chamber of His Eminence, appointed by him chief of passports in the general police, and Mr. Paolo Massani, at first the Cardinal's domestic, afterwards valet-de-chambre, and then major-domo.

And as, after having fulfilled their high functions, there remained to these two personages a little time for them to think about their own little affairs, they sold the Cardinal by wholesale and retail. Leo XII. had a knowledge of the manifold capacities of his minister and of the fashion of the Regency which he had adopted for expediting business, and was greatly struck with it. Inconsolable at the fault committed, Leo prepared himself to make a great example, by punishing his Secretary of State. And he thought so seriously of it, and with so much fixity, that he had the imprudence, in a moment of anger, to mention it.

The unfortunate! he forgot that a Cardinal is as inviolable as the Pope.

Nevertheless, His Holiness had only opened his swollen heart to his intimate friend, doctor Vincenso Todini.

This doctor was not very skilful in his profession, but, to make amends, he showed himself very brutal. Leo XII. loved him, perhaps because Todini had cured him of certain infirmities which His Holiness had contracted when he was not yet lieutenant-general of God. To this Todini, Leo XII. had, besides, confided the management of his private affairs; as also, at the same time, to a certain Father Brandimarte, who strutted with the gravity of a bishop in his Abbey de Monticello, near de la Genga. But these two reasoners, knowing that their master could dispose of the treasures of Paradise, and of the purse of his much-loved flock, *ad libitum*, thought that he had no need of his private revenues, and shamelessly stole them.

Leo began to be suspicious of it. He consequently sent a confidant to his estate, in order to discover in what condition things were. This intimate confidant of the Pope, from whom we obtained the greater part of the facts which we are relating, went, saw, returned, and presented himself at the bed of the Pope, at an early hour in the morning, to say to him, as the end of his commission:

"Holy Father, they pillage and shear you like an ..."

He was about to let slip a word, I don't know what, when he perceived that the door was ajar, and that Todini was there upon the watch. The confidential envoy of Leo XII. suspended his recital. He spoke of the rain, and of the fine weather, and made a sign to the Pope, who likewise understood. Leo rang furiously, and ordered his aid-de-chambre to close the door, and drive away every person, no matter who.

Todini, who had learned the departure of the Pontiff's agent for la Genga, and the investigations which he had made there, and of his return, and had heard the commencement of the report, did not require to know anything more. Leo XII. had then the knowledge that his managers robbed him.

Todini assisted always at the very frugal dinner of the Pontiff, and regulated, in jest, the quantity of salt which should be put into his eggs, and the quantity of water which he should mix with his wine. Upon this day, Leo XII. did not speak to him as ordinarily; and even received his services with a certain impatience. Todini understood, and resigned himself to await the explosion of the thunder.

It was then to this man, before being aware of his dishonesty, that Leo had opened his heart regarding Cardinal Bernetti, whom he had threatened to despoil of the purple, and to exile to Fermo. At this moment, in danger himself, Todini went to Cardinal Bernetti, that they might understand each other.

Leo XII., as we have already mentioned, was sick when he was elected Pope; but immediately afterwards, having begun to follow a severe regime, his health became better, and now he was almost well. Some days after the affair of Todini, Cardinal Bernetti took to his bed, protesting that he had the gout. Leo XII. went to pay him a visit, going through an interior staircase, which led from the ante-chamber of the Pope to the apartment of the Cardinal Secretary of State.

At the palace of the Vatican, the secret passages and the concealed apartments are numerous; one might say that they were expressly constructed to conspire in, to commit crime, and to escape from justice in!

Doctor Todini and Nicolino, his first aid-de-chambre — that is to say, his personal valet-de-chambre — accompanied His Holiness.

Cardinal Bernetti received the Pope with an earnestness and an effusion of affection warmer than usual; for His Eminence had, in general, rough manners — which made his flatteries more appreciated, when he put himself to the trouble of giving them. After having conversed a long time with his minister, Leo XII. became thirsty, which often happened to him: he asked for a drink. Nicolino wished to wait upon the Pontiff; but the aid-de-chambre of the Cardinal, Paolo Massani, solicited this honor, and on his knees presented to Leo XII. a glass of lemonade. His Holiness swallowed it at a draught. He talked a little further with the patient; afterwards, without taking the trouble of treating him with the usual benediction, which the Cardinal knew but too well how to understand, Leo left.

Arrived at the first landing-place of the staircase, he stopped. Todini and Nicolino thought that His Holiness had forgotten to say something to his minister. "No," replied Leo XII., a little irritated, "I am sick in the lower abdomen!" He took breath for a moment, and then continued to ascend. Once in his apartment, he lay down, and ordered Nicolino to bring him a decoction of chamomile, to apply upon compresses to the abdominal region. Todini was called in again in the evening; he came and said, "Holy Father, this is nothing!" They continued the compresses during the night. Leo XII. did not close his eyes, and the pains, far from becoming calmer, increased. At eleven o'clock next day, Todini came again and prepared himself to give his ordinary attentions to the Pontiff, who suffered from retention of urine. Leo burst into loud cries and fainted.

They did not administer any other remedies, Todini always saying, "It is nothing!" They called in no other doctors; they permitted nobody to approach the sick-bed, except Nicolino, and two days afterwards, Monseigneur Barbolami, nephew of Leo XII., and one of the four *Camerieri segreti partecipanti*, who carried to him the Viaticum, almost secretly.

This nephew had already arrived too late! Leo XII. was at the worst.

The agony of the Pontiff lasted three days and three nights. Bernetti, as was fit, having always the gout, did not have himself transported to the bed of the dying. He limited himself to sending his valet-de-chambre, Massani, four times in order to learn the news. Todini, who remained in the ante-chamber, said to him always:

"*He still lives!*"

Being impatient, Massani returned two hours later. "*Is he finally dead?*" he exclaimed, almost angry.

Todini nodded his head that Leo XII. had expired. Massani drew near to the partly opened door and saw the corpse.

They had kept what had happened with the greatest secrecy.

When Massani had assured Bernetti that Leo XII. no longer existed, the Cardinal's gout left him as if by a miracle, and he went out an hour later in his carriage.

This death — or this murder? — troubled nobody, affected nobody. The Pope is dead! long live the Pope!

So soon as the life of the Pontiff is in danger, according to the etiquette of the court of Rome, it is the Cardinal Penitentiary Major who has the right of assisting him. But they had kept the sickness of Leo so profound a secret, that the Cardinal Penitentiary learned at the same time, as did Monseigneur Barbolami, that His Holiness was sick and that he was dead. When the great bell of St. Peter and that of the Capitol announced at Rome the decease of the Vicar of Christ, there was in Rome an universal explosion of maledictions which accompanied the soul of the departed. Leo XII. did not leave one friend, not one regret.

He had only known how to punish.

The characteristic of the reign of Leo XII. was terror.

In his conferences with Prince de Metternich, at the court of Napoleon, he had not learned to love liberty, to respect human life, to recognize the rights of the people. The Roman States, and Italy in general, from this period, appeared to his eyes like a black spot, which endeavored to darken God in the person of his representatives — the princes,— and to tarnish the two ministers of Providence — Austria and the Papacy.

Austria covered Italy; she was at Venice, at Milan, at Turin, at Modena, and at Naples. They gave chase to man because this *sinner*, according to the expression of Mr. Bonald, aimed to become a *citizen*. The Carbonari were in fashion, and the axe of the executioner likewise. Leo, in his quality of God's lieutenant, then set his heart upon the work with enthusiasm, and he cut down: he hewed down in the forest of liberty, heads and principles. He was unrelenting. Of a harsh, ardent, and active nature, an obstinate and despotic character, full of unsatiated and irritable passions; a fanatic through State theory, he thought that as chief of the Catholic world he ought to take the initiative for the repression of the insurrection of the people against the principle of public authority. He ought to be imitated and followed, not preceded; and Prince Metternich recognized himself this priority of the Holy Father. Besides, Leo created *special commissions* in order to punish outside of the laws, not only crime, but the *suspicion* of crime. He violated society, which at this period demanded to be left alone, at liberty, and which believed in God and in human dignity. He governed, in one word, by that famous maxim of Cardinal Rivarola, who said:

"The *Laity* are not permitted in Rome, but simply *tolerated*."

Leo gave full power to that executioner; and in one day only, the 31st August, 1825, this man condemned five hundred and eight individuals *suspected* of having been liberals,—the greater part to capital punishment. The name of this Cardinal, even to-day, even after Cardinal Albani and Cardinal Antonelli, and the massacre of Pérouse, is a scarecrow in the Romagna. In the winter evenings, the old people relate *their fear!* At Ravenna they tried to kill him; but the blow having failed, this ferocious Eminence took for coadjutor Monseigneur Invernizzi, and Colonel Ruinetti. The carnage recommenced with redoubled zeal; and when the axe of the executioner was tired, Cardinal Bernetti ordered, by two very dry *official* lines, "to transport those accused of crime into a *malarious* district!" God will take care of the rest. Ought not God to do something for the safety and the honor of his marshal for the earth?

The reign of Leo XII. has been a great lesson to the world. It has proved that the temporal government of the Pope, whatever one does, cannot be reformed. Leo believed, and some believe to-day, that evil is in men. Leo struck the priests rudely. Did they become better? Some to-day demand of Pius IX. a little secularization; trouble lost. The evil is in the institution. But, what Pope would dare to touch the Papacy?

CHAPTER VII.

PIUS VIII.

PIUS VIII. showed himself worthy of Leo XII. for political and religious intolerance. The same men were continued in the same work.

The holy-water sprinkler had already been changed into a clerk.

The 14th of May, 1829, Pius published a general edict of the Holy Office, which must have given joy in heaven to Saint Dominique de Guzman, and to

Torquemada,— are they not both in heaven? But Pius VIII. did not live long enough to cause Leo to be forgotten; for behold, in one year after, Gregory XVI. arrived.

The Holy Ghost chose him in a hurry. Disturbances grew bold everywhere, even in Rome, at the gate and under the windows of the Conclave.

Austria pointed out the man whom they wanted; the Sacred College obeyed.

We shall speak of the revolt further **on**; let us now speak of the Pope.

CHAPTER VIII.

GREGORY XVI. AND HIS COURT.

GREGORY XVI. — the Cardinal Mauro Cappellari — was a tall and vigorous monk of the Camaldules. He had a vulgar physiognomy, always cheerful, but not very good, upon which was enthroned a large red nose badly treated by a fistula. His large voluptuous lips permitted a row of teeth to be seen, dirty but sharp, and in a condition to crunch the revenue of the kingdom of this world, and of the other of which the Son of God may invest him. An inexhaustible tear moistened his eyes, which were a little jaundiced and marbled with red veins, and gave life to them. A smile hovered over this countenance, but a beastly smile — material, gross, and buffoon-like. The voice of Gregory was strong, and when he spoke, and particularly when he burst out into a laugh, he had the habit of beating his abdomen like a drum.

Familiar with persons who approached him, always in a very good humor, he delighted in vulgar plays and plebeian farces. Sometimes he threw crowns to Signor Antonio, dean of the hostlers and chair-men, who, being short and fat, made grotesque grimaces in picking them up. Sometimes he unbridled the droll caprice of exposing the bosom of his train-bearer, Cardinal Soglia, with whom he played at blindman's-buff.

One day this play was likely to have been fatal to him. Cardinal Soglia, with his eyes bandaged, was to break a pot, in the middle of the garden of the Vatican, with a big club. If the persons engaged in the play perceived that he aimed correctly, and that he would break the utensil, they turned him round. The Cardinal then struck the air and was laughed at for missing. But while His Holiness stooped, one day, to take away the threatened pot, Cardinal Soglia raised his cudgel to strike. If a prelate had not held the arm of the Cardinal, the skull of the Vicar of Christ would have been broken into shivers — and the Roman Church would, without doubt, have had one martyr more!

When Cardinal Soglia was promoted to other

functions, his office of buffoon to the Pope was given to Monseigneur Arpi, to which was added also the office of confessor to His Holiness.

Gregory loved eating very much; he drank like a Swiss. Being a monk of the Camaldules, he frequented the taverns, and tippled without ceremony with peoples' servants, particularly if there was in the place a pretty maid-servant. Gregory, like Ferdinand I. of Naples, relished the woman who had a strong smell. He had no prejudices, and, besides, but little religion. Gregory only hated the revolutionists; and, except himself and Gaetanino, he loved neither the people, nor the priests, nor the world, nor heaven! Love he did not know; he only understood lust.

This Gaetano Morrone had been his barber when he was still a monk; he afterwards was his secretary.

Gaetanino personified the type of Frontin. A handsome man, crafty, pliant, given to compliments, understanding a word, a look, a wag, a frown, and agreeable, he knew how to please everybody. Gregory, on becoming Pope, had made him his first aid-de-chambre, and had decorated him with the order of St. Gregorio Magno. Although a layman, Gaetanino dressed like a prelate, with crimson stockings and cassock, and a three-cornered hat. He dwelt with his wife in the palace of the Vatican, where the employés lived with their wives, their daughters, their housemaids, their servants; and the priests and soldiers with their mistresses.

This palace is so constructed and complicated with corridors, with dark closets, remote and intricate apartments at the top of the house, that love and debauchery strut and nestle there as in their natural nest. At night, the Vatican is the worst place in Rome. The strangest adventures in Rome take place there; everything is mingled there. It is the *Icaria* of vice. In the twilight, busy phantoms can be seen gliding about; soldiers, servants, prelates, have all of them one color, one end, one gait. If two friends meet, they do not know each other. Some one awaits at the door a more vigilant rival, then succeeds him, or goes elsewhere, to one side, to a better story, lower down. Bad luck to him who gets angry; he is pointed out by the finger, and is excommunicated as a man who aims at scandal. Revenge is permitted. From midnight, the secret life of the Vatican is redoubled; it takes a name and a form. A current of communication is established between all its parts, which during the day are so carefully distinguished. There is no longer an apartment of the Pope, of the Secretary of State, of prelates,—neither ante-chambers, nor kitchens, nor lofts; they go from one place to another, everywhere.

It was then said that the barber's wife was also the friend of the Pope. We affirm nothing, we deny nothing. It always happened that at the fête of the baptism of Gaetanino's infant, whom the Romans called *a Gregoriolo*, or *little Gregory*, there were three Cardinals, among others, the Minister of the Interior, Mattei, and Asquini, Patriarch of Constantinople, twenty-seven Archbishops, Bishops, and prelates of all colors, Antonelli included. The Pope came out of his apartment, embraced and kissed the little monkey.

To take charge of this child, the barber had engaged a very pretty country girl from Frascati. The Pope amused himself by slipping pieces of gold into her bosom, when he met her in the gardens of the Vatican. Madam Gaetanino raged with jealousy, and the beauty from Frascati was sent back. Gregory not seeing her any longer, asked what had become of her. There was discord in the family; but the barber was constrained to recall her.

His Holiness, notwithstanding, had a carbineer for a rival.

Gregory often went to pass his evening with his barber, and amused himself with the children.

Besides, who had any right to scandalize Gregory for his amours, if he was the most honest among his Cardinals and prelates? Look further, and judge!

Monseigneur Marulli, president of the *Auditoriato della Camera*, courted publicly the Countess de Lozzeno, the Duchess de Bracciano, and the Countess of Ludolf, the not very pretty wife of the ambassador from Naples to Rome. This prelate, this pasha, so furiously accumulative, was so impudent, that one evening, at the ball given by the ambassador from Austria, Mr. De Lutzow, he presumed to place his hand on the bosom of an English lady. An attaché of the Spanish ambassador, present at this outrage, and witnessing the sudden pallor which covered the countenance of this lady, took Monseigneur by the collar and pushed him into the ante-chamber, among the servants.

Monseigneur Ciacchi loved the red Countess of Morconi, and disputed with a noble guard about her, having at the same time another mistress at his home. This woman gave to Monseigneur Ciacchi many children, which he had the courage never to disown, even when he was appointed Cardinal.

Cardinal Bottiglia made court to Madam Persiani, the wife of a druggist in the Piazza Rotonda. Every day from one to five o'clock, his carriage might be seen, filled with the priests who accompanied him, stationed at the door, while His Eminence informed himself up stairs, close to the pretty druggist, about the price of pepper and canella.

Monseigneur Matteucci, judge of the *Sacra Ruota*, now minister of the police, loved Madam Gigli, wife of a picture-merchant, who, beautiful and stupid as a statue, had gone through all the workshops, standing as a model for the Virgin. Monseigneur Matteucci, besides, borrowed money from the husband, and took from him a commission upon the pictures which he sold for him.

Cardinal Viale-Prela — dead, but lately Archbishop of Bologna, consumptive and intolerant, was not familiar himself with Madam Polidori, a relative of the Cardinal of that name. This Cardinal had loved her before him, since by a letter under his private signature he had ceded her to his confrère for the sum of five thousand crowns and a little picture, the head of a child, by Carlo Dolci. At the court of Vienna, Viale-Prela, though old, has left some traces of his gallantry.

Cardinal Piccolomini, large, fat, with the air of a musketeer, smoked twenty-five cigars a day, in hope of becoming thin. They had been obliged to dismiss him from the office of minister of war, because they had found missing from the army chest a million of crowns. To indemnify him for the interruption of these benefices, Gregory had appointed him Cardinal. Piccolomini lived with Madam Restituta; he accompanied her to the theatre in citizen's dress and into society, played at her house and with her, played for her at the houses of others, and swore like a dragoon. But Madam Restituta loved *that* dragoon, and *the* dragoons; so that it often fell out that Cardinal Piccolomini and Madam Restituta gave each other reciprocally a few blows. Monseigneur Soglia mimicked admirably the quarrels of the Cardinal and his friend, and Gregory laughed till he cried.

Cardinal Altieri frequented the Camarilla; but like a great lord, His Eminence made but little noise and great headway. During his youth he had been the darling of the Roman ladies, not on account of his generosity or his beauty, but from the elegance of his manners and the sarcasm of his words.

We have spoken of Cardinal Bernetti.

Cardinal Ugolini was intimate with the wife of Vanvitelli, the advocate — a very pretty woman, on my word! of an ugly and old husband who smoked in his pipe, drugs to kill the bugs, and was good for nothing except to eat up the revenue of the Cardinal, and to give a name to his children. This husband *in partibus* called Cardinal Ugolini, *my colleague*.

Cardinal Zurla, although Vicar of Rome, old and a monk, disguised himself in the evening, that he might frequent the bagnios. *Those ladies*, who recognized him, demanded of him his blessing, and he gave it more willingly than his crowns. He often caught a thump in the quarter of the Transtevere. Once upon a time he met his secretary, who was waiting for some one, and who having recognized him, gave the way to him, saying to him, "After you, Most Eminent." Leo XII. caused His Eminence to be surprised, thus disguised in one of the houses of the Banchi di Santo Spirito, and obliged him to pass the night in the round-house.

Monseigneur Dandolo Foscolo, Archbishop of Corfu, kept house with Madam Giuditta Mazio, niece of the Cardinal of the same name. Monseigneur Dandolo Foscolo passionately loved women, play, intrigues, and did not scorn the score. In fact he honored with his presence, for many weeks, the prison of Clichy at Paris, where he was attached to the Nunciature. Madam Pasta got him out of his trouble. She gave a concert in the salons of the Princess de Lieven, *for the purpose of drawing a soul out of Purgatory;* but, with malice savoring but little of Christianity, she caused the name of Monseigneur Dandolo Foscolo to be circulated through the auditory. The next day Monseigneur received twenty-one thousand franc-notes. He had won almost as much at lansquenet (a game of cards) with the sirens of the place; so that he gave one on account to his creditors and left the prison. After that, he had to leave Paris. Gregory XVI., according to his custom, appointed him Archbishop of Corfu.

Monseigneur Lancellotti would have been suited with his servant-girl, if Madaleine had been willing to suit herself with him. The fact was that Monseigneur Lancellotti was not precisely handsome, and that Madaleine had been at Narni. As soon, therefore, as she felt her wings free, she escaped. Twice Monseigneur Lancellotti sent the gendarmes to bring her back; finally he attached to himself a female dragoon, an old sorceress who superintended even his thoughts. Nevertheless, it thus happened one day. Monseigneur officiated at the Church of

San Carlo. On turning to say to the people, *Dominus vobiscum!* he saw the old demon in the first rank before the altar. He stopped aghast. The old woman made a sign to him to tell him: she has flown away! Monseigneur Lancellotti immediately ended the missal, quitted the altar, ran into the sacristie, tore off his sacred robes, threw himself into his carriage, and drove to the house of his friend the prefect of police. He succeeded in getting the police to recapture Madeleine. And since then, I do not know through what compromise, they have lived together without scandal.

Cardinal Grassellini was guilty, at Bólogna, of more atrocious conduct. He caused a pretty girl, of sixteen years of age, who had resisted him, to be carried off by the Inquisition. The Austrian general, Degenfeld, directed that this child should be set at liberty; but, fifteen days afterwards, this unfortunate young girl died from the effects of the harsh and violent treatment that Grassellini had made her suffer.

Cardinal de Pietro had for his friend the Countess de M——, said at the same time to be the mistress of Louis Napoleon Bonaparte. This Cardinal, when a legate in Portugal, had a quarrel on account of a lady. This lady's lover challenged Pietro to a duel. But His Eminence justly refused the challenge, protesting that he was a prelate. A prelate is not a man when he is required to fight.

Monseigneur Bedini, new Cardinal Archbishop

of Terracina, one day put in prison all the women of easy virtue in Bologne, to revenge himself for I know not what sad accident that had happened to him. Monseigneur Sibilia, for his part, being president of the Criminal Tribunal at Rome, caused all those whom he wished to compromise, women and girls, to be put in the dungeon.

Cardinal Cacciapiatti conducted himself so badly, that at the period of the Conclave of Gregory XVI., the Romans, passing in review the Cardinals from whom a Pope had to be taken, said to him:

>"Cacciapiatti! Cacciapiatti?
>Riderebbero anche i metti!
>Vi sarebbe al Quirinale
>Tutto l'anno carnovale."

>"Cacciapiatti! Cacciapiatti?
>If elected Pope, the people will laugh at ye,
>And at the Quirinal the whole year round
>The carnival and frolic will be found."

Monseigneur Belletti, at Foligno, directed the conscience of the Abbess of Madre Paola, precisely as, later, Pius IX. directed that of the Abbess de Fognano.

It was sufficient for Cardinal Tosti to squander the finances, and to enrich himself so far, that his palace at Monte Citorio was a marvel of richness and luxury. Even the knobs of his door-locks were of amber. This Cardinal had the right, and he had the taste not to pass by an ornament still more precious. He caressed in his hotel an extremely portly Portuguese, called Madaleine; and brought up there a young man taken from the hospital of St. Michel, named Giovannino. These two favorites sold the graces and favor of His Eminence.

Cardinal Marazzani, having in love ascetic tendencies, found his friends in the convents. This Cardinal died from indigestion, in eating oysters — he had eaten thirty-six dozen! — like Cardinal Diario Sforza, who died of an indigestion from lobsters; and Cardinal Vidoni, of an indigestion from sherbets. This Vidoni was such a gourmand that if, in passing along the street, the odor ascending from a kitchen tickled him, he got out of his carriage, entered the house out of which the provoking perfume came, and went to taste the dishes which had attracted him.

But the adventure which made the most noise was that of Cardinal Antonelli. Monseigneur Antonelli was pro-legate at Macerata. He lodged with Count Clerici, an elegant, handsome, witty young man, who was about to marry one of the most beautiful of the Sabine girls. The pro-legate occupied one wing of the hotel, the Count another. In order to visit each other, it was necessary to descend the staircase, cross the court, and afterwards go up to the apartments for reception. Antonelli, saying that he was very busy, saw from time to time his hosts, and only saw them; for, in the country, they love the priests like the Venetians love the Austrians, or the Neapolitans the Bourbons

Through politeness, the Countess always expressed her desire to the pro-legate to see him oftener at her soirées, where some friends came to play at faro, to talk about the news of the day, and to partake of some refreshments. Antonelli, one day, said, that crossing the court was a very great obstacle, and that he would have had the pleasure of more frequently visiting his friends, if a door could be made on the inside, so as to pass from one apartment into the other. This being very easily to be done, the next day it was accomplished.

Count Clerici had the confidence of youth.

And besides, who would have ever been able to suppose that this flower of beauty and elegance, the Countess, had had eyes for any other than the charming young man who had just espoused her?

Besides, Cardinal Antonelli is far from being handsome. There is in his form something of the wild beast, his features are rough, heavy, and coarse — a bear changed into a man, walking along. Large lips red with blood; teeth separated, gray and sharp; arched forehead, large fiery eyes with a black look, always restless and glistening with desire; a short nose; his face round, somewhat thin and wan, and of a yellow tint; when he talks he stammers, and often repeats the same word. Although tall and thin, Antonelli moves awkwardly; he is without elegance in his actions, and without eloquence. It fell out, nevertheless, that this Caliban seduced Titania.

One day Count Clerici entered the house unexpectedly, and found his apartment occupied. He forced the door open, and saw the pro-legate Antonelli where nobody but the Count Clerici ought to be. A contest took place between them. Antonelli, like Joseph, left his garments in the hands of his antagonist, and fled. The Count pursued him; Antonelli barricaded himself in his apartment. The Count commenced a siege according to rule, and prepared to scale the place. Antonelli took to the balcony, called for the police, said that the Count wished to assassinate him, accused him of rebellion against lawful authority, and issued a writ to take him before a magistrate. The gendarmes seized the unfortunate one. But the intrigue soon became public; the population of Macerata rose in insurrection. Antonelli saved himself by means of a disguise. Arrived at Rome, after this exploit, Gregory made him Cardinal. Count Clerici sued for a separation from his wife and obtained his demand. The young man is miserable: the young wife has gone to pine away in — I know not what convent.

Is it necessary for me to give other examples? No.

I have mentioned here those of which everybody speaks, and of which one can speak without indiscretion. What would take place if I were willing to name the guilty of to-day, and to repeat what is whispered in the diplomatic mansions, in the salons, in the boudoirs, and particularly in the convents of the women; finally, that which is not learned from the first comer, and which is not talked about in the cafés.

After this, was not Gregory XVI. able to pass for an irreproachable man and a saint?

Two days after the election of this Pope the revolution commenced and embraced Central Italy.

Let us relate this episode of our history: it happens à *propos* as a response to the protestations and enterprises of the dukes and grand-dukes of the Pope and of Austria.

CHAPTER IX.

THE DUKE OF MODENA, FRANCIS IV.

FRANCIS IV. of Modena was the strongest prince of the time; a Satanic mixture of the lowest vices and exalted aims; extreme in everything, violent, and inexorable.

As a man, he was possessed by the demon of speculation and usury. He overloaded his subjects with taxes until they were completely exhausted. He monopolized the corn, the wine, the oil, the food, the cloths of the Duchy, and resold them to his people. He lent small sums of money on pawn, at an interest of 75 per cent. He engaged in foreign commerce, under a fictitious name; he had armed vessels cruising on the coasts of Africa, which, kept in pay by him, made captures on his account, or half for his account and half for the Dey. He had taken everything from his people,—life, liberty, honor, property; he held them on every side. He could starve or feed them at his will.

As prince, he had a taste for the police, and he pushed this taste so far that it became a passion. He did not content himself with knowing what his subjects did against his government; he wished to know what they thought, what they said, what they ate; their aims, their passions, their family quarrels, their caprices. He penetrated to the domestic hearth, into the salons, the bed-chambers, the confessional, the closet of the man of letters, and the workshop of the artist. The material and moral existence of his people was brought to light. Notwithstanding, not being content with having made his own police, he wished to make that of the Pope, that of the Grand-duke of Tuscany, or that of Austria.

With an activity so ravenous, we easily comprehend that this man could not content himself with knowing the names of all his subjects, their ages, their tastes, and that a mind so vigorously tempered ought to have more elevated tendencies. He wished to be king no matter at what price, nor where, to enlarge this strait-waistcoat which impeded his respiration. The Duke Francis had large lungs. But he hardly saw the legal means to spread himself, to appropriate to himself certain portions of country belonging to his neighbors as small and as avaricious as himself. He had recourse then to a conspiracy.

In 1819 the King of Naples had instituted the society of the *Concistorio*, the chiefs of which were Italian sovereigns not belonging to the house of Austria. This society, encouraged by Russia, was directed against Austria. They aimed at a new partition of the Peninsula, in which the Pope would have had the Polésines, Rovigo, and a large part of Tuscany; the King of Naples, the Marches, the Isle of Elba, and some other provinces of the Pope; the Duke of Modena, with the title of King, Venetia, a part of Lombardy, Parma, and Plaisance; the King of Piedmont, the rest of Lombardy, the Italian Tyrol, Lucca, Massa, and Canara; and Russia, for her good offices, the choice of Ancona, Civita-Vecchia, or Genoa.

This society acted energetically, particularly at the time of the Grecian war, and during the contest between the Porte and Russia. But the peace of Adrianople and the countermining of Austria, who knew of this society, put an end to so ridiculous an enterprise.

The Duke of Modena, although an Austrian, had slipped in among the conspiring princes, and had been the most active. Afterwards he had tacked about, sufficiently in time to reconcile himself with Austria, and to enter into her good graces by delivering up to persecution some liberals and carbonari with a rancor and a ferocity that bordered upon folly. Austria, in fact, pardoned him; but, always fearing the enterprises of this turbulent being, they wished to have him for an accomplice.

Charles-Albert, Prince de Carignan, when the revolution burst out in Piedmont in 1821, was Regent. Yielding to the same necessities which led to the abdication of King Victor, he had promised a Constitution. This was an inexpiable crime in the eyes of Prince de Metternich. King Charles Felix having no children, the inheritance to the throne of Sardinia returned to the Prince de Carignan. Mr. de Metternich began to work upon the King in order to get him to abolish the Salic law in favor of the Duke of Modena, who was married to a daughter of King Victor.

Not having succeeded, Prince de Metternich commenced to attack him "by a system of calumnies (wrote M. de la Maisonfort, French Minister at Florence, in his despatch of the 15th of November), the focus of which I suspect is at Modena, and its propagators everywhere where there are Austrian agents." Besides M. de Metternich had said it to M. de la Maisonfort, in clear and positive terms, "We will take from him his hereditary right to the crown" (despatch of the 22d of June). And M. de Chateaubriand wrote, in his despatch of the

16th of April, 1829, from Rome, "Thus, that the Cardinal Albani has a pension from Prince de Metternich; that he is a relative of the Duke of Modena, to whom he pretends he will leave an enormous fortune; that he weaves with this prince a small plot against the heir of the crown of Sardinia: all this is true." But the Prince de Carignan, having from the commencement tried to aim at the protection of Louis XVIII., Baron Pasquier had already opposed his veto to the designs of the Austrian minister and to the hopes of the Duke de Modena.

Francis not having succeeded in raising up a throne with the assistance of the enemies of Austria nor with Austria, tried another means. He wished to coincide with the liberals, discover their intentions, and conspire with them for the redemption of Italy.

The Italian patriots maintained relations with the Cosmopolitan Club of Paris. Ciro Menotti and Misley, to whom the Duke was candid, caused his propositions to be offered to the French Club, who accepted this co-operation by promising to the Duke, Lombardy, Parma, Plaisance, Ferrara, and the other towns of Italy which should rise in rebellion and should wish to be annexed to his kingdom, *unreservedly constitutional!* The Duke of Orleans, Louis Philippe, took part with his friends of the Cosmopolitan Club. He consequently knew with the others the propositions of the Duke, who, on his side, had promised money and the men necessary in order to provoke revolution in the Peninsula, Spain and France — for the profit of the Duke of Orleans.

Francis IV. purchased his crown!

The agents of the French Club came to Modena and settled these agreements in due form.

The patriots, without doubt, wished to serve themselves with this instrument and to break it immediately when they should no longer need it; the Duke, on his part, promised all that they demanded from him with the same intention.

The Spanish patriots not being yet ready, caused the Italian revolution to be retarded. But that of France burst out — and Louis Philippe had his crown.

Then the Duke of Modena sent Misley to him to recall to his remembrance his agreement and his promises. The King of the French had forgotten all of them. And as he had become the principal support of order, he denounced all the intrigues of the Italian patriots to Austria, as well as their names, their designs, and among other things the projects of the Duke de Modena. Mr. de Metternich limited himself to sending to Francis a copy of the despatch of Count d'Appony, ambassador of Austria at Paris, in which that diplomatist gave to him an account of this conversation with the king.

Behold then the Duke dethroned for the third time; but this time he was furious; so that he said to all who desired to listen, "The Duke of

Orleans? well, yes, I know him; he is an abyss of deceit!"

In the meanwhile the Duke de Praslin, envoy-extraordinary of the French king, arrived at Modena. Mr. de Praslin came to announce to the courts of Central Italy the accession of Louis Philippe to the throne. Count Molza went immediately to the hotel where this envoy was about to put up to demand from him a copy of the letter which he had with him for his master. Mr. de Praslin replied, that he had no copy, and that he would have given the original personally to His Highness.

Count Molza left for the purpose of combining with the Duke for a reception insulting to the French envoy. But the latter, having doubt upon the subject, took post and set out at the same moment.

The Duke de Modena caused a rumor to be spread that he was not willing to recognize the French king.

In the meantime it was necessary to satisfy Austria on the one side and the liberals on the other, who pressed him to give the signal for the revolution, which had been rife for a long time. He had but to choose. He threw himself into the arms of Austria. He then awaited the shock of the revolution, which, in fact, burst forth on the 3d of February.

CHAPTER X.

INSURRECTION OF CENTRAL ITALY.

REVOLUTION is never a new thing in Italy; it is there, and has been there permanently for ten centuries. The Austrian soldier, the Swiss of the King of Naples, the galley-officers of Rome and of Piedmont, have put it down on one side, have suffocated it on the other; but when they believed it to be definitively strangled, it raises itself up, behind them, and alongside of them, and again cries out, "Long live Italy, and long live liberty!" So that the revolution in Italy is like the Christ: when they think he is in the sepulchre, he is upon Tabor. And what does it matter when they called it yesterday *Young Italy*, the day before yesterday, *Carbonari*, and the day before that, *Freemasonry;* or that they call it to-morrow *Reform*, or *Piedmontism*, or *Nationality*. All this is only but a symbol. At the bottom there is but one thing, real, powerful, electric, immortal: no more Pope, no more foreigners! In fact, question the nobility of the Roman sacristy, the lazzaroni of Naples, the valiant Lombard aristocracy, the Tuscan peasant, or the Piedmontese soldier, or those generous citizens of Venice, — you will discover that they may perhaps have fears for the constitution, for the republic, for unity, for atheism, for socialism; but all will reply to you unanimously: No more Pope, no more foreigners. This aspiration is the animal heat of the Italian life, which may be benumbed, may remain latent for a moment, but which can never be extinguished.

This revolution has often changed its centre, and its chiefs, but never its end; for its end is one of the eternal conditions of moral society,—the possession of one's self.

Now, the perception of right is universal in Italy.

Thus, as England makes of the Italian question a parliamentary passport; as the Emperor Napoleon undertook to shackle after having given the impulsion; all this is but ephemeral, and as little as it is insolent. The day upon which Italy shall be persuaded that such an event, such an European complication, or such a false alarm indicates the hour marked upon her dial to take up arms, God assisting, she will rise all alone at Palermo, at Venice, at Rome as at Milan, at Turin as at Naples. There are some deeds always ripe in the psychological history of the peoples, the putting into operation or the accomplishment of which may be deferred for a certain time, but can never be suppressed. France will be a republic; Poland, Italy, Germany, will be reconstructed, free and independent; Russia will go to Constantinople; Austria, the Porte, the Pope will be blotted out! And to what does all this tend? In faith, but to little purpose. Some fine morning the Parisian people will get up in a very bad humor, and all is done.

Austria, at this moment, is again concentrating her armies in Italy: it is very well. Her armies will, perhaps, ravage anew our fields, will bombard our towns, will slay thousands of men; but, at last, they will cover but a retreat. They perhaps will no longer fly; but they will leave, and there will be Italy. For, when we see a nation like this accept, in order to satisfy this instinct of autonomy and of vitality, even a candidature so grotesque as that of the Duke of Modena, it would be necessary to be as blind as the Prince de Metternich, as pusillanimous as King Louis Philippe, for the purpose of insisting upon provoking the cataclysm — of which 1848 has only been the prelude. The incapacity of the Prince de Metternich was fatal to Austria. He wished to make of Italy a province of the empire, when he ought to have made of it a democratic Hungary — the Kingdom of Italy; and by the attraction of liberty and unity draw in the other Italian provinces. What took place? what will now take place? Grave and incalculable misfortunes; but Austria will leave the Peninsula upon the day when Victor Emmanuel *shall be able* to cry out: "To me, Italians! Let us make Italy!" And we, the other *Know-Nothing* republicans, we shall be the first to resign; for we may deplore on seeing our mother abashed, but we cannot deny her for all that; she is a mother always, and may amend.

This is what was said by those who had, or appeared to have, faith in the Duke de Modena and the Duke d'Orleans, in 1831. This is what we say to-day.

I shall not relate here how Francis IV. was deceived by King Louis Philippe, and how he deceived the Italian patriots. The latter, nevertheless, were not discouraged. Having their eyes always turned toward democratic France, believing themselves already strong enough to display the tri-colored flag, Ciro Menotti, the chief of the patriots of Modena, resolved to give the signal for Italian action. On the evening of the 3d of February, 1831, about forty conspirators met at Menotti's dwelling to hasten the revolution, which was to take place on the 7th of February. For, from certain non-equivocal signs, it appeared that the Duke had information concerning it. And, according to the event, he had.

Joseph Ricci had besought his father, greatly compromised in the cause of Francis IV., to absent himself from Modena during the day of the seventh.

Called to the palace, menaced and constrained, Ricci had made some revelations; not enough, perhaps, to compromise his friends, but sufficient to save the Duke by putting him on his guard.

Francis IV. sent away General Zucchi, the most energetic and most dreaded of the conspirators; he ordered the suspected to be watched, guarded the city gates, and kept the troops confined in the barracks. When he knew that the principal group of the conspirators were assembled at Menotti's, he sent there his dragoons. Surprised, the patriots thought of defending themselves. They counted both upon Colonel Maranisi, who was with a band of insurgents, to fall upon the rear of the Ducal troops; and upon the countrymen, who were to penetrate into the city at night. In fact, these peasants had come, but they had found the gates of Modena closed; the Colonel had taken fright and gone to sleep in a tower; so that the forty conspirators were left alone to fight against the soldiers of Francis. Notwithstanding, the dragoons were put to flight, or they let themselves be, for the dragoons did not fire at the windows; almost all of which appertained to the party of liberty.

The dragoons then retired, when the Duke, having learned that they had wavered, regardless of the supplications of his minister, Mr. Scozia, put himself at the head of his troops, and led the artillery before the house of Menotti.

There were some families in this hotel who were innocent, among others that of Mr. Scozia: the Duke listened to nothing. Concealing himself behind a piece of wall, he commanded them to fire. The besieged riddled this piece of wall with shot, and still resisted for some time; but, having consumed their munitions, they were obliged to surrender. Menotti, who tried to glide over the eaves, was grievously wounded. Francis IV. ordered the prisoners to be thrown into the dungeon, and sent for the executioner before trying them. He already gave himself up to revenge, when, on the morning of the 5th of February, the news of the revolution in Romagna arrived. Seeing himself in danger, and knowing that all his subjects detested him, Francis IV. quitted Modena and fled to Mantua, carrying with him the dying Menotti.

Some time before, Menotti and the Duke had reciprocally assured each other's lives, by an article signed by both of them. Menotti had concealed this holographic obligation in a volume of Dante, in his library. At Mantua he reminded the Duke of their agreement. The latter demanded, as the price for keeping his promise, seventy thousand francs. The family of Menotti and the patriots collected this sum, but it was never presented to the Duke, who held his victim as an hostage and letter of exchange.

At Modena a provisional government was formed, which was immediately placed in relation with that of Parma.

The Parmasans had imitated the Modenese, and the Duchess Maria Louise had also fled toward Lombardy.

In the Romagna things took the same course.

The Pontifical States are equally as badly administered as the kingdom of Naples: but, with this difference, that in the Neapolitan States the institutions are good; and the men who ought to administer them always perverse; and that in those of the Pope, if by chance a man of good intentions is met with, he finds himself paralyzed by barbarous and superannuated institutions which compose the ecclesiastical rule. This is why the first word, under all circumstances, these revolted people speak, has always been, Reform! reform!

At the Congress of Vienna, Cardinal Consalvi, assisted by the Czar, had succeeded in separating the Legations from Austria; but she had retained there some advanced posts, by occupying the fortresses of Férraro and Comacchio. Austria regarded the definitive possession of these provinces as a question of time and opportunity.

Cardinal Consalvi, on the 14th of June, 1815, had protested against this occupation, and demanded the restitution of that part of the Legations situated on the left bank of the Po, which Austria retained in despite of everything. On his return from Venice, Consalvi, wishing to attach to himself the people, who had been habituated to a species of administrative autonomy for several centuries, promised many reforms, codes, tribunals, &c.; but, although his administration was not very tricky, he did not keep his word.

Leo XII. avoided him as being too liberal. The reign of terror, inaugurated under Pius VII., continued under Leo, and the Carbonari, whom they wished to crush, increased in number and in force. Cardinal Rivarola sentenced them, without mercy, to death, to the galleys, to transportation, and to exile.

Austria pushed on vigorously; for Austria heartily desired to show to the Italians that the happiest among them were those who were under her government. They understood perfectly, at Vienna, the spirit of the Peninsula.

In the secret instructions given by Prince de Metternich, on the 23d of September, 1830, to Count de Bombelles, chargé des affaires diplomatiques, in Lombardy, he said:

"So far as regards the interior situation of the Peninsula, Italy is without doubt the one, among all the countries of Europe, in which there is the greatest tendency to revolutions, that is to say, to accept forms of government liberal in the worse sense. In general, Italy has been materially prepared for these tendencies through the fall of all her ancient institutions, restored only in part or in name; and the desire of the Italians to obtain an independence free from all foreign influence—a desire which for one thousand years has not been satisfied—had taken possession to-day, more than ever before, of many minds. So that the tranquillity of the greatest part of Italy unfortunately cannot have but little guarantee *external to the national character*. Its inhabitants, in fine, demand another state of things and independence."

In fact, the Prince was not mistaken; for never was a revolution begun under more pacific auspices.

On the evening of the 4th of February, Professor Orioli, mounted upon a table of a café, in Bologna, had exposed to the people, and to the youth of the university, all the absurdities and immoralities of the government of the Pope. The people ran to take up arms.

Ferrare, Urbino, Spoleto, Imola, Ravenna, Cesène, Goutio, Forli, Sinigaglia, Viterbo, Fano, Rimini, Fermo, Faenza, Perouse, Jessi, Ancona, Camerino, every city of the State, followed the example of Bologna; and Rome herself would have crowned the work, if one of the conspirators had not revealed the secret to a friend of Cardinal Bernetti. So that, when Mr. Lupi, the chief of the liberals, gave the signal, he did not find any more the Papal troops which he had gained over and attached to the liberty party.

The first acts of the new government of Bologna were: the constitution of the provinces upon a more logical and juster system; the organization of the tribunal upon the French model; the convocation of the comitia in order to choose deputies and establish a form of government; and the declaration that the temporal government of the Pope in the Legations was abrogated in law and in fact.

For the rest, here is the way Cardinal Bernetti, in his note to Mr. de Saint Aulaire, of the 27th of March, 1831, related, in his own style, the progress of the revolution:

"Hardly was His Holiness seated upon the Pontifical throne, when a turbulent crowd rose in insurrection at Bologna, and uniting themselves to the revolutionists of Modena attempted to overthrow the domination of the Holy Chair. The Pontifical representation was obliged to leave; the rebels constituted a provisional government, which at first seduced the troops of the garrison and took them into their pay. This government possessed itself of the government chest, and disposed of it at will; it obliged the citizens to take up arms, to hoist the tri-colored flag, and proclaim liberty; and, declaring itself a nation and a power, decreed the forfeiture of the Pope and exercised domination over these provinces. These revolutionists believed themselves called to overthrow the Peninsula. They succored the rebels of Modena, and overran like madmen the Duchies and the Romagna, from Pesaro to Urbino, carrying rebellion into all the peaceful provinces. Unfortunately, the troops of the Holy Father all abandoned their flag and increased the revolutionary ranks. These bands marched against the fortress of Ancona, which, after a very short resistance, surrendered with its garrisons. In a few days the Marches and Ombria underwent the same fate; and a month had not passed over before the rebels were close to the capitol, where they had many friends. . . . . There remained to the government only the road to Naples, and that to Civita-Vecchia for having communication abroad; all the rest were occupied. The demagogues boasted of having powerful protection (the Duke d'Orleans); and some names formerly illustrious, to-day proscribed everywhere in Europe, were mingled in one revolution, and imposed themselves upon the population. Your Excellency is not ignorant of what family I speak (Bonaparte); but it will be ignorant perhaps that an individual of this family (Louis Napoleon) had the audacity to write directly to the Holy Father, in an insolent and menacing tone: ' *That the forces which advanced against Rome were invincible;*' charitably counselling him to deprive himself of the temporal government, and demanding of him a reply."

A sin of youth since greatly expiated!

In fact, Sercognani, to whom Queen Hortense had, a little before, made a present of a horse, advanced upon Rome; and the tri-colored flag was seen floating on the heights of Otricoli, fifteen leagues from the capitol. But, by paying him twelve thousand crowns, the Bishop of Spoleto, to-day Pius IX., made him fall back as far as Osimo.

In the meantime, the Pope and Cardinal Bernetti endeavored to intimidate the revolutionists through menaces and excommunication. They also promised clemency, but not a word of reform. The revolution spread itself.

The Cardinal Albani, after having conquered the irresolution of the Pope and shaken the confidence of Cardinal Bernetti in the success of the Sanfedistes, caused the resolution to be adopted recalling the Austrians; and on the 7th of March Cardinal Bernetti was able to post up the following notification:

"We announce with joy that there has arrived at the office of the Secretary of State the official news of the entrance of three grand columns of Imperial Royal Austrian troops at Modena, Parma, and at Pontelagoscuro, the 3 current, and that from thence these troops advance by forced marches into the interior of the Pontifical States."

Mr. de Saint Aulaire, the French Ambassador, protested by declaring:

"That the government of his very Christian Majesty was convinced that clemency and the voluntary concession of reforms, recognized as necessary in the provinces in which the revolution has spread, would be more salutary and satisfactory remedies than the support, always dangerous, of a foreign material force."

CHAPTER XI.

DIPLOMATIC INTRIGUES.

MR. DE SAINT AULAIRE'S protestation was but a form, or, at the farthest, a parliamentary weapon, at the service of Messrs. Sebastiani and Casimir Perier. They had declared that France adopted the principle of non-intervention; Mr. Sebastiani, by adding (session of 27th of January, 1831), that they would know how to make it respected; and Mr. Perier (session of 18th of March, 1831), that he would sustain this principle everywhere by the means of negotiations; for he did not concede to any people the right to force him to fight for her cause; the blood of Frenchmen belonged only to France.

Prince de Metternich had qualified the principle of non-intervention (despatch of the Chargé d'Affaires of France at Vienna, September, 1830) "from the strange pretext, by which the French government wished to introduce, for its convenience, a new law of nations, which had been never known before, and which was simply and purely the overturning of all the rules which had up to this time presided over the politics of the European States."

Notwithstanding this, the French government had agreed with Austria "that she might intervene, but after a repressive occupation an immediate evacuation." They were, besides, agreed that the French government should keep an eye on the Italian patriots residing in France, and cause all their projects to miscarry; the Austrian government, on its part, doing the same thing with the Legitimists and Bonapartists.

Mr. de Saint Aulaire, on his part, had assured the Pontifical government that King Louis Philippe would oppose all upturning, and he had offered to him the moral support of France to put down the revolutionary spirit and to oversee the refugees. Colonel Ravinetti, in a proclamation addressed to the Papal troops, spoke to them in the same way concerning the disposition of France. In fact, as soon as the news of the insurrection at Bologna arrived at Paris, the King had written to Gregory XVI., " to testify his interest and solicitude for him."

An opposition comedy against intervention was then played, to amuse the liberal party of France, but the King, underhandedly, permitted Austria to do all that she wished; and left Marshal Maison at Vienna, and Saint Aulaire at Rome, as well as Lafayette with the other members of Parliament at Paris, to protest.

The Duke de Reichstadt paid for all. He quickly died of a delicious poison — the kisses of the Archduchess Sophia!

Peace with monarchies, war against liberty and the people, this is to what the juggler of the revolution of July consented. But if France was belittled, the Prince was strengthened.

When the news of the Italian insurrection arrived in Paris, the people applauded. The Italian refugees prepared to march upon Savoy. Some of the French patriots favored the project, and all assembled in the South. At Lyons these patriots were warmly received by the prefect himself, Mr. Paulze d'Ivoi. Mr. Baune offered to place at their disposal two battalions of the National Guard.

They refused, not wishing to compromise the government, and left in small parties. "But at the moment," says Louis Blanc, in his magnificent *History of the Ten Years*, "at which some of them were about to reach the frontier, between Meximieux and the Pont de Chazet, they heard behind them the sound of horses' feet. Immediately some dragoons and gendarmes appeared, sent in pursuit of them, commanded by Mr. Carelet, a loyal officer, who spared no pains to soften the rigor of his mission. To resist was impossible; the unfortunate refugees reëntered Lyons, their hearts filled with despair."

The same fate attended Messrs. Lenati, Misley, Grillanzoni, Mantovani, Mori, Franceschini, Visconti, and Pépe, who were at Marseilles on the point of embarking, with thirteen hundred muskets, two pieces of cannon, and munitions. The prefect, Mr. Thomas, prevented their departure.

Louis Philippe kept his word.

During these transactions, the Austrians entered Parma and Modena.

The Duchess Maria Louise punished nobody, for she did not become wicked until she became old. But Duke Francis IV. became intoxicated with vengeance, declaring, "That the most sacred of a sovereign's duties was punishment." The Duke not finding the terrible Ricini sufficient, had called to his aid the Prince de Canosa. These three bloody fanatics understood each other marvellously.

The Prince was the brains; the Duke, the arm; Ricini, the axe. They commenced by organizing bands of brigands, whom they decorated with the name of soldiers, and who became assassins. These miserable creatures took an oath "to defend the invincible Archduke, who might be called the first soldier of the age; adding, that they knew individually all those who partook of the maxims of the villanous liberals, that they held themselves responsible for the life of this well-beloved father, of this great captain, by forewarning them that the justice of the soldier was no less sudden than sure."

The Duke disarmed his people, and delivered them to the mercy of these galley-slave clowns.

He immediately closed the schools, declaring that government and public instruction were incompatible. "Don't you speak of studies," said he to the fathers of families who demanded schools for their children; "give me men less instructed and more faithful to my person."

He established military commissions upon the model of those at Naples, published terrible laws, and a rescript in which he said, "that even in rendering justice, he performed a kindness." Afterwards he caused Menotti, Ricci, and many others, to be executed. The military commission condemned one hundred and four of them to different punishments — all exorbitant. Francis IV. wished to purge himself in the eyes of Austria from all complicity in the conspiracy. He wished to prove to

Prince de Metternich that he had conspired for the purpose of learning who were the factious, and baffling their plots; he wished to show that he had betrayed the guilty, and not accomplices.

Austria consented. Her soldiers assisted, arms in hand, in all the horrors of the Ducal reaction; and the court of Vienna rejoiced in seeing these States plunged in misfortune while her own remained peaceable. Nevertheless they remained peaceable because the Italian patriots themselves, in order not to violate the principle of non-intervention, had imposed upon the Lombards and Venetians the duty not to move, and had refused them succor!

But while the corps of Austrians of Marshal Frimont extinguished liberty in the Modenese and in the Parmesans, another, under the orders of Prince Bentheim, marched upon Bologna. In order not to give occasion to this intervention the Romagnol provisional government had disarmed the Modenese, commanded by General Zucchi, and recalled the insurgents who marched upon Rome. They had made some preparations by enrolling seven thousand men, one-third only of which were soldiers of the line, gendarmes, and custom-house officers. But the arms gave out. In all the insurgent provinces there were but sixty-five hundred muskets and a few thousand pikes, which General Grabinski had had forged.

Tuscany had prevented the sending of four hundred muskets and four hundred sabres purchased at Leghorn. Enthusiasm and good-will were on the side of the insurgents; but numbers, force, and discipline were on the side of the invaders. Besides, the central government was not sufficiently organized to unite the forces and views of all the insurgent cities.

On the 21st of March the Austrians presented themselves before Bologna. After a short resistance, they were permitted to enter. The provisional government had left for Ancona, protected in its retreat by General Zucchi. They fought the whole length of the road. But at Rimini, on the 25th of March, the encounter was longer and more formidable. General Geppet was twice repulsed, notwithstanding his forces were four times more numerous, and he was not able to occupy the city until night, when the insurgents had left. They marched upon Ancona, pursued for twenty-four hours by General Geppet, with artillery and a Congreve battery.

Ancona was not tenable. The garrison was composed of eight hundred men. The preparations of General Armandi and of General Busi were insufficient. It was necessary to surrender. The provisional government endeavored to come to an understanding with Cardinal Benvenuti, made prisoner at Osimo, where he wished to stir up the people, and march upon Ancona. There he was placed at liberty, and there he remained. The members of the provisional government capitulated with him; and on the 26th of March, 1831, this capitulation was published, signed by the Cardinal and by the members of the provisional government, Mamiani excepted.

Gregory XVI. did not wish to recognize it, protesting that the Cardinal " had ceased to be the interpreter of his will as soon as he had been made prisoner by the enemy." Gregory XVI. forgot that Benvenuti was free when he capitulated, and that he was supported by the Austrian army, only at a few leagues' distance.

The reaction commenced.

Cardinal Bernetti nevertheless promised *a new era.*

Ninety-eight patriots embarked upon a merchant vessel for Corfu, with papers in due form, were captured by an Austrian corvette commanded by Baron Bandiera, and thrown into the dungeons of Venice. Others, more fortunate, crossed Tuscany by forced marches and reached France.

Prince de Metternich was content. He compromised the Pontifical government by a reaction which should make it more detested, and he at last occupied the Legations.

9

CHAPTER XII.

TWO-SIDED POLITICS.

CARDINAL BERNETTI had promised *a new era;* but the Pontifical government, then as now, proved itself incorrigible, and resolved to change nothing, to concede nothing. The people were always, notwithstanding the revolution was suppressed, delivered up to the mercy of the malignant ignorance and good pleasure of the clergy. The diplomatists played then the same voluntary that they do to-day. Only the farce was two-sided: one for public opinion, for the journals, for the opposition party in France and England; the other for those behind the scenes, where the powers reciprocally deceived themselves.

The Austrians fortified themselves in the Romagna.

Prince de Metternich had promised "after the repression of the revolution an immediate evacuation." But to promise and to keep your promise, said the great statesman, are two things — between which frequently an abyss opens, sometimes a century passes — a war bursts forth, and in which diplomacy always mingles. And the latter, after having skirmished under every pretext and over every interpretation, closes the discussion, some fine day, by saying: State reason! or else, public safety!

or European police! equilibrium—fait accompli! and all the rest.

To Mr. de Saint Aulaire's note of protestation, Cardinal Bernetti had replied by his of the 27th March, 1831, in which he said, "that the succors demanded from S. M. I. R. Apostolic were not accompanied by any treaty; that the Austrian forces would not in any wise meddle in the affairs of the Pontifical government; that they would remain in the States of the Pope for the shortest possible time, and that the Holy Father, in order to establish tranquillity in his States, was occupying himself with administrative ameliorations."

It might be supposed that the Pontifical government could be believed on its word, but neither the people, nor Europe, nor the diplomatic corps ever believed it.

The abuses, or to speak better, the absurdities of this government were known. They had provoked a revolution; the Austrians had seized the occasion to spread themselves in the Peninsula. That awakened the jealousy of the government, and the dissatisfaction of the opposition in France; which might prolong the occupation and stir up troubles. It was then necessary to furnish a remedy.

The representatives of the five great Powers, authorized by their governments, assembled and drew up the memorandum of the 10th May, 1831. They admitted "that the States of the Church had need of ameliorations, to be founded on a more solid basis; that these ameliorations, which should become the foundation of a new era, ought, by an interior guarantee, to be protected from the changes inherent in the nature of all elective government. The principal guarantee was the general admissibility of the laity to the administrative and judicial functions, the judicial reform promised by Cardinal Consalvi in 1816; local administration, by the general organization of the municipalities elected by the population, and the foundation of municipal franchises; the organization of provincial councils destined to assist the governor of the province in the execution of his functions, and which should be consulted upon the interests of the province; these councils should finally conduce to the amelioration and simplification of the provincial administration, control the municipality, assess the taxes, and enlighten the government on the necessities of the province; a central establishment, charged, like a Supreme Court of account, with the control of the financial service of every branch of the administration, with large and independent powers, in order to answer the general expectation. This jury, or *administrative-consultum*, should have the stamp of stability, should be chosen by the municipal councils from among the notabilities of the country, and form a part of the council of State, nominated by the sovereign."

Austria had framed this *memorandum*. She had even caused the most liberal proposition to be introduced into it, well knowing that these things would appear to the Sacred College still worse than revolution, and if necessary, Austria would so make them appear to it. The court of Vienna knew in advance that the Pope would not accept of it. In fact, Mr. de Metternich had underhandedly counselled him by his ambassador, Mr. de Lutzow, and by the minister of Russia, Mr. de Gagarin, to repel this *charter*, knowing besides that this would prolong the agitation, and therefore the necessity for the intervention of the imperial troops would thus be justified.

But the session in France was about to open. Mr. Casimir Perier was likely to find himself opposed to the opposition, who could refuse him the budget of foreign affairs. It was necessary that he should attain a result, and he stood firm.

"We have suffered," said Marshal Maison to the Prince de Metternich, "your limited and transient occupation, in order to re-establish the Pontifical authority, and always by protesting. The end of this exceptional invasion is attained; the repression is complete; there is no more either rebellion or trouble; the evacuation ought therefore to take place."

There was nothing to be said in reply, the rather as the King said in confidence in the ear of Count d'Appony: "Once the session is closed, if there is need, you are close by, you will cross the Po, and do what you will."

The Prince de Metternich likewise did not show himself too hard.

But Cardinal Bernetti, although *in petto* well satisfied in disembarrassing himself from the Austrians, desired to be assured that he would not be left to the mercy of the revolutionists, whom he did not intend to conciliate by any concession. He coveted a guarantee of impunity for the government, on account of the non-execution of the *memorandum*, and demanded an assurance that he should not be abandoned.

Cardinal Bernetti understood that a new intervention was more dangerous than the first, because nothing authorized Austria to constitute herself, as was said in the debates, on the address of Mr. de Lafayette, "*a European supervisor.*" Thus to the note of Mr. de Saint Aulaire of the 2d June, he replies: "His Imperial Majesty has left the Holy Father judge of the time that the imperial troops should remain in the Pontifical States. He is then free to entertain or to reject the desire of the royal government of France. The Holy Father, however, demands this evacuation; but then only as your Excellency shall be authorized to prevent every species of danger which might result therefrom, by publishing an official act in which your Excellency expresses the lively regret with which the French government would learn of new troubles, the execration with which it would regard any one who should dare to be the author and provoker of it; and in which it should recognize the necessity in which the Pontifical government would find itself of again calling for foreign intervention and succor, without the country opposing the least obstacle thereto, and finding therein the least subject of quarrel."

The government of Louis Philippe having, first of all, concerted this strange note with the Prince de Metternich, had the impudence to accept it. In consequence of which, on the 15th July, the Austrians quitted the Legations.

Cardinal Bernetti was not sorry for it, for he kept his eyes upon the tactics of Mr. de Metternich. Through his agents, the great Austrian Chancellor already was commencing to form this society, Ferdinandea, which prepared the ground in the Legations for the definitive occupation of Austria. Through his special agent, Mr. Sebregondi, a friend and compatriot of the Pope, Mr. de Metternich endeavored to turn Bernetti out of the Secretaryship of State. Through the Austrian ambassador he placed obstacles in the way of the execution of the *memorandum*. And while the Austrian generals were loudly proclaiming in the midst of the populations the necessity for reform, through his dispatches, Mr. de Metternich showed himself devoted to the interests — to the preservation and to the tranquillity — of the States of the Church.

It was necessary, however, to do something. Cardinal Bernetti saw himself confronted by three exigencies. That of the people who demanded reforms and services and solid guarantees, and who had still the power to enforce them. That of liberal France and England, who wished firmly the execution of the *memorandum;* and that of the Sacred College, of the Sanfedistes, and of the three Northern courts, who hardly wished to accord anything, or to make only illusory concessions.

Gregory XVI. aimed to satisfy the exigencies of the people, by the formation of Swiss regiments and bands of brigands, which were picked up from the prisons of Civita-Vecchia, of Civita-Castellana, and Fort Saint Angelo, and which were called companies of the *Centurioni.* He soothed the demands of France and England by oily words, and by promises. Austria, the Sacred College, and himself, understood each other. So that Cardinal Bernetti believed himself to be sufficiently strong to publish the edict of the 3d of July.

Gregory XVI. eluded the *memorandum* in it in the most impudent manner. He declared that the municipal councils should not be elected by the people, but appointed by his legate, the prefect of the province; that these councils should not have the initiation, and that no proposition should be deliberated upon without having been previously submitted to the superior authority; that the delegate of the province could not approve the *procès verbal* of the sessions; that the laity should be excluded from the government of the Legations; that each province should be declared a legation.

On the appearance of this edict the public spirit revolted. The pro-legates themselves did not dare to publish it. The National Guards took up arms. Deputies from the provinces assembled together at Bologna under the presidency of the pro-legate, and on the 22d of August they decided "the absolute suspension of the publication of the edict of the 3d of July in the province of Bologna, and the suspension of its execution in the provinces of Romagna, where it had been already published."

A deputation was immediately sent to the Pope to supplicate him to accede to the voice of his people, and to grant the desired reforms.

At the same time the National Guard refused to take the Papal cockade, and no more money was sent to Rome.

The Pope listened to the commission of the deputies from the provinces, and promised, by equivocal words, that he would advise upon it. But as soon as he was sure, by means of the support of Austria, of being able to borrow three millions at 65 for 100, and that he had collected some troops, he changed his tone. The National Guards were ordered to take the Pontifical cockade; the universities and the schools were closed; the taxes were increased; the lawful order was declared disturbed, and, after having called anew for the intervention of Austria, the regulations of the 5th and 31st of October and those of the 5th, 15th, and 20th of November for the administration of justice were published.

By these regulations, and that of the 5th of November (Title x., Book 7, and Art. 11, Book 8, and No. 24 of the Preliminary Dispositions), political offences were judged by a supreme commission, without appeal, composed of ecclesiastical judges and presided over by a Cardinal; the inculpated were refused the liberty of a defence and the calling of witnesses, or to be confronted with their accusers! the encroachment of the ecclesiastical upon the civic tribunals was confirmed; every privilege of the ecclesiastical tribunals was sanctified, establishing for the priests every immunity, the right of asylum in sacred places, and, by special provision, as to the same offences, that they should be condemned to a less severe punishment; finally, even in the Legations, the tribunal of the Holy Office was established, which until then had never performed its functions but in Rome.

The indignation of the provinces was at its height. All the judges, advocates, attorneys, notables of every class assembled together in order to protest, and a deputation was sent to the Pope, in order to beg of him a suspension of the execution of these fatal edicts.

At the same time, they caused an address to be presented to the diplomatic body, in which they revealed the practices of the government which, principally in the dioceses of Montefeltro, Pesaro, and Rimini, raised and armed the peasantry, for the purpose of throwing them upon the peaceable citizens by exciting them to plunder.

The Pope gave notice that he would not receive the deputation of the departments, and on the 10th of January, 1832, Cardinal Bernetti notified the representatives of France, Austria, Prussia, and Russia of the resolution taken by His Holiness, to send troops into the Legations, to dissolve the civic guards, and to put an end to anarchy; reserving to his sovereign clemency the right to punish or to pardon, " and counting upon their aid, if the troops, meeting with resistance, should have need of it in order to make his legitimate authority prevail."

On the 12th, the representatives of the four Courts replied, each one separately, that the Pope was entirely right; that he was plainly within the laws; that they desired all that he desired; that the people were wrong in not being satisfied with the government of the Holy Father, and that they approved in advance, no matter what was done, ready to aid him by force, if he required it.

Mr. de Saint Aulaire especially made himself noticed by his conservative zeal, terminating his note thus: " If it should happen that the Papal troops, in their *wholly pacific* mission, should meet with a culpable resistance, and that some factious persons should dare to commence a senseless and fatal civic war, he made no difficulty in declaring that these men should be considered as the most dangerous enemies of the general peace, and that the French government, faithful to the politics so often proclaimed respecting the independence of the States of the Holy Chair, would employ, if necessary, every means to assure it."

We see that the *memorandum* had no longer any existence for the diplomatic body.

Cardinal Albani commanded the crusade; Baron Marschal, an Austrian, directed the military operations.

The National Guards of Bologna, Imola, Faenza, and of Forli would not listen to reason. They marched by the way of Césèna, whilst a deputation went to Cardinal Albani at Rimini, in order to beseech him to prevent the shock of civil war.

Albani would listen to nothing. Blind and ferocious, he was bound to finish it in any manner whatever.

His troops likewise were put in motion, and on the morning of the 20th of January, 1832, they were in sight of the civic guards. The latter had encamped near to Césèna, on the declivity which commanded the two routes which led to the town from Lavignano and from Cesenatico. They numbered 1800 men, without able commanders, badly armed, uninstructed in the management of arms, and without plans or reserve. The Pontifical troops, which came by the way of Cesenatico, were composed of about 4500 foot soldiers, 500 cavalry, and eight pieces of artillery. Arrived in the presence of the patriots, the combat commenced, and lasted two hours. The civic guards were beaten and dispersed. The Pontificals entered into the town in triumph, but without resistance. Notwithstanding this, it was given up to every species of excess, the faubourgs were sacked, the Church of Nôtre-Dame of the Mount was pillaged, and the convents of the nuns were invaded, and horrors committed in them.

The next day, and likewise without resistance, they penetrated into Forli. The peaceable population, the timid people, had gone to meet them, to receive them as brothers. A brawl took place, provoked expressly by the Papalists, who killed one of the common people. All at once the brigands, ranging themselves in order of battle, commenced to cry out: "Kill! Kill!" and, firing a volley, threw themselves with the bayonet upon this crowd of women, children, and old men, massacring a hundred, and wounding others in proportion.

Afterwards the town was sacked.

In the meanwhile, Cardinal Albani entered into Forli. They told him of the butchery; he called it a *sad accident*, as Mr. de Saint Aulaire had called the executions *Papal measures*. The Cardinal ordered 1500 francs *to be taken from the treasury of the town* and given to the wounded and despoiled.

The same thing afterwards took place at Ravenna, on the evening of the 7th of February. And another encounter of six hours took place on the 21st between the liberals of the lower Romagna and the Papalists coming from Ferraro.

In the meanwhile a part of the civic guard had deployed again upon Bologna with three pieces of artillery, which they had at last procured. This guard, united with the civic guard of Bologna, awaited the police of the Pope.

They did not dare to show themselves.

On the 19th of January, the Austrian General proclaimed at Milan his new intervention. On the 24th, the Imperial troops, encompassing in their midst the Papalists, entered Bologna. Cardinal Albani also entered there, accompanied on one side by Colonel Marschal, and on the other by Prince de Canosa.

He came in good company and acted accordingly.

The Austrians conducted themselves in an exemplary manner, and were everywhere received as liberators. They endeavored not to confound themselves with this scum of Papal bands. They even did more. When the population of Bologna assailed this rabble, and covered it with mud, stones, and hisses, upsetting even its Colonel in the mire, pursuing it to the barracks, where a fierce affray took place, the Austrians at first left them alone; afterwards they re-established order by chasing from the town *this gang of galley slaves* — the legions of the Holy Father!—as the Austrian commandant called them.

CHAPTER XIII.

THE DUPERS DUPED.

EVERYBODY believed that this affair was for the moment arranged. Austria appeared satisfied; King Louis Philippe believed himself relieved from embarrassment; Prussia, Russia, and the Italian princes rubbed their hands; and the Pontifical government breathed. The Italian people, being considered as nothing in this affair, they scarcely disquieted themselves about the state of its soul or the condition of its body. A singular, unforeseen incident, a stroke of audacity of Casimir Perier, an adorable perfidy of Cardinal Bernetti, happened to complicate the situation.

The debates upon the address to the Chamber of Deputies in France had been stormy. General Lamarque had moved that the evacuation of the Austrians, still occupying Ferrara, had not been complete; and Mr. de Lafayette had drawn up his amendment, terminating, " We regard the evacuation of the Roman States as definitive; and hereafter France will not consent, and will not suffer, as any one shall, the violation of this system of non-intervention." Mr. Sebastiani had stammered out some very confused words, without making any positive verbal engagement; but he had permitted the depth of his thoughts to be clearly perceived, that if the intervention should be renewed, things would not take place altogether as they had done.

But the intervention had been renewed; again they were about to find themselves in opposition to the Chambers. It was by all means necessary to take an honorable determination.

Casimir Perier had followed attentively enough the progress of foreign affairs to foresee that the Austrians would not delay to re-occupy the Romagna. General Sebastiani being sick — at that moment he had the portfolio — Count de Rayenal counselled him.

Some time previous, Casimir Perier had written to Mr. Saint Aulaire, "That His Majesty, King Louis Philippe would have seen with infinite pain a new intervention; and that he should constantly be careful to seize every occasion to convey it to the knowledge of the government of the Holy Father and to that of the diplomatic corps."

Mr. de Saint Aulaire did not fail to create the opportunity, and to express these dispositions of his court. But attention was scarcely paid to it; for King Louis Philippe was regarded as King Log.

The morning of the day upon which the news of the entry of the Austrians into Bologna arrived, Mr. de Saint Aulaire renewed his complaints and protestations to Cardinal Bernetti. Then, to give more force to it, he permitted himself to say that if things went on thus, France would find herself under the necessity of occupying in her turn some point in the Pontifical States. This declaration was simply an eloquent impulse of the ambassador: nevertheless, Cardinal Bernetti suspected that Mr. Casimir Perier wished to discover, by this adroit inquiry, the intentions of the Pontifical government. The Cardinal had also received some news, and he already knew in what manner the Austrians were behaving at Bologna, and the treatment which they had permitted to be inflicted, under their eyes, upon the Pontifical soldiers. He was very angry. He replied then with spiteful emotion to the Count:

"Ah, bah! You will not do it!"

The tone with which the Cardinal said these words struck Mr. de Saint Aulaire. He opened his eyes; and once at home, immediately forwarded to Paris his conversation with the Cardinal.

This despatch was likewise a thunder-bolt to Casimir Perier.

The next day, Mr. de Saint-Aulaire again saw the Cardinal, and gave a little more consistence to his proposition. He gave it as the probable form of the decision which the cabinet of the Tuileries might make. The Cardinal had during the night reflected gravely upon the proposition. He was always greatly incensed at the conduct of Prince de Metternich, who never neglected any occasion to set himself down definitively in the provinces which he had coveted for so long a time. Bernetti had foreseen all the advantage which he might draw from a simultaneous occupation by Austria and France, and had calculated that the only means of neutralizing the Austrians was to call in the French. Thus he replied still more brusquely and dryly than the day before:

"I say to you that you will not dare to do it!"

"But if we dare to," insisted Mr. de Saint-Aulaire, "what will you do?"

"Nothing!" coldly replied the Cardinal: "when a thing is accomplished, there is nothing more to be done in opposition to it."

Mr. de Saint-Aulaire knew enough about it. He broke off the conversation and returned home. Some hours after he reiterated in writing, under some pretext, the same question, by giving it more and more the appearance of a communication from his cabinet. The Cardinal understood that the ambassador desired a written document.

He did not hesitate to satisfy him, and threw upon paper the reply that he had given to him verbally.

Immediately the verbal reply and the letter of the Cardinal were despatched to Paris.

Casimir Perier was enchanted with it. He did not breathe a word to the King, and gave the order for the expedition to Ancona.

But while the expedition was preparing and the last despatches from Rome were arriving, Mr. de Rayenal, with the consent of the king, opened with Count d'Appony, and directly with Mr. de Metternich, the same negotiation. Only Mr. de Rayenal presented it to the Prince as a distant probability, and perhaps as a governmental necessity for the French cabinet. The Austrian Chancellor, at this overture, broke out into loud exclamations. But Mr. de Rayenal replied, that he had only to choose between this measure or a Laffitte cabinet, which would have embraced Europe. Mr. de Metternich, who, at bottom, was not as brave as he chose to appear in the eyes of Marshal Maison, in order to frighten King Louis Philippe, understood that there was scarcely time to jest; consequently, changing his tone, he replied: " Yes, simultaneous occupation with us as has been done in Greece and Belgium, in the proportion of the English forces in opposition to yours in the Scheldt; but a disciplined corps, under the most exact instructions, and under officers that can be relied upon; the flag of the Holy Chair everywhere, with some hundreds of men; the tri-colored flag shut up inside the barracks; finally, entire liberty to the Pontifical agents in the administration and police of the cities, as the imperial troops have done."

Thus were affairs situated with the Prince de Metternich. Negotiations were carried on at Rome. For, on both sides, the Prince and Casimir Perier had given instructions to their ambassadors to come to an understanding with the Holy Father in order to put in execution this possible decision of the cabinet of the Tuileries without chafing too much his susceptibilities, convenience, and interest. While these things were going on, the news arrived of the occupation of Ancona, at the same time that General Cubieres arrived, who was to conduct the negotiations.

But this is the way the thing had taken place.

As soon as the preparations for the little flotilla had ended, Casimir Perier had embarked eleven hundred men under the orders of Colonel Combes. He had given the command to the captain of the ship, Gallois, by remitting to him despatches, which he was to open when out at sea, to learn where he was to go and what he was to do. Casimir Perier took these precautions in order that he might not be opposed by the King. At the same time, with the consent of the King, he had sent General Cubieres to have an understanding with Cardinal Bernetti, to soften the blow, and to take command of the troops. But it happened that the journey of the General experienced as much delay as the flotilla had experienced of propitious winds. Arrived at three miles from Ancona, Captain Gallois stopped, and waited for two or three days the orders from Paris or Rome. Finding that his new instructions were delayed, that the effervescence of the population of Ancona was at its height, and that hostile preparations were being made in the fortress, he took upon his own responsibility to accomplish the operations, and on the night of the 22d to 23d of February, 1832, he disembarked upon the shore a part of his troops. The soldiers reaching the town at a running pace, burst open the gates with the axes of the sappers of the 66th, and entered.

In a moment the posts were surprised, Colonel Lazzarini, who commanded them, was made prisoner, and the troops disposed upon the square in such a manner as to command all the streets of the town, which rises like an amphitheatre from the shore. At noon Colonel Combes and the remainder of the soldiers were disembarked, in spite of the cannons on the mole which opposed them. They advanced upon the fortress, occupied by Colonel Ruspoli with 600 men and 36 pieces of artillery. But not a shot was fired. Casimir Perier had caused an agent to precede the flotilla, who should advise him of the public feeling in Italy; and Mr. Ditmer had succeeded very perfectly.

The fortress capitulated. The pro-legate refused to sign any paper, and retired. Immediately the tri-colored flag floated over the whole city, in the midst of the frantic acclamations of the populace, who fraternized with the French, and received them more like brothers and saviours. In the evening the town was illuminated; there were banquets, patriotic songs; and a staff officer, mounted upon a café-table, his naked sword in his hand, announced that the 66th was the avant-guard of the liberators of Italy. The enthusiasm was at its height; the more so as they saw the political prisoners, who were confined in the fortress and elsewhere, already placed at liberty.

This news, these details, were a thunder-stroke to everybody — to the Prince de Metternich, to the Pope, to King Louis Philippe, to the English Parliament — all furious against this sortie of Casimir Perier. But the one who appeared the most irritated was exactly the one who had played the angry man — Cardinal Bernetti. Cardinal Albani exclaimed, in full Consistory, " that since the Saracens, they had never seen anything like it ! "

Cardinal Bernetti wrote a very lively note, in which he said to Mr. de Saint-Aulaire : " His Holiness demands that the French troops that have in an hostile manner penetrated into Ancona leave without delay." The Pope ordered that the Papal authorities should leave Ancona for Osimo immediately, taking away everywhere the Pontifical arms and flag, and excommunicating the town and its occupants. Count Aberdeen demanded from Earl Grey, " if it was to favor Austria, or to succor the Papal government, that England had tolerated the expedition to Ancona." Prince de Metternich only, seeing himself fooled, moderated his anger.

He declared (correspondence of the French ambassador at Vienna) " that the measure itself, and the circumstances which had accompanied it, ought necessarily to make it an European affair, every cabinet being equally interested in questions which such an audacious violation of the law of nations provoke." And in order to decry the French, he ordered to be spread profusely the order of the day that General Grabowski, commandant of Bologna, had published, and in which he said: "That the French expedition could only be directed upon the same principles which had induced the troops of His Imperial Majesty and Royal Austria to enter into the Legations."

The imperial troops were nevertheless ordered to contract their circle and to augment their contingents: so that this handful of French were watched and kept under the eye and the muskets of fifteen thousand Austrians. Mr. de Saint-Aulaire, General Cubieres, and King Louis Philippe could answer nothing but, "Fait accompli! orders transgressed!" They affirmed that Captain Gallois had acted on his own responsibility; that he would be punished and dismissed; and that all should be repaired and every satisfaction given.

Casimir Perier replied to the King:

"Either that, or take back my portfolio!"

And he replied to Prince de Metternich, by the King's order, by sending to him the letter which Cardinal Bernetti had written to Mr. de Saint-Aulaire, in order to prove to him that the French expedition was desired by Rome, and that they pretended an anger which in reality they did not experience.

Prince de Metternich was appeased. He understood that Bernetti was his enemy, and that it was necessary to take away the ground from under his feet in order to crush him. His agent Sebregondi in fact undertook the work, and, having failed in 1833 and in 1835, succeeded in 1836, as we shall see.

Prince de Metternich gave ridiculous proportions to the occupation of Ancona—so far as the French soldiers nevertheless were willing to comply with them, for they did not comply with them always and in all things. He caused Gallois and Combes to be dismissed; repulsed every idea of reform; stifled every complaint; and was severe toward the liberals: in a word, the Grand Chancellor caused ignorance and barbarism to fall again upon the Roman States; closed the schools, opened the dungeons, corrupted men, children, and women, and cursed progress.

Lord Seymour, the English ambassador, understood it; and quitting Rome, where he had nothing more to do, addressed his well-known letter, under the form of a protest, to the diplomatic corps.

To this severe letter, Prince de Metternich replied:

"That it appertained neither to Austria, nor to any power, to dictate laws to the Sovereign Pontiff . . . . that the Italian governments saw in similar concessions an imminent danger to the safety of their own States; that these concessions were, in the eyes of the malcontents themselves, arms to destroy the government and to excite troubles . . . . that each new concession made, whether to the demands of the malcontent subjects, or to the request of a foreign nation through diplomacy, would be a derogation from the independence of the Sovereign Pontiff . . . that he had placed some experienced Austrian functionaries at the disposition of the Pope, in order to assist him in his difficult circumstances; and that His Imperial Majesty, holding the conviction that the proposed concessions for changing the Pontifical proceedings had only in view, in the opinion of those who claimed them, but the freeing them entirely from the power of the Holy Chair, through regard for the repose of Italy, the Emperor considered himself obliged to refuse his support to such demands."

And all was said!

CHAPTER XIV.

DISMISSION OF BERNETTI.

GREGORY, who feared so much the revolutionists, should have pampered Cardinal Bernetti, and have placed this precious Minister under glass. It did not thus take place, and for a reason. Bernetti, who was ambitious of power but for himself only, did not love Austria, though using her for himself. But Austria is the Holy Ghost of the Holy Chair. Prince de Metternich hated Bernetti, who had fooled him. He had frequently advised Gregory XVI. to dismiss him and find a better.

But Gregory, who perhaps recollected the fate of Leo XII., had always eluded the demand of the all-powerful Austrian Chancellor. Finally, one day, the latter caused to be intimated to him very honestly, this: "Holy Father, your Cardinal Bernetti does not please me; I do not want him! I cannot reckon blindly upon a man who is capable of saying publicly to France: Clear out! and in secret: Remain! He must be changed; he must."

Bernetti had gone to Naples, in the hope of getting a concordat from His Sicilian Majesty. Prince de Metternich would have wished immediately to replace him by Cardinal Lambruschini, more of an Austrian than Austria herself; but the French ambassador moderated the Teutonic heat. They were then obliged to make Monseigneur Capaccini officiate *in the interim*, who was very able and a great Austrian, who would have taken his orders from Cardinal Lambruschini.

It was in 1836. Gregory XVI. this time wished to rid himself of the Cardinal who treated him like a master. Bernetti had his famous gout, and Latour Maubourg was absent. The Pope then went to pay a visit to the Cardinal, taking good care to ask for a drink; and, in a very gay tone, said to him:

"Cardinal, we have thought of your health."

"Ah! how good Your Holiness is!" exclaimed the Cardinal.

"The affairs of State," continued Gregory, "are a burden to Your Eminence."

"But by no means, Holy Father, by no means," repeated the Cardinal.

"Yes," replied Gregory, "yes; the affairs of State are too heavy for Your Eminence's age. We are going to disembarrass you. Let Your Eminence take the trouble to present me with your resignation; I am ready to accept it."

"Impossible, Holy Father," said the Cardinal, with a slight saturnine smile.

"How impossible, Cardinal? how? Nevertheless . . ."

"Impossible, Holy Father, I tell you," replied the Cardinal; "the gout hinders me from doing it."

Gregory XVI. breathed. He had given to the *impossible* of the Cardinal a political signification. Gregory then left, hissing out an *ite missa est*, according to his habit when he was gay or tipsy. Arrived at the Vatican, Gregory XVI. commenced at once to write a long letter. He wrote a page of it; then he drank; then he sent his major-domo, in the evening, to ask concerning the health of the Cardinal and to remind him of the resignation. Cardinal Bernetti did not reply to the cajoleries of the major-domo, but in a jovial tone related to him his history, recalling all the services which he had rendered to the Holy Chair. The Pope received this answer and went to bed.

Next day he finished his letter, adding to it another page of caresses and of flatteries, and ended thus: "Cardinal, I accept the resignation of Your Eminence."

Gregory then ordered the Dean of the Sacred College to be called, Cardinal Pacca, and gave him the commission of bearing his letter, without saying anything.

Seeing that it was a decided affair, taken on the sudden, before he had prepared his defence, Bernetti hesitated no longer. He resigned his place, cured of the gout, and sent his resignation. And as he had received some days before a decoration of I know not what Order, in which there is an animal with horns, he showed it to his friends, and said:

"You see it! I have left the ministry with a horn!"

Cardinal Lambruschini succeeded him: and *verus incessu patuit Deus!*

CHAPTER XV.

TRAVELS OF GREGORY XVI.

CARDINAL LAMBRUSCHINI was a monk also, like Gregory XVI. Tall, full of aristocratic haughtiness, headstrong, of a piercing wit, obstinate, hardly sensible to skilful flatteries and to women's smiles — for tears found him like steel — he willed what he willed. He understood men, business, the proprieties of life; he was not a stranger to the intrigues of the courts of Europe, having followed the diplomatic career; he was initiated into the principles of the Holy Alliance, and gave to them the consecration of the Papacy. Legitimacy was his natural religion; France, his *delenda Carthago est;* Italy—impenitent Spartacus—a rebel and atheistical land, which it was necessary to temper again by discipline, by force, and by punishments.

In choosing this Secretary of State, Gregory XVI., who had believed that he was ridding himself of a master, gave to himself a tyrant.

In fact, Gregory had such fear of him, that as soon as he saw him peep over the threshold of his chamber, he exclaimed:

"It is very good, Eminentissime; it is very good; it is remarkably good. Your Eminence has done marvellously! Go on; go on!"

And he signed without reading! and if he was tipsy he immediately came to his senses; if he lay snoring under a tree in the garden, at the noise of his Cardinal's steps he quickly jumped up as active as a young man of twenty years of age. But His Holiness became tired. The notion seized him to travel into the Provinces.

This desire thwarted Lambruschini enormously; it thwarted the Consistory. Gaetanino had so over-excited this old man's brain that there was no way of making him give it up. The journey was decided upon.

Gregory desired to see Ancona. Thirty carriages, and six wagons to carry the silver plate, accompanied him on the journey. He was followed by four ministers, by prelates, by major-domos, with *maîtres d'hôtel*, with buffoons; further, by two prelates, *camericri segreti*, by Arpi the trainbearer, by an almoner, — although Gregory had never given an alms in his life! — by the crossbearer, the director of the posts, the grand *ecuyer*, thirty of the noble guards, all the carbineers, four *monsignori*, masters of ceremonies, among which was that Monseigneur Brancandore whose exploits Aretino would have blushed to relate, four valets of the cape and sword, the doctor, Gaetanino, and the cook, Salvatore Fancelli; then an army of domestics, scullions, makers of ices, grooms, purveyors, and four *bussolari*, or officers destined to open the door for His Holiness. Afterwards came the Cardinals, the Bishops, the canons, the monks, who attached themselves to the cortege all along the route, and forty-five musicians — the music of the dragoons — who should play when the Pope dined.

Gregory loved very much the polka and the Neapolitan *tarantella;* he regaled himself with them during the two hours that his dinner lasted.

The principal occupation of this journey was good eating. In the morning he took chocolate, or even a breakfast *a la fourchette;* at one o'clock, dinner; in the evening, supper. Between whiles, coffee, ices, brandy, cakes, and sweetmeats in abundance.

Gregory ate a good deal, and drank immoderately. He sealed his dinner with two bottles of champagne. These dinners were so richly served, that it suffices to say that the dinner of the lowest domestics was composed, besides the entrée and dessert, of ten courses, and a bottle of champagne for each person. At Loretto they consumed, in three days only, for the salt for the ices, 600 crowns! (3,240f., $648, gold.)

In the intervals of the repast, Gregory visited on foot the churches and convents, gave benedictions, talked small talk in the convents of the nuns, related smutty stories, fabricated miracles, and amused himself. The people and the State were scarcely remembered by the sovereign of the Church. There was no business, and particularly no pardons; those persons who went to visit the Pope were literally robbed by the domestics in the ante-chambers, who demanded and exacted gratuities.

Everybody shunned the dwelling of the Vicar of the poor Christ: one was pillaged there as in the forest of Bondy.

The most remarkable events of this journey were these: at Loretto the Pope had an indigestion, and at night they carried his sheets, escorted by torches, carbineers, noble guards, and many Bishops in ceremonial robes. It would have required but little to have made them expose them to the admiration of the faithful. They inspected the saucepans of the *Sanctum Sanctorum* of Gregory XVI.—the kitchen. They scolded the cook. Monseigneur Barbolami had a manual correction administered to the scullions; finally, Gregory cast out this unfortunate indigestion, a little of it upon everybody—but principally upon the revolutionists! It had been a scandal and sacrilege to avow the truth. A Vicar of God who ate like a porter? Fie then! that would have been a Protestant calumny! Besides, at Jessi, the people finding themselves mistaken in their expectation of an amnesty, organized an illumination with tri-colored lamps. This so frightened Gregory, that he made everybody stay up during the night, the dragoons under arms; and next morning he left before daylight.

The journey lasted a month and a half, and cost 400,000 crowns — or two millions of francs! ($400,000 in gold.)

Three years later, in 1843, the Holy Father wished to make a second journey to Terracina. There he received the visit of Baron Rothschild of Naples. This little man, as ugly as he was rich, having no more of a nose than he had of charity, brown as a rusty penny, a most charming spoiled child, impertinent as a nobleman's lackey, presented himself to His Holiness in white satin breeches, like Charles X. at the coronation of

Rheims, in a dress embroidered with gold, and decorated with all the decorations of Europe which he had gained as gratuities with his loans. His Eminence, Cardinal Tosti, seeing the Messiah of the public debt of Europe, solicited the honor of carrying the hat and sword of the descendant of the tribe of Judah, who permitted him to do it. He would even have taken off his boots, as the Vicar of Louis XIV. did Lauzun's, if he had not worn pumps with diamond buckles.

At Civita-Vecchia, Gregory wished to go a fishing — doubtless in honor of St. Peter — and to bless the galley-slaves. For Gregory had a passion for blessing, particularly when he was a little tipsy. At Rome, whenever he had any difficulty in his digestion, he went into the ante-chamber and drenched with benedictions the carbineers, the Swiss, the pack of lackeys, and even the frescoes on the ceilings.

When the galley-slaves of Civita-Vecchia were in the presence of His Holiness, they began to cry, properly: "Pardon! pardon!" Gregory XVI. blessed, passed on, and accorded no pardon. He could present them with the gift of an eternity of happiness in paradise, but would not remit them a few years from jail.

Afterwards Gregory went to eat the red mullet, cooked *à la maître d'hotel*, which he had caught a few hours before.

On this journey the suite of the Pope caused to

be brought in 70,000 crowns' worth of smuggled goods.

And this journey, made against the wishes of Lambruschini, as we have said, cost 80,000 crowns, which Cardinal Tosti placed at the orders of His Holiness, without counting what the treasury since had to pay.

Besides these journeys, Gregory went every year to enjoy his villéggiatura at Castle Gandolfo; he made an excursion to the Capucin Convent of Genzano, to eat the famous lenten dinner that these Cordeliers served up to him, and paid some visits to his neighbors, the Barberini, Orsini, Torlenia, who would have willingly escaped them. In all these journeys Gregory XVI. was received under a canopy, to the sound of bells, the houses decked with flags, and the people in their best clothes. They expected *mirabilia* from this man, whom they kept, said some one, cloistered like an odalisque, and whom they considered as ignorant of his people's misfortunes. He was now in a position to see for himself. But the journeys were finished without any other inconvenience than a few drunken fits! Gregory amused himself greatly, and gave himself up to a comparative study of the wines of his States. The municipalities ran into debt, and ruined themselves to make much of him, in the hope of an amnesty; but the amnesty did not enter into the order of ideas of the Vicar of God. He returned to Rome, and all continued as it had done before. *Animalia ibant et animalia revertebantur!*

Only, as Cardinal Lambruschini perceived that Gaetanino and his wife were not sufficient to distract His Holiness any more, he added to them some Capucins, who, by their grotesque tricks and their convent jests, amused him very much.

Gregory pleased himself mostly in seeing them tipsy, and making them roll in the basins of cold water in the gardens of the Vatican.

In the meantime Lambruschini reigned and governed.

But as he was not able to perform the whole labor of the reaction, he invested with his irresponsibility and with his whole power, Virginio Alpi, Colonel Freddi, Atilio Fontano — men who would have been pointed out as *braggadocios* of the South in 1816 and 1817 in France — and, above all, Nardoni.

CHAPTER XVI.

FILIPPO NARDONI.

NARDONI, a Colonel of the carbineers, is one of the most influential men of the real court of Rome, one of the principal wheels in this government of charity and honor. Behold under what circumstances he began to dawn upon the scene.

Brigandage, as well as smuggling, is a normal element in the social life of the people of the Roman States. These two crimes are a protestation against the government of the priests — an opposition. I should almost say an opposition party, for brigandage and smuggling are in reality only the communion of the people raised in opposition to the communion of the tonsorial caste. This is the reason why a brigand and a smuggler are not considered as dishonorable persons in the Apostolic States.

In 1841, I assisted in getting a cause ready for trial at Bologna. A handsome young man presented himself as a witness. The judge asked him: "Witness, what is your profession?"

"*Tirino!*" (smuggler,) answered the young man — as if he had said, advocate or doctor! And the register wrote down *tirino* without changing a muscle.

In the provinces of Campagna and Marittimo, a young girl would repulse as a coward a young fellow who should demand her hand before having been *à la macchia*, (becoming a brigand.) In these provinces, likewise, at this epoch, everybody was more or less a brigand, or had something in common with them. When any one did not take the musket, as a principle, or did not go to demand protection from them against the persecution of the police, as carbonaro, he became a receiver of stolen goods, a treasurer-merchant, spy, colporteur, or simply a plenipotentiary between the *men of the mountain* and the gendarmes, between the chief of the band and the Pontifical pro-legate, who was going to govern the province. They agreed upon the quota of booty each should take, and all was arranged. The pro-legate slept, the gendarmes went to give chase to the brigands in the village taverns, and the gentlemen of the mountain labored in peace.

These brave men generally respected the poor, and commonly the laity of the country. They sought in preference ecclesiastical game; but chiefly the birds of passage — the foreigners. At length this forced tax enraged the priests; and the diplomatists made remonstrances, in order to guarantee the free passage of their fellow-citizens who were too proud to have their passports viséd by the ambassador of the Gasparone at Rome, when they wished to proceed to Naples or through Tuscany. Leo XII., who then reigned, had no more taste for the brigands, because he thought them the accomplices of the liberals. He then resolved to strike a grand blow.

The province of Frosinone was the centre of the brigands' kingdom, and for this same reason was the place most desired by the prelates who wished to make a fortune. They first put into their own pockets all the extraordinary expenses which they were allowed for the repression of brigandage, and afterwards they honestly gained their part of the benefits. Leo XII. had sent delegate after delegate to Frosinone; but, except some unfortunate little beggars, or some modest carbonaro, whom they had hung with a flourish of drums and trumpets, disguising them like brigands, never had a real, pure-blooded, authentic brigand mounted the Jacob's ladder of the gibbet. Hungry for this *rara avis*, Leo XII. appointed Monseigneur Zacchia delegate for Frosinone. He allowed him a suite of police and gendarmes that would have tempted a king of Naples; he gave to him full powers and a blank order upon the treasury. Monseigneur Zacchia had, besides, the command of the military forces of the province. He packed carefully in his trunks a large provision of good intentions, and commenced his journey.

Arrived at Frosinone, the Antonelli family descended from Sonnino, and went to pay him a visit. The conference between Monseigneur Zacchia and the father of His Eminence Jacopo Antonelli lasted many hours; after which Filippo Antonelli returned to the mountain. Monseigneur Zacchia, who was in train to be installed, ordered the trunk in which he had placed his good intentions, in order not to derange them, to be thrown into the granary. This excellent prelate was then soon seen commencing his journey for the purpose of visiting the province. He was seen zealously employing himself in the chase of the wild boar and the carbonari, giving and receiving sumptuous dinners, receiving presents and never making any, surrounding himself with pretty women, amusing himself, entertaining, making himself to be entertained and treated splendidly, making himself likewise to be paid splendidly by the treasury and by the communes for the expenses of the journey, and that of the princely cortege that followed him; but of the capture or pursuit of brigands there was not even a pretence.

Leo awaited this royal game!

At last, tired of waiting, His Holiness sent to seek the Colonel of the carbineers, and obliged him to speak openly. This honest man, to whom Monseigneur Zacchia had granted too niggardly a portion, confessed everything. He said that the brigands, the receivers of stolen goods, and Monseigneur Zacchia formed only one and the same family. Leo XII. at once dismissed his delegate and recalled him to Rome.

The fate of this prelate was curious. Dismissed by Leo XII., Gregory XVI. properly appointed him governor of Rome, and superintendent of the police. One day Monseigneur Zacchia took the singular fancy of rendering justice in the famous lawsuit of the infamous Don Abo. It was a simple fancy upon his part; but it cost him dear. Gregory took the thing as a piece of irony, as a personal insult, as an outrage to his government, as a revolutionary act, and dismissed him without mercy, by creating him Cardinal. His Eminence was not able to be consoled for his disgrace, and died from chagrin.

Leo XII. sent into the Campagna and the Marittimo Cardinal Pallotta, as legate *à latere*, with the full power of a sovereign. This Cardinal fixed his residence not at Frosinone, but at Ferentino; he made the Bishop of this town his chamberlain, gave himself a guard of honor mounted on horseback, and aides-de-camp, surrounded himself with a court more numerous than that of the Duke of Lucca; and after having addressed an order of the day to the troops, a proclamation to the brigands, and a manifesto to Europe — so curious that a copy of it will bring four crowns — he began his circuit through the province. Leo XII. feeling all the ridiculousness of his legate, which was made a subject of mirth in the Roman saloons, hastened to recall him. Cardinal Pallotta, wounded, refused to obey; and he even undertook to offer an armed resistance to the orders of the Pope, when an officer of the carbineers and new categorical orders from the Cardinal-Vicar, determined him to return to Rome.

Perceiving that his prelates and Cardinals were incapable, Leo XII. thought that, in order to put an end to the brigands, he would have to invest a layman with a special command. A layman! he immediately reflected, and what will they say in Europe and in the States? That the priests are good for nothing, and that the States must be secularized! Softly; that will carry us too far. No laymen!

By dint of thinking on it, nevertheless, Leo discovered a combination that settled his business. He knew that Monseigneur Benvenuti had an intimate friend, Giacinto Ruinetti, colonel-commandant of the first regiment of carbineers. This Benvenuti was a good man, a gourmand, a sluggard, not affected in fact by his self-love, in short, an easy and accommodating character. He appointed him then pro-legate of the provinces of Campagna and Marittimo, but on condition that he should take with him Colonel Ruinetti, and blindly follow his counsel in the business of exterminating the brigands. Benvenuti promised everything that the Pope desired, and he and Ruinetti set out.

This latter had for his secretary the quartermaster Filippo Nardoni. This honest lad had been twice condemned — once to the pillory for having robbed, a second time to the galleys for having forged a passport. He had succeeded in escaping from the galleys. Having made up his mind to change his conduct, and to serve as a hunter of game, he had arranged with the police, and had entered into the gendarmerie. Tired, however, of being quarter-master, he was desirous of becoming an officer. The Cardinal-Minister of war deeming the demand incongruous, had refused it. Nardoni in the meanwhile longed after the epaulets.

He began by showing himself greatly attached to

Colonel Ruinetti, and very devoted to Monseigneur Benvenuti. But the cunning fellow quickly learned, that while he was equally protected by his two chiefs, he would remain eternally quartermaster. It was necessary that he should render his services to one of these at the expense of the other, should compromise himself with one of them against the other: with which should it be? Here was the difficulty. The choice might become dangerous — Nardoni did not lose his wits. He decided to devote himself to both; but secretly to each. Thus he began to calumniate Monseigneur Benvenuti, near to Ruinetti during the day, in the office of the Colonel; and in the night, he disguised himself as a *ciocciaro*, a peasant, and went to relate to Monseigneur Benvenuti every possible evil about his colleague. In brief, the two friends, the gendarme and the Bishop, soon became embroiled, and began to write to Rome against each other secretly, and often by anonymous letters. Nardoni wrote the despatches for both sides.

In the meanwhile, the extirpation of brigandage went on. They had taken some brigands, and had duly hung them; they had also hung some receivers of stolen goods, hunted the remainder of the bandits from place to place, and had hemmed them in on the tops of the mountains, which were covered with woods, and were very precipitous. In a sense the expedition promised an happy issue, when the dissension took place between Ruinetti and Benvenuti.

Jealous of each other, each one fearing lest the glory of the success might not be attributed to him, they slackened their pursuit. The brigands took breath; they even gained courage, and commenced to fight against the gendarmes. The matter failed; but Nardoni was appointed an officer.

It is known how Monseigneur Pellegrini accomplished his design upon Gasparone by capitulation.

Such were the beginnings of Nardoni. This promised well.

For the Neapolitans who have seen Campobasso, Morbillo, Campagna, Mazza; for the Sicilians who have seen Cioffi and Maniscalco—monsters—Nardoni might pass for a St. Vincent de Paul; but, for the Romans, the wretch was scarcely less atrocious.

Cardinal Lambruschini, so careful of his autonomy and of the entire and irresponsible exercise of his authority, had not, nevertheless, the initiation of the police. This initiative appertained to Austria; and it was only upon this condition that he was appointed and remained Secretary of State, as certain letters found in his house have proved, and which I had in my hands, at the period of his flight from Rome in 1848.

The grand Provost of the Austrian police in Italy was the Duke of Modena: the soul and brain of this Duke was the famous Prince de Canosa, ex-minister of the police of the court of Naples. It was then from Modena that Lambruschini drew his inspirations and Nardoni his examples. Austria had nothing to complain of about Nardoni; but the Roman people were more difficult to please.

Nardoni, in fact, had so just an opinion of his own merits, that after the death of Gregory XVI., during those four months in which Pius IX. had the eruption of liberalism, he cut off his hair and his mustache, changed his name, and escaped to Malta.

In 1849, when the conspiracy took place at Gaeta against Roman liberty, Nardoni, who had always maintained the secreted sons of the Police of the Sacred College, and knew at his fingers' ends all the *Sanfedistes* of the State, took the packet-boat *Marie Christina* for the purpose of returning to Civita-Vecchia. He then attempted what but lately Anviti essayed to do at Parma. Arrived at Catania, a traveller who had recognized him went on shore and denounced him.

A man kept himself constantly in his cabin, lying down, carefully enveloped in the bed-clothes. He called himself Mr. Mussoni.

"Mussoni, it is very well now," said the Captain of the National Guard to him, who went to arrest him on the packet-boat; "but formerly? Ha! recollect yourself! Have you never been anything else?"

"It is possible, sir; still, I do not believe in the metempsychosis myself," replied Mr. Mussoni.

"But I do, myself," replied the Captain; "I say to you that you were formerly Mr. Nardoni."

"Sir . . . ."

"Let us go; get up, and follow me."

"But you are mistaken, sir, ..."

"Do you prefer that I should make the people of Catania come on board by chance?"

"Ah, damnation!" he then exclaimed; "shall I then never again find upon the earth a foot of ground willing to support me?"

"Pardon, sir," replied the Captain, very politely. "I am going to prepare seven feet of it for your service."

While these things were going on, the people of Catania grumbled, and wished *son Delcanetto de Rome!*

Mr. Gagliani, who had made the capture, capitulated. He promised to produce Mr. Nardoni, provided that they would not do him any harm. The people agreed.

Alongside of the guard was a poultry merchant. Mr. Gagliani took an enormous open work cage, in which the merchant kept his turkeys, enclosed his prisoner in it, and suspended the cage to a window, as a grisette does her lark. The joke saved the man. All Catania ran to see Plato's strange *biped without feathers;* and the children amused themselves by throwing cheese at him to make him peck at it.

Mr. Nardoni, reassured, perpetrated puns.

Finally, they took him from this pillory in the evening, and reconducted him secretly on board the vessel. Mr. Nardoni left for the purpose of conspiring for the interest of the reaction, and he is at this moment chief of police at Rome, greatly in favor with Pius IX., who plays with him his little match at billiards, when Monseigneur Stella is with Madame Adelaide.

Nardoni had in his trunks silver, papers, plans, and arms; and the terrible revolutionists, who caused so much fear to the *universe*, did not even search the trunks of the friend of Antonelli and of His Holiness.

The system of Lambruschini and of Nardoni and Company aroused again the public execration, and drove the people to despair. Attempts at revolution commenced. At Viterbo, in 1839; at Bologna, in 1843; at Rimini, in 1845; .... there were some insurrectionary efforts, which were put down, and punished by frequent condemnations to death, and to the galleys for life. I shall not recount the details of these troubles, and of this terrible reaction. Mr. Farini has done it; and everybody knows the beautiful work of Massimo d'Azeglio, *I Casi di Romagna*. My recital would then only be a repetition, even where it might enter into the plan of my work to discuss them. The name of Gregory XVI., when uttered, accompanied with an epithet of contempt up to that time, is no longer heard but with a cry of malediction.

Gregory knew nothing, and wished to know nothing about it.

He desired to die in peace. He saw nobody;

the few, rare individuals who went to visit him, made a solemn promise not to speak to him about business. If, perchance, any one failed in his promise, at the first word which he dared to utter, the Pope commenced crying, " Treason! murder!" and the unlucky one who had undertaken to trouble the tranquil beatitude of God's Lieutenant, was driven out, battered and bruised.

Yet this vegetable life had one magnificent moment. It was when it was no longer the Sovereign of Rome who acted, but the Pope; when it was no longer the Monarch who spoke, but the Vicar of Christ. The Pope of the Western Church addressed himself to the Pope of the Eastern Church — the Czar of the Vatican to the Czar Nicholas. Let us recall it.

CHAPTER XVII.

POPE AGAINST POPE.

AFTER having suppressed the Polish revolt, the Emperor Nicholas had perceived that the danger would always continue, would always be threatening as long as there should be any Catholics in his dominions; and that these Catholics, as one part of their duties, had displaced a resident sovereign by a foreign sovereign. It was necessary at all cost to redress this anomaly, and to blot out this enormity. He thought about it, and consequently correspondence with the Court of Rome was opened.

"The last Polish Rebellion," wrote Prince Gagarin to Cardinal Bernetti, in his despatch of 20th April, 1832, "which has presented so menacing an aspect, might have easily acquired an immense expansion if it had not been repressed by the troops of His Imperial Majesty; that the Holy Father may be convinced that in supporting the rights of his throne he will defend in the most strenuous manner those also of religion. The suppression of the revolt in Poland has been an immense service rendered to all powers, upon which rest at this moment the guarantees for the preservation of social order. The return of similar alarms will menace the whole of Europe with evils that will push it towards an abyss, the depth of which would terrify the imagination to look at, and from which the power of the Emperor has for the moment preserved it."

Imbued with these principles, cut off from the world which could have opened his eyes, and circumvented, Gregory then launched his famous encyclical of the 9th June, 1832, by which he outraged and condemned the Polish revolution.

"We know," said he, "that these calamities (revolution) have had no other origin and have been executed only by certain *fabricators* of lies and deceits, who, under the name of religion, in this miserable age, rise up against the legitimate power of princes, filling their country, torn from all dependent ties, with grief and mourning."

And he gave orders to watch with great attention, and to apply every care " lest the cheats might teach more of these novelties and false and erroneous doctrines," (nationality!) *ne dolosi homines ac novitatum propagatores erroneas doctrinas, falsaque dogmata!*

This was all that Czar Nicholas demanded for the purpose of undertaking a strange and rude persecution against the Polish Catholics, and preaching the Greek religion. It was all that he required to oblige the Catholic clergy of Poland to condemn as sacrilegious the national war, and to confound it with that of religion.

The treaty of Warsaw, of the 18th September, 1773, had said, Art. 8, " And his said Majesty (the Czar) and his successors will not make use of their sovereign rights, to the prejudice of the *statu quo* of the Roman Catholic religion, in the aforementioned countries."

The religion of their fathers remained then recognized in the dismembered nation. The ukase of 16th of December, 1812, nevertheless, ordering the Bishops, under pain of death, not to correspond with the Pope upon religious affairs, had safely guarded the authority of the Prince, and eliminated the intervention of a foreign prince in the conduct of his subjects. But this no longer sufficed.

They saw the necessity of suppressing Catholicism, which, rebellious in England, an agitator in Germany, an oppressor in Italy and Spain, a conspirator against liberty in France, fatal everywhere! confounded itself with the national idea in Poland. They undertook the work, but with a zeal so unskilful, that State reasons took the semblance of fanaticism. Protestations commenced. The nobility of Vitepsk, the priests of Novogrodek, the united Greeks of Uszaz and those of Luborriez, the Jesuits, — the clamor of the Catholics was universal.

"For some time," said the nobility of Vitepsk in their petition to the Emperor, "every means has been employed to draw the united Greeks to the dominant religion. . . . The means employed fill the soul with terror." The parishioners of Uszaz added, that, having protested their desire to remain faithful to their religion, "the commission commenced pulling out our hair, striking us on the teeth till the blood came, striking us upon the head with blows, putting some in prison and transporting others." So that one might have said, that Poland was thrust back to the first days of Christianity, to the age of Nero and Domitian, as they have been depicted by the Catholic historians, with so much emphasis and gross exaggeration.

Entire populations remained without a clergy and without churches. In the memorials addressed to the Pope by these populations, the Jesuits said:

"Would you desire to see a congregation assembled together for prayers? Go into the villages during the night, approach the closed church, there you will hear at their doors whole families prostrate groaning in the darkness. Their tears are the dew which precedes the dawning of the morning. . . . Every measure tends to uproot the religion, as well as the language of our ancestors; a Catholic, in the Russian Empire, is almost below a Jew; a Polander, below a Calmuck. . . . Minds are vacillating . . . . and the Holy Chair has not one word of blame against the apostates nor encouragement for the faithful. Cause our cries of distress to be heard at the feet of the Holy Father."

Gregory, moved by these pitiable declamations, at last awoke from his sleep; and at first Cardinal Bernetti, and afterwards Lambruschini, commenced to write notes upon notes, and complaints upon complaints, to the Court of St. Petersburg.

This court kept silent. At last, fatigued, Count Gourieff, in the month of May, 1833, sent an insulting note, in which, among other things, he said: "The clergy of the orthodox Church have no serfs, and cannot own them; the Roman Catholic clergy, on the contrary, possess good peasants who work for them, and a great number of which profess the religion of the majority of Russian subjects. . . . That as to the treaties of 1773 which you invoke, we have but a few words to say in reply. The clergy has betrayed the confidence of the government! It has inculcated in the youth principles hostile to legitimate authority and to established order; it has taken an open and active part in the last revolution."

We call again the attention of Count Cavour to the ukase of 1812 and to this note. These precedents are eloquent, and a great indication of the mode in which the Court of Rome must be treated. And who shall dare to say that Russia is revolutionary?

The Pope then addressed himself directly to the Emperor, who answered him by an autographic letter on the 3d of December, 1840. The Emperor Nicholas, without promising anything, on the contrary, advised him to use what influence he had left to persuade the Polish Catholics to a blind obedience to their master, and added: "I should not know how, very Holy Father, to terminate this letter without expressing to you the sincere interest which I take in the maintenance of tranquillity in the provinces governed by Your Holiness. Heir to the throne of the late Emperor Alexander, I am equally so to his pacific and conservative principles, and I love to keep in remembrance the active part that my brother of glorious memory took in the restoration of the temporal power of the Holy Chair."

The Court of Rome then published a manifesto to Europe upon her differences with Russia and upon the sufferings of the Polish Catholics. The Czar was affected by it. They commenced, in consequence, to provoke an agitation in the Romagna, in which the name of the Duke de Leuchtenburg was pre-eminent. The Duke de Leuchtenburg had some possessions in the Romagna. They endeavored to come to an understanding. At last, in 1846, the Czar came to Rome.

CHAPTER XVIII.

THE POPE AND THE CZAR.

GREGORY XVI. received Nicholas in the Palace of the Vatican.

In order to reach the Pope you must cross seven ante-chambers. The first filled with those Swiss so grotesquely dressed, whose livery was designed by Raphael in a moment of spleen; the second filled with grooms, chair-men, and lackeys; the third with carbineers and the Capitol guards, now no longer in existence. Upon one side of this antechamber is a door which leads to the hall of the Consistory, another which opens upon the landing of a special staircase for the use of the police. The civic guard occupies the fourth ante-chamber; the fifth is occupied by a chevalier of Malta, a Swiss officer, and two valets of the sleeve and sword; the sixth is possessed by twelve noble guards; and finally, the seventh by Monseigneur, the master of the chambers, two prelates *camerieri segreti*, an officer of the noble guard, and two *bussolari* at the door, by which the hall of reception is entered.

The latter is not large; longer than broad, with a ceiling with gilt roses, and two windows opening upon the Piazza of St. Peter. As to the furniture, there is only a desk with a silver inkstand, an armchair, and a large Christ. No looking-glasses, no canopies, no chairs, nothing vulgar or profane. The richness of the apartment consists entirely of the marbles of the floor, and of those which incrust the walls, the tables of precious marbles, the gilt and richly sculptured bronzes, the carpets, the Mosaics, and the sacred pictures of Raphael, and others.

Gregory XVI. was dressed wholly in white, with a surplice richly embroidered, and with slippers, likewise embroidered in gold. On seeing the Czar he rose and stood for a moment, then he advanced two steps to meet him. Nicholas remained also an instant upon the door-sill, struck perhaps with the austere grandeur of the place, perhaps with the aspect of this dying old man, whose head was calmly reclining upon his chest. At last he advanced without saying a word.

How the times of the Papacy have been changed, since Alexander III. had placed his foot upon the head of Frederick Barbarossa! Moral power always remains the same. Everybody is seized with respect by the whole aspect of this scene, of Oriental draperies, of people throwing themselves upon their knees, embracing the feet, and demanding the benedictions, of this old man, who sometimes is caught himself by the comedy which he plays. Even when we do not believe, when we are no Catholic, and that, accustomed to the service of the court, we laugh at these mummeries, we are dazzled by the Persian and Babylonian ceremonies of the Court of Rome — as at a play we become affected by a misfortune skilfully represented by an actor, knowing all the time that the misfortune is not real. Gregory complained with much dignity and with sorrow, of the sufferings of the Polish Catholics. He made the Autocrat of sixty millions of inhabitants hear the voice of justice, and of grief, stifled in the midst of his peoples, and he thus terminated:

"Sire, a day will come when we shall both of us appear before the tribunal of God, to render an account of our actions. I, overwhelmed by years, shall precede you; but I should not dare to sustain the look of my Supreme Judge, if I had not undertaken the defence of a religion which God has confided to my care, and which you oppress. Reflect upon it well, Sire! God has instituted kings that they might become the fathers, not the executioners of their peoples!"

This was the first, this was the last noble and courageous act of this nature broken by the cloister's rule of passive obedience. Gregory XVI. felt that he was about to die.

CHAPTER XIX.

THE END.

IT was the end of the month of May, 1846. The legs of Gregory were swollen, and his strength was nearly exhausted. One day he, who had entirely secluded himself from the exterior world, found under the pillow of his monk's bed the book written by Massimo d'Azeglio upon the "Affairs of Rimini." Then he could read about all the atrocities which his people had suffered, what they demanded, and what they proposed that they might withdraw from so abominable a government. Gregory was staggered by it as with a stroke of lightning. Immediately he commenced writing a brief ordering the Cardinals to assemble in a secure place, and contrary to the apostolic constitution, to appoint his successor during his lifetime, that the rights of the Church might be saved.

He then took to his bed.

Gregory had loaded many with benefits, particularly his barber and Cardinal Mattei, who even lived in the palace of the Vatican. But as soon as his favorites saw him in danger, as soon as they perceived that this crowned head was menaced by death, and that this man no longer had largesses to bestow, silence took possession of his dwelling. In the immense halls of the Vatican no other sound was heard but the distant and monotonous one of the sentinels who mounted guard. Those magnificent and solemn chambers wore the aspect of a tomb. The Pontiff, stretched upon a cot-bedstead, saw no one. The long and splendid days of the month of May passed away without this old man being able to exchange a word with a living being. The nights with their shadows succeeded still longer and more sad.

One day, Gregory was burning with thirst. Hearing the footsteps of some one, he called. It was one of the kitchen domestics. The Sovereign begged him to stop a moment and talk a little with him. The perpetual silence frightened him. He then ordered his confessor and buffoon, Monseigneur Arpi, to be called. And the confessor buffoon, who owed everything to Gregory, not only could not find one pleasantry to amuse his master, but did not even know how to frame one word of consolation to assist him in mounting the Golgotha of the dead. He hastily saluted him, stopped for a moment and secretly administered to him the sacrament. For the more the malady of Gregory increased, the greater were the pains taken to conceal it.

They feared a revolution like that of 1831. In the States of the Vicar of God revolution is always *en permanence*.

Gregory, immediately afterwards, commanded his barber, Gaetanino, to be called. Gaetanino had vanished from his master's bed, carrying with him his riches. Gregory desired a consultation of doctors; but Father Vernaud, a brother of the Hospitalers, his ordinary physician, assured him that he was in no danger. He asked for the Cardinal Lambruschini and the Cardinal Mattei; their Eminences sent back word that they would come on the morrow.

The morrow!

Afterwards, he saw no one.

Yet he was thirsty! he was hungry! this Vicar of God.

For three days Gregory had taken nothing. Upon the candle-stand alongside of his bed he found a piece of lemon-peel. Gregory nibbled it and swallowed the pieces.

The sentinels themselves were kept at a distance that their footfalls might not disturb the void and solitude that had been made around the dying. And — he, who could still speak to Rome and to the world, *urbi et orbi!* had with him not a relative, not a friend, not a servant. He, who still could say to three millions of subjects: be free and happy. Yet the Pontiff held his tongue that he might not attack the heritage of that oligarchy who left him to die in despair.

Gregory the XVIth died of starvation.

The Archbishop Ruggieri of that new count Ugolino, was Cardinal Lambruschini, who concealed the agony of Gregory from everybody, that he might have time to cast his nets, and familiarize his clients, and thus in his turn secure for himself the nomination of Pope.

In the ages passed, Vicars of Christ had been assassinated, in the houses of their mistresses, with a blow from a hammer. Vicars of Christ had been strangled, hung, dead from age, knocked on the head with stones in a riot, dead in exile, killed; but it was reserved for the nineteenth century to see a Sovereign Pontiff die from hunger, in the palace of the Vatican, in his own capitol, always reigning, through the desert which his ministers had created around his person.

The autopsy of the dead body proved that Gregory had only in his shrivelled stomach *three pieces of lemon!*

Not even broth from his kitchen.

Yet he left millions to his nephews, souvenirs to his favorite, Cardinal Mattei, and immense riches to his valet Morroni, who had been selling him for fifteen years.

Behold then the Pontifical government. To whom does it belong? Behold the Pope. No ancestors, and no heirs. *Pulvis et umbra sumus.*

Let us recapitulate.

Gregory had reigned for sixteen years. What had he done? What remains of his career? Like his predecessors, Gregory, as their successor, desolated a people. For sixteen years, three millions of Italians remained exposed to the aim of the carbincers and sbirri of the Vicar of God. And evil was to him that budged.

Industry, commerce, science, agriculture, learning, morals, fine arts, everything, all had stood still, all had languished in the kingdom of the Vice-God — the brothel and the scaffold excepted. He failed in all his promises, falsified all his deeds, perjured himself in all his oaths, denied to the people all their rights, prevented every expansion of the understanding, and trampled under foot every dignity of the State. Three millions of Italians were a body to be taxed, and nothing more. To annihilate this people, France lent her counsels, Austria her arms, Prussia and Russia their moral support, England her silence, and Spain cried bravo! and the Italian princes hung on to the Pontifical mantle that they might double the weight of the Successor of Peter. They undertook to strangle Italy without noise, and without danger. Gregory gave them God for an accomplice. Notwithstanding, like Italy, the people of the Roman States did not die; and not a year passes without a sign that they do not wish to die. Pius VII. had garrotted them, Leo XII. had slashed them, Gregory had crushed them under the axe of the executioner, and under the feet of foreign soldiers; they had bled everything until it was pale, prostrate in the mud, prostituted, sold, brutalized, exterminated;—for what purpose then was it useful? Gregory had found revolution at the door of the Conclave that chose him;

Pius IX. in his turn found it there, upright, in arms, more decided, and more alive than ever. Gregory had reigned for the Austrians; Pius IX. will reign by the Austrians and the French.

Had Gregory only gained one sympathy, abolished one abuse, cured only one wound, reformed one institution, suppressed one privilege, made for his people one step, one only! upon the road of progress and civilization? No. He had increased the public debt, taxes, public immorality, injustice, and every misery of the most miserable people of Europe. For sixteen years of his reign there rose up but one great cry of malediction, and an insatiate desire of vengeance.

An alternation of revolts and their suppression. Such was the reign of Gregory the XVIth.

CHAPTER XX.

SITUATION OF AFFAIRS.

WHEN on the first of June, 1846, the bell of the Vatican tolled the knell which announced the death of the Pope, the astonishment was universal. It was like the case of Leo XII., whose sickness was concealed from every one, and whose death was suddenly made known. The Sacred College, in particular, overflowed with indignation against

Cardinal Lambruschini and Cardinal Mattei. It denied the reason of their perfidious conduct; and Cardinal Micara, the Dean of the College, overwhelmed them with irony and cruel reproaches. From that moment, excitement reigned everywhere — among the people — in the Sacred College — among the diplomacy.

The creation of Pope, at this period, was a matter of supreme importance. The Papacy, perhaps, was never before placed in a more difficult position.

In 1829, Cardinal Bernetti, a man of clear perceptions, said to Mr. de Chateaubriand, "that the temporal Papacy was at an end, and that he should have during his lifetime to assist at its funeral." Leo XII., Pius VIII., Gregory XVI., had increased its responsibilities and rendered its continuance impossible. All felt it, but they also saw that they could not annihilate an authority, which from the fourteenth century had taken its place among the sovereign powers of Europe, without causing trouble and provoking commotion. A change in Italy was necessary. It was first necessary to drive out the foreigners, the Janissaries, the fruit of this institution. But Europe, constituted as it was in 1846, was hardly prepared for so radical a change. She was not even in the following year, when the first muttering of the revolution had re-echoed beneath the Italian skies. Indeed:

"No territorial and political connection on the

other side of the Alps is advantageous for us," said Mr. Guizot in the Chamber of Peers, on the 3d of August, 1847; and governed by this opinion, he had written to his ambassadors at Vienna and at Rome. "Assure Prince de Metternich," wrote Lord Palmerston to Lord Ponsonby at Vienna, the 12th of August, 1847, "that her Majesty's Government is of the opinion, that it is necessary to adhere to the stipulations and conventions of the Congress of Vienna, in Italy, as well as everywhere else in Europe, and that no change must be made in the territorial boundaries stipulated in that treaty without the consent and concurrence of the parties thereto."

"The Emperor is firmly resolved, that what concerns the state of the possessions assigned to the different Italian States by the laws which he has guaranteed; that he will do nothing that is contrary to what his duties and political interests prescribe." Letter from Count de Nesselrode, the 24th of February, 1848, to Baron de Brunow at London.

Prince de Metternich, in his despatch to Count Dietrichstein, of the 2d of August, 1847, laid down: "The Emperor, our august master, has no pretension to be an Italian power; he is satisfied with being the chief of his own Empire. Such parts of this Empire as are situated beyond the Alps, he intends to preserve. The Emperor seeks nothing in any direction, out of his actual possession. What is in his possession he is prepared to defend."

Now, the Sacred College knew the opinion of the Cabinets of Europe, as to the overturning of the existing order of things, and consequently it was reassured as to the maintenance of the temporal Papacy. But it also knew that all the subscribing powers to the *memorandum* of 1831 partook of the notion that some reforms were necessary, even urgent, and all agreed not to prevent them.

Prince de Metternich did not show himself opposed to them, neither as to the principle, nor as to the opportunity. Indeed, the French minister of foreign affairs, having one day let fall in his salon, that the Lord Chancellor marched at the head of the partisans of absolute resistance, the Prince quickly replied to Mr. d'Appony:

" That he believed in the triumph of moderate ideas in those countries which, like France, had gone through many revolutions . . . because liberty then is a compromise which acquires the value of a benefit. . . . But he did not believe in the success of a just mean, in the phase in which the Italian States were found; because it was not the close, but the commencement of a revolution. That it was not true that he was a partisan of absolute resistance . . . . that there was nothing absolute but truth; that politics concerned the conduct, which was no foundation for the absolute; that his resistance to the revolutionary spirit had sometimes been active, as in 1820, sometimes defensive, as in 1831; for the present he was a looker on; because what was taking place in Italy was as much a revolt as a revolution; that revolts were easier to be repressed than revolutions, — they have a body which we can lay hold of; that revolutions were of the nature of spectres; and that it was necessary, in order to regulate our conduct respecting them, to wait until they are clothed with a body."

Persuaded of the truth of this principle, the action of the country and of the diplomatic body was the same. The people acted upon the Conclave that they might obtain reforms. The diplomatic body dreamed of sending forth from the Conclave a Pope, less absolute and less blind than the preceding one, a Pope who should satisfy in a certain degree the public mind.

In all the cities of the State they commenced signing petitions for reforms, for the vigorous execution of the memorandum, and for a general amnesty. These petitions were filled with the signatures of those persons most remarkable for their social and intellectual position. That from Bologna alone contained 1753 names, all of the nobility and citizens. For they refused the signatures of the lower orders to prevent the least suspicion of democracy.

The people indeed willed otherwise. What they wanted was apparent when they chose representatives by universal suffrage, who proclaimed the republic and the abolition of the Papacy!

The citizens in 1846 understood the situation of

affairs; they concealed in their hearts their desire for a constitution, if they had this desire, and demanded reforms.

The diplomatic body, that likewise understood what Mr. de Chateaubriand had comprehended in 1829, had written to Mr. de Pontalis, to wit: "That diplomatic action and the intrigues of the court no longer are of any use in determining the choice of a Pope or in prescribing him; the diplomatic body, I say, is satisfied with exercising its right of exclusion. It also serves as a nucleus for certain caucus combinations; volunteers its advice or gives counsel, listens with impatience to the zealots about the independence of the conclave; and that is all."

Finally, owing to this circumstance, every manifestation remained smothered in the germ from the celerity with which the nomination was conducted. They were afraid of a revolution which might have succeeded while the Holy Chair was vacant, and the people were agitated by their emotions. For from petitioning to action the distance is short. The imprudence or too great zeal of a provincial pro-legate had sufficed to provoke trouble.

The most active among the diplomatists, and almost the first to do anything, was the French ambassador Mr. Rossi. Mr. Guizot had left him without special instructions. Mr. Rossi profited by his right of exclusion against Cardinal Lambruschini, who was known to be supported by the eldest branch of the

Bourbons and the friend of Austria, and gave his support to Cardinals Gizzi, Falconieri, Soglia, and Micara.

"And since when has the Holy Ghost become reasonable?" responded Micara, when Mr. Rossi spoke to him of his choice.

Cardinal Bernetti was the candidate of the courts of Prussia and of Russia.

The minister of Austria alone remained inactive, at least in appearance, awaiting the instructions which Cardinal Gaysruck should bring him. But he took the responsibility of excluding Cardinal Gizzi, and of ordering a reinforcement from Ancona.

Indeed, there immediately arrived five battalions with munitions of war.

The faction of Cardinal Lambruschini was actively engaged in endeavoring to gain the sympathy of the diplomatic corps. And as they knew that the Sardinian and French ministers were the most opposed to them, they intrigued most actively to secure them. Cardinal Mattei went so far as to demand ingenuously the open support of Count Rossi, revealing to him that the Cardinal already counted upon an imposing party, that twenty Cardinals had already made an engagement in his favor.

Mr. Rossi promised him his support; but at the same time secretly cautioned Cardinals Bernetti and Micara concerning the plots of Cardinal Lambruschini, and everything that those acting for him had avowed. So that Lambruschini, believing himself already Pope *in petto,* labored to complete the number of his electors among the Cardinals of the *flying squadron,* skeptics — more men of the world than of the Church, who were still fluctuating, promising to them favors and offices according to their respective desires.

CHAPTER XXI.

THE CARDINALS BEFORE THE CONCLAVE.

AFTER the death of the Pope, the Cardinal Chamberlain ordered a medal of the vacant Chair to be struck with the exergue, *non relinquam vos orphanos!* Afterwards, according to custom, a provisional government of three Cardinals was formed.

First they proceeded to the verification of the Pope's death.

The Chamberlain clad with a crimson cassock — the mourning color of the Cardinals — presented himself, in company with the city authorities and the delegates of the Sacred College, before the bed of Gregory XVI. He struck the forehead of the Pope three times with a little hammer; he called him three times: Mauro Capellari! Mauro Capellari! Mauro Capellari! Then declaring that Gregory XVI. was dead, and that the Holy Chair was vacant, he broke, with the little hammer, the ring of the Fisherman, *annulum pescatoris*, and ordered the customary funeral.

While the corpse remained exposed in the Sistine Chapel, the Sacred College assembled themselves under the presidency of their dean, the Capucin Cardinal Ludovic Micara.

How strange and terrible a man was this Cardinal! One of those types of men supposed to have been lost with the sixteenth century, tall, pale, with a broad, bold forehead, thin face, black eyes, a scorching and aggressive look, a white beard descending to his chest, one, in short, to inspire an artist, and to move a woman! Intelligence, will, boldness, courage, sparkled in his eyes; from every gesture an overpowering magnetic emanation was disengaged. Micara was something of Jules II., of Paul IV., of Sixtus V.; the speech of Savonarola, the keen irony of Alexander VI. A man also of pure manners, unconstrained behavior, contempt for useless ostentation, inflexible as brass, a frankness almost amounting to brutality, the absolute and peremptory air of one who has passed his life upon the field of battle, — an aggressive spirit amounting almost to arrogance, and of stern principles. Had this man reached the Papacy, the world would have felt him. We should have seen the Papacy of the Middle Ages revived; crusades against the Austrian Empire, religious wars, the abolition of the Jesuits, an Evangelical reform of the Sacred College, and I know not what else!— the democratization of the Papacy, or the *dictatum papæ* of Gregory VII. Perhaps the fantastic fooleries of the *Primate* of Gioberti! Certain it is, that he would have broken that stupid mould of the Papacy which has existed since the sixteenth century; he might perhaps have made a scourge of it, but he would have made something. He would have galvanized it for a century more, or would have killed it.

"Reflect well upon it, people," he said to the Romans who applauded him on his way to the Conclave; "reflect upon it well: with me thou shalt neither want bread nor the gallows!"

He then met Cardinal Lambruschini and Cardinal Mattei, whom he loaded with accusations on account of their conduct. He pronounced the boldest philippic against the government of the deceased Pope and his ministers, which he also had done during the lifetime of Gregory XVI. in the consistories in the presence of Gregory himself. He called Mattei and Lambruschini traitors to God, false to the people, felons to the Sacred College, whose rights they had usurped. But his contempt and irony were especially terrible when he came to the examination of those prelates who should have been sent as delegates into the provinces. He described them as men with blemishes, or nobodies, in every way unworthy, and elevated through favor or simony. He called them all lackeys.

The words of the Cardinal Capucin excited a tempest in these meetings. From that time it was perceived that misunderstandings existed among the Cardinals, and any one could enumerate them.

Cardinal Micara, with his ferocious eloquence, reviewed the whole situation; afterwards he came to a partial examination of the subject of reform, of amnesty, and of the future. On all these questions he stirred up the profoundest depths of the hearts of these old men, each one according to his respective nature.

During these discussions the partisans of Cardinal Lambruschini commenced deserting. He saw himself openly abandoned by two of his creatures, Cardinals Piccolomini and Fieschi. The situation became clearer.

From these preparatory meetings it was apparent that the Cardinals went into the Conclave divided thus:

The party of resistance at any price, absolutists, Austrian, opposed to all progress, to every concession, to every change. This body favored Cardinal Lambruschini.

The party which I shall call the citizen party, who were in favor of some reforms at once, of an amnesty to a small extent, of a little commercial liberty, a little of the *memorandum* corrected and revised. This party divided its votes between Cardinals Falconieri, Soglia, Gizzi, and Mastai.

Finally, the very small party of Cardinal Micara, who demanded radical reforms, slow but progressive, and forming a system of complete democratization and moralization of the Papacy. It was, as Micara said to me, the Mountain of the Cónclave.

In the midst of these three parties a small number of indecisive Cardinals fluctuated, which was called the flying squadron, who, forming a just medium, dreamed of a Papacy more laical than ecclesiastical. This party had Cardinal Bernetti for its chief, and in its suite Opizzoni and Patrizi. It held in its hands the fate of the battle, and we shall see that it was this party which decided it.

During the time which preceded the entrance into the Conclave, these parties were working, each one engaged in intrigues, at first using the influence of money, afterwards of women. Some signed compromises, some engaged themselves through promises, some sold their suffrages. Scarcely any one *gave* them! As is always the case, the election commenced by jockeying.

The people also acted, but in another way, upon the minds of the Cardinals, by manifesting a willingness to end the policy of Gregory XVI. by encouragement, flatteries, and menaces.

These men were divided into four factions; but the people and the diplomacy laid down these two propositions: *statu quo*, with the determination of resisting revolution, by aiding Austria as in 1831; or else, progress, reform, amnesty, relying upon the favor of England, upon the Italian people, and to a certain extent, upon France.

The Cardinals on their way to shut themselves up in Conclave, could hear the voice of the people speaking sufficiently loud. "Take care, then! no monks, no foreigners!" They could understand what they meant when they greeted with frantic applause Cardinal Gizzi, who had driven from his province the extra-judicial commissions, and who passed for a liberal; and the Cardinal Micara, who at the head of the opposition struggled through his whole life against Leo XII. and Gregory XVI. We shall see what account they took of it.

CHAPTER XXII.

THE CONCLAVE.

THE Cardinals entered into Conclave upon the 13th of June.

The diplomatic body went to compliment them. It was the duty of this body to express to the Conclave its wishes, which ordinarily consist of commonplaces. But upon this occasion Mr. Rossi, who was delegated by his colleagues to speak, broke through routine, and made himself the organ of the crowd, whose groups he had just passed through, and whose aspect and voice he had seen and heard. Mr. Rossi exposed with severity the miserable situation of the Roman States, the faults of the recent government, the urgent wants of the people, and the necessity for reforms. He formulated the wish, in the name of the Italians and the diplomatic body, that the Conclave should choose a man capable of comprehending the greatness of his position, the exigencies of the times, and the wishes of the people.

Cardinal Micara laconically replied to him, "that the Sacred College knew its duty, and that it would perform it."

The doors of the Quirinal were then closed.

All of the windows had already been plastered up, to intercept all communication from without. But the first care of the Cardinals, who were interested in keeping up these communications, was to contrive, with the assistance of their servants and of the Conclavists, the making of a small hole in the still fresh plaster, through which a pack-thread might pass, that by this means they might send and receive letters.

The dinners of the Cardinals were sent to them from without upon hand-carts, escorted by a butler in a carriage bearing the arms of the Cardinal for whom the viands were intended; — then could be seen the splendid dishes and plates of some, the meagre fare of others — these were compared, commented and jested upon. All the dishes were in turn examined by a commission of Bishops, in the dress of the Pontifical ceremonial, under the supervision of Prince Ghizi, who, by hereditary right, is the guardian of the Conclave. They disemboweled the poultry and the fish, they broke the eggs, they examined the bottles, they peeled the oranges, they examined the soup-tureens. . . . But notwithstanding all these precautions, means were always found to convey a message and to receive a reply.

Indeed, Cardinal Lambruschini, it was said, sent the news of his trouble, after the second scrutiny, to the minister of Austria, and solicited the arrival of Cardinal Gaysruck, Archbishop of Milan, a person of great influence, particularly with the Neapolitan Cardinals.

His Eminence received a reply, under the double ticket of a bottle of champagne, to prolong the contest, as the Cardinal was on his way.

Cardinal Piccolomini, it was also said, sent to Cardinal Bernetti, in the carved handle of a knife from which the blade had been broken, the solicitation of a Roman princess, an old friend of the Cardinal, requesting him and his friends to give their votes to Cardinal Mastai.

In the meantime, after having said the *Veni Creator* in the chapel, the Conclave opened and held its first session.

We have sketched the manner in which the Cardinals were divided on the outside; nevertheless, once within, once abstracted from exterior influences, the position of affairs became modified. The influences acted only from a distance, and greater interests took the place of private animosities and ephemeral ends.

The great cause of the Papacy was admitted.

The Conclave then separated under two banners. One, under that of an inflexible Papacy. The other under that of a Papacy of reform.

Lambruschini stood as the candidate for the first. He had employed his time so well, during the sickness of Gregory and afterwards, that he entered into the Conclave almost Pope, with a compact, strong, and active party. He then looked haughty and smiled.

The party of the Papacy of reform presented four candidates, nay, even five with Bernetti, to wit: Falconieri, Soglia, Gizzi, and Mastai.

Cardinal Micara had frightened, by the formidable attitude which he had taken, this corrupt and decrepit body, that feared to revivify and fill again the world astonished at its existence. It particularly feared the austerity of his principles, and the simplicity of his manners.

The Sacred College was composed of sixty-two Cardinals, fifty-three of whom were created during the long pontificate of Gregory XVI. And it was this which inspired with confidence Prince de Metternich, who manifested under these serious circumstances an incomprehensible inertia. Fifty-one Cardinals entered into the Conclave.

It appeared impossible for the Cardinal of Spain and the Cardinal of Portugal to be present on account of their old age, and the distance to be travelled. But Lambruschini counted upon the arrival of the Cardinals of Milan, of Genoa, of the Patriarch of Venice, of the Cardinals of Salzburg and of Malins, whose votes were promised him, as well as two of the three votes of the French Cardinals — the votes of the Legitimists.

It required, for the validity of the election, two-thirds of the suffrages of the Cardinals who were present.

Cardinal Lambruschini, as well as Austria, expected a great deal from Cardinal Gaysruck, on account of his experience in the tricks and intrigues of conclaves, and the influence he could exercise by making himself the centre and leader of the conservative party. But nothing had been prepared at Vienna, and it was only after the news of the death of Gregory, that Prince de Metternich resolved upon and sent his instructions to the counsellor charged with ecclesiastical affairs at Milan. The long conference which Cardinal Gaysruck had with this agent, who communicated to him the principles and exclusions which should prevail in the new election, was taken notice of at Milan.

Besides Cardinal Gizzi, whom the Austrian Minister at Rome had vetoed with his own authority, for the sole reason that this Cardinal was the candidate of the liberals, it was known that Cardinal Gaysruck bore also the exclusion of Cardinal Mastai. So that, if the Austrian Cardinal had arrived in time, Mastai would not have been nominated for Pope. Prince de Metternich foresaw that this Eau de Beaumont of the Papacy would do as much mischief to Austria by his liberal fancies as by his sympathies and his reactionary infatuation.

The Romans, in order that they might ridicule Gaysruck, presented to him the first portrait of Pius IX.

But Gaysruck had hardly reached the frontiers of Tuscany, when he received the news that the Pope was elected.

CHAPTER XXIII.

HOW A POPE IS MADE.

FROM the result of the first balloting, on the 13th, Cardinal Lambruschini could form a pretty correct judgment of the position of affairs. He compared the strength of his party with that of his competitors; his party recognized their strength and became bold.

In the face of an opposition so marked in principle and design, great precautions should have been taken not to wound the self-love, the interests, the timorous consciences and the indecision of the passive Cardinals. The partisans of Lambruschini were devoid of tact. Sure of their victory, they marched towards it with flag displayed, almost doing violence to the indecisive. So far, the candidature of Lambruschini was rather a moral one. They knew that this man was the highest incarnation of the system whose triumph was desired. But a Cardinal who has been Secretary of State never presents himself as a candidate, knowing that he is detested by all those whom he has neglected. But this candidature, already so imprudent in itself, was compromised by openly proclaiming it.

They should have temporized, lost some votes, wearied the impatient, allured the avaricious, used resistance, demonstrated the Cardinal to be the last resource, and seized the first propitious occasion to nominate him at once. They should have watched him as a reserve, drawn to him lost votes, set up against him a ridiculous rival, thrown away their suffrages upon Cardinals whose election was impossible, in order that they might present him as a bargain, a compromise. But no. The partisans of Lambruschini, inexperienced in conclaves, immediately proclaimed him their chief, and gave him their votes upon the second ballot.

When, upon the morning of the 14th of June, the Cardinals proceeded to the chapel to deposit their votes, the name of Cardinal Lambruschini was heard seventeen times. The other suffrages were divided among Falconieri, Mastai, and Soglia.

And, a strange thing! not a vote for Gizzi, who was, notwithstanding, as we have seen, the candidate of the people and of a part of the diplomatic body, and who was the most salient expression of the system opposed to that of Lambruschini. This proves how little the Sacred College cares for the public wishes, what consideration it has for the situation of the State. But it was solely because he passed for a liberal, and that he was designated by the people, that he was forsaken.

In examining the ballot, it was discovered that one of them had the fold broken open, under which the name of the voter was found. Then Lambruschini declared the balloting void, and that it was necessary to recommence.

The opponents of Lambruschini desired to maintain the ballot, and a lively debate took place. But the rules were clear. It was necessary to vote again.

Cardinal Micara, quite sick, remained in his cell. The questors, again going to procure his vote, told him what had taken place.

"Ah bah!" said he, "ask His Eminence and his party if they want a midwife."

In the meantime the suffrages were again collected. But this time Cardinal Lambruschini had badly calculated. His seventeen votes on the first ballot were reduced upon the second to fourteen.

"The first time," remarked Cardinal Bernetti, "the Holy Ghost was absent."

The position of affairs became more serious. The aggressive and united attitude of the reactionary party excited alarm in the opposition, who were scattered and showed themselves weak and tranquil, confiding rather in the justice and good sense of the Cardinals than in their own energy. They, nevertheless, saw their adversaries boldly stand up and accept their challenge.

The Cardinals went back to their cells silent and thoughtful, with the presentiment that a combat was about to take place. The Papacy itself was the cause, and the evil genius of Italy baffled Cardinal Lambruschini.

If this man had succeeded in being Pope, the fate of the Holy Chair, perhaps, would have been immediately decided.

Night set in, and the vast palace of the Quirinal again fell into silence and shadow. But it was precisely at this hour that the real battle began.

The balloting had placed Cardinal Gizzi *hors de combat*. The opposing candidates were now reduced to three: Soglia, Falconieri, and Mastai. Cardinal Fieschi, who was one of the questors, and Piccolomini — the two chief deserters from the Lambruschini party, — made known to Cardinal Micara the position of the liberal party. The Cardinal counselled them to select from the three candidates, the most transparent, the least known, the

14

least compromised by any precedent whatever, and the biggest fool (*lo più zuccone*), and to rally upon him alone.

They could without trouble have given their suffrages to a man who was all these things, having been nothing until then, and under whom the whole world might have hoped for something, or not have been afraid.

The question thus laid down, Cardinal Soglia, who already had a physiognomy, was banished. Much beloved, in his legation of Osimo, this Cardinal had showed a certain leaning towards liberal principles, and he might awaken the fear or anger of those tried Cardinals who had refused their votes to Gizzi.

To this advice Cardinal Bernetti, the greatest fox in the Conclave, added that of making haste. They should take away from the enemy the possibility of receiving reinforcements from the Cardinals who were about to arrive. They should deprive them of the opportunity of converting the Cardinals who might desert through the allurements which the Lambruschini faction brought into play. He advised the hastening of the election and the carrying it by assault the next day. Cardinal Soglia, through the persuasion of Cardinal Piccolomini, withdrew his name as a candidate; and Cardinal Amat de S. Fillippo, obtained the renunciation of Cardinal Falconieri, who resigned his votes in favor of Cardinal Mastai.

The latter possessed all the qualities that Cardinal Micara desired.

But to secure the election, Cardinal Fieschi, who exercised during the night a feverish activity, slipped to Cardinal Bernetti the letter of the old Roman princess, of whom we have before spoken. He also supported the letter by certain promises, causing him perhaps to have a faint glimpse of the portfolio of foreign affairs, and stirred up his old hatred against Cardinal Lambruschini. In a word, he decided him to carry his flying squadron — ten votes — in favor of Cardinal Mastai.

The whole night was passed in these conferences.

In the interior of the Quirinal, Cardinals Fieschi, Amat, and Piccolomini, were seen, through the whole night, gliding like spectres through the darkness from cell to cell, in search of suffrages, of counsellors, of adherents; promising, exciting doubts, giving replies, making propositions, combating refusals, exciting desires, carrying messages from Cardinal to Cardinal, from one corner to another of this immense edifice; then working the packthreads on the outside to call reinforcements, to contrive intrigues, to crush cabals. Everywhere was movement, fear, agitation, restlessness, hope, discouragement, impatience, the pleasure of a vote gained, the vexation of a vote refused.

There were a dozen of Cardinals that they had not even tempted. Those had not placed the cross of St. Andrews upon the door of their cell to signify that they were fixed in their decision; but they were so compromised, so detested, so despised, or sold, or servile, that they were called *the band of the Sanfedistes*, and they did not even do them the honor of calling upon them.

On the other side the activity of Cardinal Vannicelli, of Cardinal Mattei, and of Cardinal Massimo was immense. They also hastened from cell to cell to attract adherents; they also corresponded with those outside and sent and received messages.

Massimo had the effrontery to present himself in the cell of Cardinal Micara, and to request his vote for Cardinal Lambruschini. Micara replied: " Rather to Nardoni, my dear! we have had enough of the reign of the police; let us try something else."

Bernetti, on the contrary, promised Vannicelli his vote in favor of the reactionary candidate, and to confirm him in the opinion that he promised seriously, he laid down certain conditions, which the other accepted in a trice.

He also withdrew from the temptation of the Austrian Cardinals all his friends who voted with him, and sent to them his order in favor of Cardinal Mastai.

CHAPTER XXIV.

A QUARTER OF AN HOUR WITH THE HOLY GHOST.

AT last the morning of the 15th of June arrived. The traffic which had lasted all the night, ceased, and the Cardinals, with slow steps, silent and pre-occupied, wended their way towards the chapel.

There was something solemn and sad in the air which they breathed. The wearied countenances of these old men, broken by the night which they had passed in watching, if not in prayer, the anxiety and hope of some, the fear of others, the august character of the action which they went to accomplish, the grandeur of the invocation which they addressed to the Eternal, the Aurora which saluted the city, still asleep at the foot of the immense Quirinal,—all, in fine, the hour, the men, the functions, and the attitude of the parties and the position of the leaders, set a serious and majestic seal on the great drama which was about to unfold.

Soon the voice of Cardinal Micara was heard, who, although seriously ill, was carried into the chapel by his own directions, and there delivered, in his poetic and powerful words, an allocution to the Sacred College.

"The sudden election of the Pope," wrote Mr. Scarlett from Florence to Lord Aberdeen, on the

26th of June, 1846, "has been principally attributed to the determination of the younger Cardinals, to commence voting before the arrival of the foreign Cardinals, aided by an energetic appeal made to the Conclave, by Cardinal Micara, President-in-chief of the Apostolic Chamber.

"In opposition to the interests of Cardinal Lambruschini, who wished to demonstrate the necessity of awaiting the arrival of the foreign Cardinals, Cardinal Micara declared that the period had finally arrived when the government should no longer be submitted to foreign influence, but should be conducted in a manner more in harmony with the progress of the age. This discourse produced a profound impression, as well by the tone in which it was spoken as by the subject-matter; and principally because it was the speech of a man universally respected, and whom the Transteverins called with an emphatic voice to occupy the vacant throne."

After this discourse the excitement was extreme. They collected the votes.

The questors, to whom the duty appertained of opening the ballots, were Cardinals Mastai, Vannicelli, and Fieschi.

The counting of the votes commenced.

Cardinal Fieschi read the names in a loud voice. Not a breath disturbed the silence. The eyes of fifty-one electors were directed to the lips of the reader.

The name of Cardinal Mastai Ferretti began to be heard. No attention was paid to the first votes;

but when the name was proclaimed for the tenth time, when it was repeated the twelfth and afterwards the fifteenth time, accompanied with the smile of Cardinal Fieschi, and the joyful regards of the Cardinals for reform, every eye was turned toward this man, who, pale and trembling, opened the ballots, and passed them to be read by Cardinal Vannicelli.

The latter, sombre and gloomy, repassed them to Cardinal Fieschi.

The name of Mastai resounded the twentieth time; then twenty-five was counted, then thirty.

Mastai spoke no longer. He stood motionless. At the thirtieth time he seated himself, and besought Cardinal Fieschi to be still.

Mastai was afraid of being attacked with a fit of epilepsy.

But the Cardinal, on the contrary, continued raising his voice with more solemnity, with more emphasis. At the thirty-third vote, Mastai Ferretti fell senseless.

It was the number of votes necessary to elect a Pope.

Nevertheless they counted as far as thirty-six.

Mastai had fainted upon the tiara.

Cardinal Diario Sforza, who was placed between Cardinal Lambruschini and Cardinal Polidori, whom Scarlett mentioned to Count Aberdeen as one of the possible candidates, then turned towards the former, and said to him in his Neapolitan patois:

"Ha! what says Your Excellency? We have chosen *the king of the Popes!*"

He had voted for Lambruschini, but Lambruschini had miscarried, and Polidosi, a reformist, heard it!

Behold their Eminences!

Cardinal Diario had died from an indigestion caused by eating lobsters, as we have said.

It is impossible to describe the joy of the party who gained the victory. The Conclave no longer had the air of an august congress, but of a hall of school-boys at play. They threw themselves on the still senseless Cardinal Mastai, and amid the noise of frantic exclamations and impassioned and disordered emotions, they carried him to the altar.

"After the monks the ladies!" cried Cardinal Micara, shrugging his shoulders, seeing the body in a swoon pass before him. "Long live St. Peter!"

And Cardinal Bernetti turning towards his neighbor, Cardinal d'Angeli:

"Let us go," said he; "the Papacy is f——. The last one stained it with blood, this one will prostitute it."

In the meanwhile they invested Cardinal Mastai in the Pontifical robes.

When, by the aid of Cardinal Oppozzoni's snuffbox, he returned to life, he found himself Pope. Immediate proclamation and adoration was then demanded.

The conduct of Cardinal Lambruschini was admirable for steadiness and dignity.

Cardinal Mastai, fatigued and white as the laces of his aub, was left alone, incapable of speaking a word.

From this tumultuous agitation in the chapel, it was quickly understood in the Quirinal that the Pope had been elected; and when the dinners of the Cardinals were brought, some indiscretions spread abroad the news of it in the city. It was then that Cardinal Lambruschini received the letter from the Count de Lützow, of which we have spoken. He threw it to one of his conclavists, remarking, "The imbecile."

The news spread throughout Rome; everybody hastened in the evening to see the smoke from the pipe of the stove in which they burned the ballots. But when they perceived that the usual hour was passed in which this white little cloud rose above the pipe of one of the cross-aisles of the edifice, the commotion in the city became extraordinary. The carriages of the diplomacy and of the nobility, and an immense crowd of people had gathered, as was common, to see the signal of what passed within. Seeing nothing, the belief in the election was confirmed.

Besides, they knew that of the three costumes which should on the morrow be used at the ceremony of the adoration of the Pope, neither the one to fit a tall nor medium-sized man had been called for. The rumor then spread that Cardinal Gizzi, a very small man, had been elected.

At the house of this Cardinal, and in the family mansion at Ceccano, the domestics stole some things, and broke the remainder.

In the town, consequently, the rejoicing was at its height. They had a Pope in accordance with the times and the public desire! This is why, on the morrow, the population of Rome and of its environs crowded all together to the square of the Quirinal, occupying the roofs and the windows of the surrounding edifices.

In Rome they passed the night in fêtes, in felicitations, in exchange of hopes. The families of those who had been condemned threw aside their mourning; profusion and smiles reigned everywhere. At last the hammer was heard demolishing the curtain of masonry, which concealed the gallery of the Quirinal.

The plaster was still fresh, for since Gregory XIII., no Conclave had lasted for so short a time.

Complete silence reigns; fifty thousand eyes are turned towards a space of a few yards in extent. The partition falls, and finally the Pontiff is seen upon his portable throne (*sedia gestoria*), surrounded by his court of Cardinals, Bishops, and Prelates, splendidly and picturesquely dressed — something of the Oriental, dazzling, striking to the most hardened imagination, and which would be grand were it not theatrical. Then a Cardinal advances to the front of the gallery, and with strong and sonorous voice proclaims Cardinal Mastai Ferretti Pope, under the name of Pius IX.

He on his side, filled with emotion and very pale, blesses the people, fallen upon their knees mute with stupor and astonishment. The cortege of the Pope passes, and the people ask:

"But who then is this Cardinal Mastai Ferretti?" Who? I am about to tell you.

CHAPTER XXV.

PIUS IX. BEFORE GRACE.

TOWARDS the middle of the sixteenth century, a manufacturer of combs at Breschia left his country, where he had hardly gained a subsistence, to establish himself at Sinigaglia. The name of this artisan was Albert Mastai. Fortune smiled upon the emigrant, who at first found the comforts of life, then a family, and finally a home in a land in which he was not born, but which was nevertheless Italian ground.

The stamp of adventurer stimulated the courage of the comb-maker's descendants; success increased their ardor. They consequently were seen to leap their ignoble limits and to glide among the small nobility of the province. For in the provinces, very often the best of blazons is a purse of five pounds.

Turbulent, haughty, and encroaching, never

passive in civil commotions; keeping up with the ideas of the age, always in the front ranks, never lagging, or among those who take a step and then stand still; on the watch for fortune's favors; the Mastai family began to have weight and influence in the town, and soon they ruled it. To this was added the marriage of Gian-Maria Mastai with a Ferretti of Ancona. She brought to him a rich heritage, a better known name to annex to his own, and the title of Count. And now behold the Mastai family launched into the province.

Girolamo Mastai-Ferretti espoused Catharine, a young lady of the Counts of Sollazzi. A tall, beautiful, and good woman, Catharine loved her children almost as much as she did the gossipings of the upstart nobility. From this marriage, Gian-Maria Mastai Ferretti, whom they had just elected Pope, was born in 1792.

The celebrated astronomer Inghirami, towards the commencement of this century, superintended a college of the Scolopi at Volterra. The Scolopi are the most bitter and formidable enemies of the Jesuits, — perhaps through the jealousy of trade, although the method of education and instruction of the former is hardly better than that of the latter; perhaps, also, from the maxim, that the gown hates the gown. To this college Gian-Maria, still very young, was sent; not because he gave indications of precocious intelligence, or presented a character which needed a guide, but because his father experienced a species of remorse for having neglected the education of his other children, and his mother, a very pious woman, desired to sow in his heart those religious principles which she saw were altogether forgotten at that time.

Authors who write the biographies of celebrated men, generally make of their heroes little prodigies, even from their childhood. I am humiliated for mine. Gian-Maria proved himself to be anything else than a prodigy.

Gian-Maria was pale, frail, small, in a condition of permanent convalescence. From the age of seven he was subject to epileptic convulsions, the attacks of which were almost without intermission.

Father Inghirami, loving him a little, took care of him. He took pity upon this organization, smothered in its development, and outraged by an implacable malady. The little Mastai was then spared labor and difficulties; and so much the more as his character appeared to be very pliable and very loving, so that he even disarmed the little despots of the school. This perhaps increased the tendency of Gian-Maria towards sloth. Inghirami knew how to read the character of man, as well as the book of the Firmament. He understood that there was something thoughtful and poetical in the indolence of Gian-Maria; but he, notwithstanding, judged that this young man was incapable of becoming anything. Then, as the fits were more frequent, and as Gian-Maria came out of one attack only to fall into another more frightful and hideous, Father Inghirami wrote to his parents to withdraw him from the college. Notwithstanding Gian-Maria did not return to the paternal mansion until towards the year 1812 or 1813.

Our hero had learned very little of Latin and of Greek at college; but, unknown to himself, he had acquired taste by reading the great poets, and frequently he had translated the sufferings and desires of his soul into verse, which was not very bad for his age. His mind had taken a romantic turn, which, assisted by an extreme nervous mobility, has since given to him the character of a very passionate and enthusiastic young man. He then returned to Sinigaglia.

His native town, at that time, formed part of the Italian kingdom. The period was distracted with Napoleon and with military and warlike ideas. Gian-Maria sang the Battle of Austerlitz and enrolled himself in the ranks of the Freemasons. He lived among the soldiers. He felt himself attracted towards France, excited by the exploits of the great Captain. His eyes turned towards the epaulets. He then began to educate himself, more conformably to his secret desires and to his birth. He betook himself to the practice of arms, displaying therein great aptitude and great agility, on account of his lank and slender form. He frequently rode on horseback, and was an excellent rider. He studied music, and played, not without a certain grace, upon the flute and violoncello. Finally, wishing to arrive at the pinnacle of the science of the barracks, he became very adroit in blacking a pipe by smoking, in emptying a bottle with elegance at one draught, and passionately fond of billiards and foot-ball.

By these exercises his health was improved. He adopted a costume half citizen, half military, a little like a journeyman barber, but supremely elegant for a provincial beau. He wore a coat *à la Polonaise* with black frogs, a red cap, pantaloons with a band, large turned-down shirt-collar with a red cravat streaming in the wind, spurs, a flower in his button-hole, and a cigar always in his mouth. Being a very pretty fellow, amours and adventures came at the same time. But, nevertheless, like all handsome young men, he was not very happy in his love. Although a poet, musician, skilful in chivalrous acts, with an attractive beauty and a smile upon his lips which opened all hearts, an easy and seductive speech, a soul filled with passion and tenderness,—there was only Lena, the daughter of a small merchant, who understood him, and who loved him to distraction. She loved him so far as to sacrifice to him everything, parents, youth, honor, and beauty.

Nevertheless, Gian-Maria pursued the chase elsewhere. He felt the tender fidelity of this mistress, which all the youth of Sinigaglia envied him; but he used her for a lever to awaken the haughty jealousy of Elena, the patrician daughter of Prince

Albani, who afterwards married into the house of the Litta of Milan.

Elena possessed a dazzling beauty; and was, besides, witty, a coquette, a bird upon the branch, a bee who sucked the dew from flowery calices and passed carelessly on. She perceived the young man's ardent love, and perhaps at first shared it. Unquestionably she encouraged him, for very often in the gray polonaise of Gian-Maria the tuft of myosotis was seen, which the evening before had been remarked like a constellation on the bosom of the belle. But the nature of this woman was not in sympathy with the tender and poetic one of the young man. She then was not able to understand his soft and feminine character. This, perhaps, was fortunate for Gian-Maria. His parents encouraged his love, that a marriage so desirable might take place. Elena only felt her heart moved by the glittering of epaulets; only attracted by the jingling of the trailing sabre. In the home of Prince Albani everything was found that was most elegant and exalted in the city. His salons at that time were filled with soldiers.

One day a journey was proposed to Loretto. Elena was one of the party. There also was a young man of Cesene, flag-officer of a regiment then in garrison at Sinigaglia. This officer frequented the society of the Albani, and Elena had very often felt the hand of the soldier tremble in her own when they danced the gavotte. On the way to Loretto, they were overtaken by a storm, — the fortune of Dido and Æneas! The officer did his best to shelter and protect the young girl from the sudden storm. But in this situation distances approach each other, familiarity takes place, the expression of gratitude is heard, and — the love, in circulation in their heart for some time, bursts into a kiss, and spreads like a fire.

Gian-Maria was forgotten, turned perhaps into ridicule; she had broken with him.

Lena always remained constant to console him. But Lena did not suffice for him. Hers was the love that yielded; he sought for that which resisted. For distraction Gian-Maria plunged into dissipation; worst of all, he gambled. But as the monthly pension of seven or eight crowns which his parents gave him did not suffice, he played with skill and with avidity; he even went so far as to be accused — unjustly, without doubt — of cheating at play. In all cases he played with great good luck; and if he did not cheat, he learned the science so well that when at Rome he played at faro with the old princess Ghigi, who, at least, passed for one of the most adroit players. This lady always inquired before inviting her party: "Well, Mr. Abbé, how shall we play this evening?" "Only as Madam, the Princess, shall wish," replied Mastai. And he won from her considerable amounts.

Nevertheless, play could not make him forget Elena. He then was smitten with his foster-sister,

15

Miss Morandi. She, perceiving that he took her as a makeshift, in return tried to pay him back a little. This passion, however, which had commenced in sport, soon became serious, particularly when Morandi made her successful début at the theatre and married Mr. Ambrozi, a tenor of some renown. Then the actress, less haughty than the girl, consoled this big baby for his love of Elena, — who, at the end of the reckoning, was only a portion for him.

This new flame stirred up some tempests in the family. They had admitted him to Elena because they dreamed of a marriage flattering to their self-love; but Isabella, his sister, could not pardon him the love of a citizen Miss.

Strange rumors were spread abroad respecting these relations between the brothers and sisters of the Mastai family. Their tenderness was believed to be more than fraternal; and in truth the conduct of neither the one nor the other was free from reproach. The sisters of Gian-Maria, very light in their conduct, assiduously coquetted with the Neapolitan officers that Murat at that time led into the Marches. General Pipé loved and was loved, so he told me, by this Isabella, who showed herself so jealous of, and who was so beloved by Gian-Maria.

CHAPTER XXVI.

ALL FOR THE BEST.

THE Napoleonic epic finished, Pius VII. returned to Rome. They then seriously thought of obtaining a situation for Gian-Maria, who led a life so irregular and so perfectly useless. He was sent to Rome that he might follow some career.

Gian-Maria had two uncles at Rome; one the Bishop of Pesaro, the other, Paolino Mastai, president of the Tribunal of A. C. (*Auditoris Cameræ*), and canon of St. Peter. These two uncles ought to assist him. The family assigned him a monthly pension of fifteen crowns, which was afterwards raised to seventeen crowns and a half. Arrived in the city, Gian-Maria rented a little room, a very poor one, alongside of St. Ignazio, and went to dine with Monseigneur Paolino.

This honest man had his face covered with pimples and scabby crusts; then he ate all his food without salt, eating a great deal of everything. Thus this excellent canon died from an indigestion after having eaten a whole sheep. Gian-Maria then lived very poorly with his uncle: so much the more as the latter did not love him much, and that he could not look upon the hideous countenance of his uncle without feeling sick at the stomach. He ate little and fled to his own apartment as soon as the dinner was over. In this manner he economized his small amount of money to gamble with and to clothe himself.

Gian-Maria soon became one of the most fashionable and elegant of the young men of Rome. He saw the most attractive salons of the nobility opened to him. The women were crazy for him, and he for the women. He chiefly frequented the Ghigi, Pianciani, Colonna, Doria, and Potenziani palaces, connected himself intimately with Count Vincenzo Colonna, whose wife Dona Clara he loved to distraction; which however did not prevent him from showing himself an assiduous chevalier with other ladies, from continuing many gallantries and becoming the hero of many adventures, which today are still related at the soirées of the Roman princes. He played a great deal, cheated everybody, above all, as we have mentioned, the old Princess Ghigi, who amused herself at this strategy in order to imitate Henry IV.

After the Congress of Vienna the organization of the guard of nobles for the Pope was spoken of.

This guard is composed of eighty horsemen, chosen from the noble and poor families of the State. They have twenty-five crowns (one hundred and thirty-five francs) per month pay, a handsome uniform and a fine horse at the expense of the State.

Twelve of them, in turn, must mount guard in the sixth ante-chamber of the Vatican, and accompany His Holiness whenever he goes out. A private guard has the rank of captain; the sergeant that of colonel; the lieutenants are major-generals. This guard for parade costs the people sixty thousand crowns per annum. Gian-Maria wished to become one, and exerted himself in order to succeed. Through his female acquaintances, and particularly through his uncle, it was not difficult for him to procure a recommendation for his candidacy. Cardinal Consalvi sent it to him; and Gian-Maria believing himself already appointed, strutted everywhere and showed this letter. But soon the Secretary of State was informed that Gian-Maria was epileptic. This not being agreeable to Cardinal Consalvi, he made him return the letter of designation. This was a thunder-stroke to the young man, already proud of the place; but particularly because all Rome would now know the reason why it had been refused him. Then desolate, he thought of quitting the laical world, and of entering upon the career of the prelacy.

To be admitted to this career, a species of inquest must be submitted to, after which a statement must be reduced to writing in which are set forth one's morals, social condition, and pecuniary circumstances. The prelacy is a species of ecclesiastical guard of honor to the Pope, a nursery from which are taken almost all the agents of the government. Gian-Maria was successful in the inquest, on account of the influence of his uncles and the Roman princesses. He then took the costume of an abbé, and was as elegant an abbé as he had been cavalier.

Mastai commenced the study of the laws, and frequented the chambers of the advocate Garriossi. And as in the new phase of his existence the advantages of play were diminished, and the small pension derived from his family did not suffice, his uncle, Monseigneur Paolino Mastai, endeavored to obtain for him the situation of coadjutor to Monseigneur Maccarani, canon of St. Peter.

This honest man lived upon the revenue of six or seven thousand crowns which the canonship yielded, and he gave to his coadjutor two or three hundred crowns per annum. The latter was obliged to fill his place in the chair, read the breviary, take a vow of chastity, refrain from luxurious dishes, in one word, act the canon in all the points and severity of its function. It was as hard as comical for the young man; but finally he resigned himself, and awaited his appointment. Indeed, the appointment was already written, and the proper officer, the *dateria*, was just about to forward it to him, when they also learned of his fatal malady and its frequent and fatal attacks. The bulls were not delivered.

This fresh blow threw him into despair. He first began to blaspheme, then to weep. He saw the implacable spectre of this evil always before him, barring the road everywhere. He rushed out to drown himself in the Tiber. A friend of his childhood, the advocate Cattabene, his countryman and his neighbor, met him in this exasperated condition as he was going along the Campovaccino. Mr. Cattabene commenced to console and turn him from his sinister project; and by talking, mingling together the serious and the agreeable, he led him to the door of the canon Storace, the confessor of Gian-Maria.

This canon was a booby, whom the penitent himself turned into ridicule, telling the absurd questions which the canon asked him at his confessions, and the still more absurd explanations that he, Gian-Maria, returned. Mastai had no confidence either in the good sense or counsels of this man; nevertheless Mr. Cattabene led him there.

At that time this canon superintended the hospital of *Tata Fioranni*, near the Argentine Theatre, — a hospital into which they collected the little street beggars, and where they brought them up and gave them a trade. The Rev. Storace, touched with the distress of the penitent, proposed to him, if he was willing, to take his place in the government of the hospital, and, in a word, become its superintendent and prefect.

There were fifteen individuals in the establishment. Gian-Maria accepted, — and behold him installed! He then cast aside the habit of the gallant abbé and took the costume of a provincial priest, with coarse shoes, a cassock of coarse cloth, wretched cap, something indeed so grotesque that he was the first to ridicule it. He also abandoned all his old acquaintances in fashionable life, except a little citizen Jewess, secreted alongside the *Ghetto*, whom he constantly saw.

Gian-Maria, upon quitting college, had almost abandoned his studies; he now recommenced them with ardor. He particularly applied himself to the ecclesiastical sciences under the direction of the Abbé Grazioli. He was grieved in not being able to do more, chiefly in not being able to write, on account of his malady. But, living in the hospital and leading a wiser and more regulated life, his malady began to decrease, and the attacks to diminish. Then Gian-Maria believed in miracles! He redoubled his activity against those poor creatures abandoned by the world, confined in this place and confided to his discretion. He was at this time 22 or 23 years of age.

CHAPTER XXVII.

PIUS IX. DURING GRACE.

PERCEIVING his health ameliorated, and believing that it was the grace of God which called him by this unhoped for cure, he decided to enter into orders. He proved by a doctor's certificate that his malady had left him, and obtained the dispensation to take at once all orders as far as the priesthood. Indeed, a short time after, he performed his first mass at St. Catharine of Ferrari, at which his father and some of his friends and compatriots assisted, who had come to Rome expressly for this purpose.

Launched in his career, his ambition excited him. He spoke with great facility, and his speech was vivid, sympathetic, and flowery. He was anxious to become a preacher. Gian-Maria began by preaching short sermons (*fervorini*) in the Church of St. Charles. It was a brilliant success.

Odeschalchi, not yet, at this time, a Cardinal, heard them speak of this young man and desired his acquaintance.

Odeschalchi was a missionary contractor. Chief of a troop of missionaries, he had formed a connection with Piatti, a missionary agent who speculated in the same species of public shows, and who threatened to compete with him. At Rome, preachers are engaged for a night sermon, for an harangue in some public place, or for the buffoon little discourses, which are called instructions, in the same way that a theatre agent or an *impressario* engages a tenor, or soprano, a bouffe, or a baritone. These two speculators commenced by admitting the young debutant to their friendship; afterwards they took him into co-partnership.

Cardinal Testaferrata, Bishop of Sinigaglia, wrote

this year to the firm of Odeschalchi, Piatti & Co., to engage for the season a troop of missionaries for his diocese. It was in the year 1819 that this troop was formed. And as a success was likely to follow from the début of the converted Mastai, in a place where he had been known as a libertine, gambler, and rowdy, they enrolled and sent him. They had calculated admirably upon his success. Never indeed had a prima-donna or acrobat had one like it at the famous fair of Sinigaglia. The people made fools of themselves. The women, chiefly, were filled with enthusiasm for the young Mastai. The female penitents crowded to his confessional like flies to honey. They wished to hear him, to see him, to fumble him, to breathe his breath. Madam Simonelli felt a more than Italian passion for him — a passion more moorish and tropical. She ran after the young saint like an object falling by its gravity. Madam Ferretti, a fool, a visionary, a St. Therese without her mysticism, as pretty and as impassioned as Simonelli, prophesied all manner of things for him, even the Papacy.

Miss Ferretti, abandoned or but slightly appreciated by her holy confessor, after his departure went and shut herself up in the Convent of Gubio, and there wept her unappreciated love, her unsatisfied passion.

During the mission, the Abbé Mastai reserved the night-preaching for himself. And truly there was something picturesque and fantastic in preaching in a church plunged in obscurity, where the pale and handsome countenance of the inspired young man was only illuminated in the pulpit by a few wax candles. He poured out the poesy and passion which burned in his soul upon a silent and affected audience. But still stranger were those nightly representations upon the great government square, with the windows lighted by thousands of candles and filled with animated faces. The square was crowded with an impassioned and enthusiastic mob. This multitude lived only upon the breath of this young man, who was raised upon a trestle with an immense Christ hauled up on a level with him, and alongside of him a death's-head with a piece of candle stuck into the skull. Gian-Maria wore a black cassock festooned to his side, with a woollen girdle, a surplice with a long, embroidered ruffle, an open shirt-collar, and a violet stole. His hair long behind, short before, encompassed a very pale and handsome face, shaved extremely smooth. His voice was sympathetic, and sonorous as a metal cord. The words fell from his fresh and rosy lips, smiling even in anger. His gestures were picturesque, animated, profuse, but graceful. His pose was altogether elegant, pliant, almost statuesque. Mastai did not preach, he acted. He performed in the pulpit as he had acted in the little comic operas, and in the dramas of Metastasio in the Theatre of Sinigaglia with amateurs. He had always taken a female part. Now he scourged himself with ardor, he plunged his hands into the burning alcohol to demonstrate the fiery flames of purgatory. There were some strange scenes, and furious invectives against those who ridiculed these juggling feats. On the Place Doria, the people dragged some young men from the billiard-table that they might listen to the sermon; and on the government square they came near knocking down the jailer, who in compliance with his orders closed the shutters of the prison, and prevented the prisoners from seeing the sight.

Finally the mission was ended; Mastai returned to Rome, crowned with laurels, and on the road to a happy future.

It was at this period that he saw himself obliged to hasten to Naples on account of his sister Isabella. Very pretty, Isabella had been carried off, or rather she had followed a lover to Naples, with whom she had lived for some time in that city. Afterwards, abandoned or discontented, she had separated from him, and had fallen into the most poignant distress. From disgrace to disgrace, disaster to disaster, Isabella had arrived at the lowest point to which a woman can attain.

> Lorsque, mes sœurs, vos pauvres filles
> Le soir, pour avoir un jupon,
> Vont vendre l'amour en guenilles
> Au diable, votre âme en répond,
> Saint Père, au moins, soyez bon père,
> Ou je f....le saint-siége au feu !
>   BERANGER, "*Le Fils du Pape.*"

Gian-Maria received from his much-loved sister a touching letter, and hastened to withdraw her from the frightful mansion into which her misery had thrown her.

Soon after his return to Rome, he had to leave the hospital of *Tata Giovanni*. He had a dispute with his colleague, D. Pio Bighi, on account of his excessive severity and partiality. The quarrel took place at table. D. Pio Bighi, who was angry, dressed the hair of poor Mastai with a tureen of soup, and even began to aggravate his correction. Mastai went to complain to his protector, the Cardinal de la Genga, who was afterwards Leo XII. To extinguish the scandal, the Cardinal lent himself to the request of Mastai, who desired to leave Rome for some time.

Pius VII. was disposed, about this time, to send to Chili a politico-religious mission, of which Mgr. Muzio, Bishop of Civita de Castello, was the chief. Mastai solicited from the Cardinal de la Genga the place of secretary to the mission. His versatile fancy was pleased in advance in dreaming of long voyages, of the ocean, of the tropics, of savages to be converted, of frequenting courts, of facing martyrdom, of a new world, and of the liberty of nature. They wrote to his mother, who was opposed to it, frightened with the state of her son's health. The Cardinal-Bishop of Sinigaglia went to calm the fears and alarms of the countess, and avowed to her that a Cardinal had spoken to Pius VII. of her son for this expedition. Vanity vanquished the tenderness of the mother; the patrician conquered the woman.

The Cardinal-Vicar, Annibal de la Genga, in truth, foreseeing a refusal from Cardinal Consalvi, Secretary of State, had demanded and obtained quietly from Pius VII. the nomination of Mastai. The Pope agreed to it, and spoke of it to Consalvi. The latter, much embarrassed, informed his SS. that the *dateria* had already forwarded the brief which designated for the place coveted by Mastai, the Canon D. Giuseppi Sallusti. But the word of a Pope could not fail, and the matter had to be arranged. Cardinal Consalvi gave it into the charge of Monseigneur Muzio. "At the first attack of epilepsy," said his Eminence to the Legate, "cast him wherever you will, and let D. Giuseppi Sallusti exercise the functions of Secretary to the Vicar Apostolic." Mgr. Muzio understood and obeyed. Behold them, then, set out and awaiting, at the port of Genoa, the hour of their departure.

During these transactions, Pius VII. dies, and Cardinal de la Genga, the protector of Mastai, is elected Pope. Mgr. Muzio, before going, wished to wait for the nomination of the new Pontiff. He was then obliged to embark and take Mastai with him. The Apostolic Legate always counted on this fortunate epilepsy which should disembarrass him. But the epilepsy did not come. Neither the fatigues of the voyage, nor the confinement which they had to undergo at the Balearic Islands, nor the sea-sickness — nothing could provoke it. After a frightful voyage, they arrived at Buenos-Ayres. From thence, to reach Chili, they had still to undergo a long journey by land, very hard, incommodious, on mule-back, sleeping very often on the ground upon a bullock's hide, without supper, or God knows what kind of a supper. At last they arrived at Mendoza. The next day the mission proposed to make its entry into Chili. It was impossible, now, to dismiss Mastai; Mgr. Muzio could not present himself with two secretaries. It was then necessary to make some arrangement, and Mastai had to be contented with the place of private secretary to the Apostolic Legate. The so much desired epilepsy finally came, but too late, very light, and when Mgr. Muzio had not required it. Mastai afterwards said that the passage of the line did him a great deal of good, having had, during the whole time that he remained in Chili, only one attack of his complaint. The mission began.

The Abbé Mastai preached to the natives, and played also his ordinary part of night-preacher. The Chilians did not show themselves as enthusiastic as the inhabitants of Sinigaglia; perhaps because they had not been touched by grace, perhaps because these republicans, lacking elegance, loved their orators of the tribune, or *las corridas de toros*, more; perhaps, finally, because the troop was not happily in tune, and did not harmonize. In short, the religious enterprise was a failure.

Mastai did his best to make the political mission also a failure. He was introduced into the midst of high Chilian society. By his handsome face he seduced the women; by his title of Count he dazzled these skin-deep republicans, who were at heart haughty Spaniards. He deceived his companions with raillery; he caricatured his rival Sallusti; he alarmed the politicians, frightened the high clergy, awakened everybody's suspicion against the concealed design of their mission. At the same time Mastai embroiled the legate with his secretary; he made both of them commit blunders, by purposely arranging things for this end, in his quality of private secretary. For a *coup-de-grace* he rendered Mgr. Muzio ridiculous; and here is the way he did it.

The Augustines of the province of Chili had all obtained secularization through the Vicar Apostolic. There remained only in the convent the provincial, the cook, and a dog. The provincial seeing himself left alone, solicited secularization in his turn for himself, for the cook, and for the dog. Mastai wrote out the decree with the greatest gravity in the world, put into his pocket sixty *douros*, twenty *douros* for each, and presented the decree to his master for his signature, who signed always without reading. The next morning the journals published the decree for the secularization of the dog! After this humbug the place would no longer hold them.

The Bishop of Civita di Castello, a matter-of-fact

man, did not hesitate for an instant in speaking of their return, at first discouraged by their want of success, in the end frightened. The natives, whom they wished to convert, understanding nothing of their language, of their grimaces, of their doctrines, put themselves to expense in order to martyrize them: the politicians, suspecting their mission, prepared to expel them. The Bishop of Civita di Castello, who hardly cared to be served up as *roast beef* to the natives, nor of being expelled like deputies — without abandoning the place, engaged his passage and that of his troop for Europe. Mastai, possessed of the Spirit of God, and relishing revenge, was willing to remain at all cost.

He wished to be a little martyrized here and there, provided that they did not touch his face: he was willing to throw the whole disrepute entirely upon his colleagues. He believed perhaps truly in all that he spoke. In virtue of speaking to others, Mastai had ended by being intoxicated with the words and principles which he taught: having formed a party in highest Chilian society, he flattered himself with success when Monseigneur had failed. The latter, whether he understood, or whether he believed, dragged Mastai by force from that accursed country, and six months after their arrival they again embarked for Europe. On their return, Leo XII. recognized the courage and the skill employed by the young missionary, as also his thirst for martyrdom. Leo XII., of a savage nature himself, sympathized with enthusiastic and elevated characters. He valued ability highly. He relegated Monseigneur Muzio to his bishopric and Sallusti to his estate of S. Vito, and offered to nominate Mastai prelate. Mastai refused the *mantelletta*. The Pope insisted with more earnestness, but Mastai remained firm. Then they offered to him the presidency of the hospital of S. Miche at Ripa, (1825,) which he accepted.

In this rich hospital they gathered the magdalens, bad children, and poor children, who were instructed by teaching them the liberal arts. Excellent artists have come out of this hospital, of whom we shall name here one only, the most eminent engraver of the age, one of the most honorable and one of the most beautiful characters of Italy, Mr. Calamatta.

Mastai took this superintendency with the title of President, and employed a severity often stained with cruelty. Gian-Maria was a man who over-did everything through too much zeal or through too much ardor. In 1827, Leo XII. nominated him Archbishop of Spoleto, his own country, and already Cardinal *in petto*.

CHAPTER XXVIII.

POLITICS AT SEE-SAW.

EVERYTHING went wrong in the exercise of this new office. The Archbishop Mastai was detested; he displeased everybody. Of a violent, sanguine, intolerant character, always cruel towards the weak, he displayed a zeal not belonging to the times; he manifested a rigor arising from insolence amounting to madness. In a word, he conducted himself so badly, that when the Revolution of 1831 broke out, he was forced to fly. He nevertheless distributed a good deal in alms, although much inclined to avarice! But these charities were accompanied with so much roughness, that they almost took the form of an outrage. Reassured, however, he returned shortly afterwards, and it was he who suborned Sercognani, whom Louis Napoleon afterwards accompanied to the conquest of Rome. The head of the corrupt gang, and his first fears quieted, Mastai subdued a little the petulance of his character and showed himself more moderate; so much the more, as his brothers implicated in the Revolution were pursued. He then called to mind thoughts once endeared to him, when young and a layman, and the principles of 1789, which he had sucked in during his childhood. Struck by this inward return to aspirations, which he could no longer openly avow, he protected the liberals; he saved some, by hiding them as far as he could from the Pontifical inquisitors. Nevertheless, that he might not awaken suspicions, he ordered a revolutionist who had been buried by his parents in consecrated ground contrary to his orders, which were the orders of the Pontiff, to be exhumed. The family of the deceased again placed the body in a tomb in the Church, and threatened the Archbishop. The latter remained tranquil, contented with having shown to Rome that he did not partake the sentiments of some members of his family.

Notwithstanding, on account of his brothers, Cardinal Testaferrata treated him very badly, when Mastai went to meet him at Civita Castellana, to compliment His Eminence on his return from the famous Conclave which gave to the world Gregory XVI.

The new Pope at first believed that Archbishop Mastai was an accomplice in the liberalism of his relations, and regarded him with an evil eye. But he afterwards learned that it was Mastai who had treated with Sercognani, and had removed him from Rome. He had, besides, the proofs that Sercognani could have marched upon the Eternal City and made prisoners the whole Sacred College assembled in Conclave. Gregory then experienced a sudden and lively sympathy for the Archbishop, praised him a great deal for his conduct in tacking in such difficult times between two streams — between the priests and the people, and wished to reward him. He withdrew him from the diocese of Spoleto, where Mastai only received a revenue of from three to four thousand crowns, and nominated him Cardinal and Bishop of Imola, which yielded a revenue of nine thousand crowns, (50,000 francs, $10,000.)

At Imola, Mastai conducted himself in the same way as at Spoleto, but was less violent. In order to conceal what he might feel in his heart, he broke off every kind of relation with his family, who were marked upon the book of the police as liberals, dangerous, and opposed to ecclesiastical government. But at the same time he closed his eyes upon the conduct of individuals imbued with liberalism, and concealed all with his responsibility. He principally showed himself exceedingly opposed to the *centurioni*, that species of armed police who, commanded by that corsair in a red robe, Cardinal Albani, desolated the Romagna. This attracted to him the esteem of the people, and caused the irritability and brutality of his character to be forgiven.

Wonderful to relate, he was inexorable in the extreme with women whose conduct was light! But was that, however, of His Eminence Mastai, less irreproachable? Alas, no!

Upon the occasion of an apostolic visit, he had remarked, in a convent of nuns, in a little village lost in the midst of the mountains, an abbess who had touched his heart. It was the abbess of Fognano. This convent was in the dependency of his suffragan, the Bishop of Faenza, Mgr. Folicardi. Mastai, whether he was jealous of this Bishop, or that he did not wish to have his mistress under the direction of another, intrigued at Rome, paid some money, and succeeded in detaching Fognano from the diocese of Faenza and having it added to that of Imola. Mgr. Folicardi from that time swore implacable hatred against Mastai. He wrote report after report to the Pope upon the scandal of the visits of the Cardinal to the abbess. But Gregory, always insensible to this kind of sin, took no notice of them. Mastai, when afterwards Pius IX., persecuted Mgr. Folicardi and his family with bitterness. The love of Mastai for this abbess survived for the age and conveniences of the tiara. While upon a journey into his States, which Pius IX. made in 1855, he deviated from his route that he might visit the abbess and breakfast with her.

But this seductive La Vallière was not the only one to inflame *the angelic soul of Pius IX.* (style of the Catholic journals). Dona Clara Colonna likewise had waited for times and events. On his return from Chili, Mgr. Mastai brought only one souvenir. It was a paroquet for Dona Clara! This gallant has since, for many years, been the delight of a convent of nuns. The passion for Dona Clara had been the most violent of Mastai's. All Rome related the follies which he had committed for this pretty person. When Mastai, still a layman, presented himself to Pius XII. for the purpose of obtaining the letter of nomination for the noble guard, His Holiness said to him:

"My child, *caro giovani*, you are afflicted with two cruel maladies: you are epileptic and amorous. Enter into orders, *fatevi chierico*, and you will be cured of both."

Mastai obeyed; but it cured neither his infirmity nor his love. Dona Clara was married with the Count Vincenzo Colonna; but she always exercised a marked influence upon her sweetheart, and she promoted and tugged him through the whole of his career. Indeed, she was the cause of his being nominated to the chair of Ipoleto and to that of Imola. She solicited the purple for him; she advanced the necessary expenses for his installation to the Cardinalcy, and also did the honors of the house in the fêtes which accompanied it. Doña Clara was beautiful, though fat; she wrote verses, and was a Liberal. In the uncertainty which seized Pius IX. as soon as he was made Pope, as to what conduct he should pursue, Dona Clara powerfully co-operated with Mgr. Corboli and the Canon Grazioso, confessor of Pius IX., to decide him in favor of reform. He listened to them; and the Catholic world, for one year, believed that the Holy Ghost guided by the hand this Vicar of Christ; and the political world was struck with stupor, seeing in the Apostolic chair a Pope who amnestied, reformed, almost spoke of liberty, and placed himself outside of the terrible fascination of Austria. The universal illusion did not last long. Mgr. Corboli died, and was replaced by Antonelli; Grazioso died, and Mgr. Stella, a billiard-player, took his post; Dona Clara died, and the Countess de Spaur appeared.

Mademoiselle Thérèse Giraud, a very pretty woman, caused her husband, Dotwell, an English antiquary, who left her his fortune, to die with chagrin. She was afterwards married to Count de Spaur, minister of the king of Bavaria. Dona Clara, that she might have opportunity for frequently seeing the Pope, made him adopt the custom of giving audience to women. The Countess De Spaur thus commenced to visit His Holiness to intrigue in favor of Austria and in favor of herself. The Abbess of Fognano lived at a distance; Dona Clara was dead; there was a vacant place to be taken. The Italian Du Barry was not the woman to neglect it, or to suffer it to be filled by others. Handsome, insinuating, gay, full of resources, a verse-maker, conversing on the fine arts, relating the rumors of the city and of the salons with great wit, she became the Egeria of the Vice-God, put her hand to the fabrication of dogmas, of encyclicals, apostolic letters, to politics, and especially to diplomacy. It pleased her to hold Count Rossi in check, to defy the Liberals, to serve Naples and Vienna. Her elegance, her conversation, her person dazzled Pius IX., who finished by disguising himself as a domestic and following her to Gaeta, in 1849; for His Holiness left Rome rather for the purpose of being with this Abigail than from fear of remaining there, or from withdrawing himself from the increasing pressure of the revolution. Cardinal Antonelli afterwards drove away this woman from the Vatican, through jealousy of her influence, and advised the Holy Father to pay court to the Immaculate Conception. It was more pure and almost as moral, and Pius IX. obeyed. Pius IX. always obeys somebody in everything.

Mastai dispensed in his diocese a large amount of money in charities, and, in general, he appeared good, disguising his likings, thanks to the Canon Sarretti, his vicar, an excellent and learned man. Pius IX. rewarded this mentor and friend very badly. Notwithstanding, it was to the course that Sarretti made him pursue, to the road that this man made him traverse, that the Bishop of Imola owes the name of being liberal and just which opened the way to the Papacy. But we always forget those whom we have used as a footstool to mount on. We are never willing to remember the disrespectful times when we were nobodies.

Mastai, to make amends, always showed himself devoted and even servile towards the Cardinals of Bologna, of Ravenna, and of Forli.

His Eminence Gian-Maria Mastai-Ferretti occupied then the Episcopal Chair of Imola, when he was presented to the Conclave, which nominated him Pope.

But what was the situation of Italy on the morning of the advent to the throne of this new Pontiff? What kind of Pope would it have required? What kind of a man was Pius IX.?

CHAPTER XXIX.

WHAT EUROPE DESIRED.

THIS was the situation of Europe and of Italy. Among the sovereigns there were epileptics — the King of Naples, the Emperor of Austria, and the Pope; three were women; three were capricious and dreamers — the King of Prussia, Charles Albert, and the King of Sweden; a lymphatic fox was on the throne of Belgium; George Dandin was on the throne of France; and only one man who by his character, dignity, and intelligence graced monarchy — the Czar! The other sovereigns were crowned plebeians. But what did Italy wish at this period, and what was the attitude of the European cabinets opposed to her?

What the Italian States then demanded can be summed up in one word: Reform! Under the cry for reform was perhaps hidden the idea of a constitution; in the bosom of the constitution the principle of nationality was concealed. The feeling for the republic formed the worship of a few chosen men, who, convinced à *priori* by the study of political science, or cured by experience of the prejudice that a King could respect liberty, saw no other issue to the Italian question. The mass would have agreed. It would have been satisfied with a *true charter!* It was almost what had been demanded in the famous protestation of Rimini; in the petitions of the Lombard congregations; in the petitions to the Grand Duke of Tuscany; in the wishes expressed to Charles Albert, and by the partial insurrections of the Two Sicilies.

These necessities of the country and these wishes were trodden under foot by the Italian sovereigns; and were opposed by the foreign powers.

They all saw that the revolution was included in these demands; they all saw that this dreaded revolution dawned upon the horizon; but rather than satisfy it they were decided to run the chance and the danger of suppressing it.

Immoral and inexorable, the Princes of Europe did not recognize in the Italian people any right, any maturity of ideas, any elevation of soul in aspiring after liberty. The secular atonement, for its abuse of force, in past ages, ought still to endure for ages. They did not count for anything that this people had formerly provoked in Europe the affranchisement of the commons; that it had given birth to the Renaissance. They thought it worthy, at most, of a few judicial and administrative reforms, a code of judges, and a mayor selected by the police!

Among the Northern courts, Prussia, the most liberal, was the least hostile. Baron Caunitz thought:

"That the College of the Cardinals was destined to form a species of ministry; but that it was not necessary that all the other offices should be in the hands of the clergy." *

He greatly regretted that the jealousy of Austria rendered the task which the Pope had undertaken more difficult, and that this power had assumed an attitude of provocation and menace in Lombardy, in order to have a pretext for intervention.†

And in his despatch to Chevalier Bunsen, his ambassador, he added:

"His Majesty is penetrated with the utility, with even the necessity of certain legislative and administrative reforms which the actual state of Italy demands. The sympathies of our august master are bestowed upon the sovereigns of that country, who have undertaken the task, often perilous and thankless, of accomplishing these reforms. But at the same time, the king is also persuaded that the work of reforms such as he wishes, that it may not become a fruitful source of trouble and confusion, requires in Italy the constant maintenance of good relations and perfect understanding among the governments who participate in the supreme

---

* Despatch of Mr. Howard to Lord Palmerston, Berlin, Aug. 17, 1847.

† Idem, of the 9th September.

authority of the Peninsula, in order that all pernicious discords, all violent conflicts among them, may not turn to the misfortune of Italy, and finally surrender it either to oppression or to anarchy."

The policy of Russia was framed for resistance, without evasion and without restriction.

"In a conversation which I have had with Mr. de Nesselrode," wrote the Minister of Naples at St. Petersburg on the 13th March, 1847, to the Prince de Scilla, "His Excellency has expressed to me, in his own name as well as in the name of the Emperor, the satisfaction which is experienced here for the impassible and strong attitude which the King, our august master, opposes to the lawless movements which for some months have agitated the Italian Peninsula. His Imperial Majesty beholds with profound regret the enthusiasm to which the other Italian Princes appear to yield, because, in weakening the principle of sovereign authority, in a country already strongly inclined of itself to clamorous perturbations, this authority gives way and anarchy succeeds to the peaceful and lawful state. His Excellency the Count de Nesselrode has also expressed to me the wish that His Majesty the King, our august master, might will to persist in his system of dignity, to accord, if it be necessary, to his people what in his wisdom, His Majesty the King believes urgent and necessary, but in the plenitude of his power and of his spontaneous will; although in this sudden fever for amelioration, which the Italian people appear to be seized with, His Imperial Majesty sees rather an exterior excitement, for the removal of influence, than a real and felt want. For a nation does not pass from one day to the next, from a state almost of satisfaction and tranquillity to tendencies of radical revolutions, at which Italy seems to aim at this deplorable moment. . . . . . . The support of the Czar to resistance, and to the firm conduct of Austria, is assured in advance."

The policy of Prince de Metternich upon his side was very hard, especially at the beginning.

"The Prince de Metternich," wrote Lord Cowley on the 17th of June, 1846, to Lord Palmerston, "disapproves of a general amnesty, and desires that the institutions, that they appear too willing to give to the Roman States, may be restrained within the limits laid down in a memorial presented by the ambassador of Austria to the deceased Pope. He desires to be supported in these remonstrances by the ambassador of France and Rome."

Mr. de Metternich moreover maintained:

"That the revolution was complete at Rome and in Tuscany. For a revolution takes place when the government of a State is deprived of all its powers, and of its whole governmental action; and what, at this moment, was demanded in Italy, was the destruction of the elements of government under the pretext and in the name of reforms." *

* Despatch of Lord Ponsonby to Lord Palmerston, July 30, 1847.

He added:

"That Central Italy was given over to a revolutionary movement, at the head of which were the chiefs of the society that for years had undermined the States of the Peninsula; that under the banner of administrative reforms the factions paralyzed the lawful action of authority, and aimed at the fusion of the Italian States into one body politic: not for an Italian monarchy, because the possible King of this monarchy did not exist on the other, nor on this side of the Alps; but in the creation of a republic, very probably federative, like that of North America and Switzerland."*

Mr. de Metternich wrote to the Grand-Duke of Tuscany: "In order to read him a serious lesson upon his conduct, and to teach him, that if His Imperial Highness ever undertook to establish a civic guard in his States, he would make them rather to be occupied by Austrian troops, as well as every other small Italian State that should follow his example." †

Afterwards the Prince de Metternich ordered his minister at Turin to present this same despatch to the King of Piedmont, and wrote to Count de Lutzow at Rome:

"The revolutionary factions nourish sentiments of

---

* Despatch of Prince de Metternich to Count Dietrichstein, of August 2, 1847.

† Despatch of Lord Abercromby to Lord Palmerston, Aug. 19, 1847.

hatred against our Court, which is the natural consequence of the constancy of our efforts in favor of supporting moral principles and conditions which form the base of social life and public repose. The spirit of faction is a lying spirit, and we are the tried adversaries of this spirit." *

The Prince sought to excuse himself for the Sanfediste revolt which he had provoked at Rome, which had been put down, and of which the diplomatic body itself accused him. So that in the despatch which he wrote to his ambassador at London, the 27th September, 1847, after having laid down the principle of the exterior and interior independence of the Italian Princes, he endeavors to prove to Lord Palmerston: "That in spite of the inexact and contrary information received by His Lordship from the different points of Italy, the Imperial Government was incapable of disowning these principles." Afterwards, whether he had finally understood the true position of Austria, or whether he had thought the time had arrived for casting off a useless mask, he uttered a cry of distress and sent fresh troops into Italy.

"The spirit of subversion, which under the flag of reform is appearing in some States of the Italian Peninsula, has taken for its watch-word hatred against the Austrian power. The reasons which lead the conductors of the movement in this direc-

* Despatch of Prince de Metternich to Count de Lutzow, Aug. 15, 1847.

tion are too palpable to need any explanation. Thus we limit ourselves in admitting the fact and in not losing sight of the consequences. The events for which Switzerland to-day serves for an arena, will augment the intensity of the disturbances in Italy, and they will thus have an influence upon the situation of the government and parties in the Peninsula, as well as materially upon that of the Lombardo-Venetian kingdom. Thus the Emperor looks upon himself as bound, by the interest which he owes to his crown and to his subjects, to augment the armed force in that kingdom."*

To this note, communicated to the cabinets of Europe, Lord Palmerston, who was not duped by it, replied by his despatch of the 28th of December, to Lord Ponsonby at Vienna.

"The government of Her Majesty believes that the sentiment of hostility against Austria which prevails generally throughout Italy, has its origin principally, if not altogether, in the mistrust as to the intentions of Austria, and to the apprehension that the Cabinet of Vienna meditates an intervention in the interior affairs of the Italian States, in order to avert or retard the ameliorations and reforms which the sovereigns have been constrained to make, and which the people consider as essential to their well-being and prosperity. This hostile sentiment is founded upon fear, and Her Majesty's

* Despatch of Prince de Metternich to Count Dietrichstein, Dec. 14, 1847.

Government knows that this fear has no foundation. But Her Majesty's Government feels some apprehension lest this reinforcement of troops in Lombardy may confirm the erroneous opinion of the Italians as to the intentions and design of the Austrian Government, and augment their fears, and give a new impulse to the pre-existent sentiments of hostility. Her Majesty's Government does not see any danger as to the tranquillity of Italy being compromised, . . . and it expresses its regret that the apparent calm of the Lombardo-Venetian kingdom has not inspired the Austrian Government with the conviction of its continuation."

The political action of Lord Palmerston in Italy, at this period, has been singularly exaggerated. Perhaps the conduct, counsels, desires, and views of his agents, who were in a position to feel the rebound of Italian sentiment so powerfully developed, and who were in a position to see clearly all the miseries of the Italians,— perhaps, I say, the support of the English diplomatists, raised the energy of the people, and made it hope for a more tolerable future, guaranteed by freer political institutions than were promised by the reforms. Nevertheless, the English Government not only did nothing to encourage the Italians, but it opposed them by employing even menaces. In his despatch to Lord Ponsonby, of August 12, 1847, Lord Palmerston recognized the inviolability of the treaties of 1814 and 1815; he recognized the independence of the

States and of the sovereigns at the same time as the urgent necessity of reform in all the States, particularly at Naples and Rome. In his despatch to Lord Abercromby, of November 27, he lays down the principle "that a nation can voluntarily leave to the discretion of the Crown the choice of modes and the form of measures; but it is equally demonstrated that this confidence is accorded to the crown solely and entirely under an agreed condition, to wit: that the Crown will, in good faith, apply itself in progressively introducing into the administration of the nation those ameliorations which the reasonable wants and desires of the nation may demand."

And he wrote to Lord Minto, on the 18th of September, to advise this policy to the Italian sovereigns, whom he might see on his journey across Italy, establishing as the basis of the English policy, "That Her Majesty's Government was profoundly impressed with the conviction that it was prudent for sovereigns and their governments to continue in the administration of their affairs a system of progressive ameliorations; to frame a remedy for the evils whose existence they shall have recognized after investigation; to renew from time to time the ancient institutions of their countries, for the purpose of rendering them fitter for the gradual development of intelligence and for the growing diffusion of political knowledge; and that Her Majesty's Government was of the opinion, that if an independent sovereign judges it opportune to make in his States changes in the laws and institutions of his nation for the good of his people, no other nation had any right to oppose him in it."

And as the Prince de Metternich appeared to make some restrictions upon this point in his despatch to Lord Ponsonby at Vienna, by the 11th of September, 1847, he renewed this declaration with much force and clearness, and terminated with these remarkable words:

"Whatever may be the reports which the Government of Her Majesty may have received, regarding the last transactions and the recent diplomatic communications in Italy, he was persuaded that the Austrian government could not imagine, nor have authorized any fact in opposition to these principles, and that the Austrian government could not have any intention, neither with the King of Sardinia, nor with the Pope, of converting, it matters not what measure of *interior legislation* or administrative reform of these sovereigns, into an occasion of aggression upon their territory or their rights. For in this case, the Government of Her Majesty would profoundly deplore an event which it would be impossible for Great Britain to regard with indifference; and the territory of these States could never be violated without leading to consequences of great gravity and of extreme importance."

Lord Palmerston did not then confine himself only to reforms, but he spoke of legislative ameliorations, and threatened Austria if she opposed the regular progress of affairs.

We have seen, then, Prussia acquiesce in the reformist movement of Italy, Austria submit to it, Russia repel it, England provoke it: we shall now see France accept it.

CHAPTER XXX.

WHAT FRANCE DESIRED.

THERE were doubts and suspicions regarding the policy of the Cabinet of the Tuileries at this period. The English ambassadors at Vienna, at Berlin, and at Turin, had done nothing but denounce it to Lord Palmerston, as the accomplice of Austrian policy. And it appears that, on account of this concubinage, it was also disgraced in France. There was most certainly something strange — because we find that Mr. Guizot, in his correspondence with the ambassador at Rome, almost always made use of private letters, and seldom of despatches. It was said that it was a matter of business between him and M. Rossi, and that it had hardly any relation to the French nation. Perhaps it was not in accordance with the King, and he endeavored, by this unusual form in a constitutional government, to manage the honor and interests of the country, by wholly retaining the portfolio and flattering the contracted policy of the

King. Nevertheless, the policy of M. Guizot was not so retrograde and Austrian, as it has been said, and, if he remained behind England, he was in advance of the North. Let us do justice to every one!

We have seen what part M. Rossi had taken in the election of the new Pope. Thus, when he was presented at his first audience, Cardinal Ferretti, the Pope's relative, whispered in his ear:

"Be quiet, Mr. Ambassador; we shall have the railways, the amnesty, and everything will work well."

As if there had been an illusion as to the nature of the Papacy! And it was not only the people who were mistaken, but the diplomatists themselves, the most skeptical men, such as Mr. Rossi.

"The amnesty is not all," he wrote to Mr. Guizot, the 18th July, 1846; "but it is, in fact, a great step. I hope that the new furrow is opened, and that the Holy Father will know how to continue it, in spite of any obstacle which they will not fail to oppose to him."

The obstacles, in fact, presented themselves; and they were in the character of the man, as much as in the essence of the institution, in the interests of those who had fallen, in the inexperience of those who had risen, and in the urgency and multiplicity of the necessities of the people. Mr. Rossi saw Pius IX., and said to him:

" Your Holiness has commenced a grand pontificate. You will not permit so fine a work to miscarry. Our policy is known. We highly applaud everything which consolidates the independence of States, the prosperity of nations, the peace of the world. . . . . When we add to all this, that, after all, there is nothing more done; that, up to this time, there have only been promises, projects, and commissions which work but little, — we shall not be surprised to learn that the country begins to be suspicious and irritable. It does not accuse the Pope of duplicity, but it suspects him of weakness. . . . . Thus, I have replied to the Holy Father, that every delay in the accomplishment of the promised ameliorations would be henceforth a certain cause of troubles; that if, on the contrary, a commencement of their execution came to reassure their spirits, I did not doubt but that they would leave to the Holy Father all the time necessary for the purpose of proceeding with proper slowness and maturity. I added that the creation of a central government and of a cabinet appeared to me the measures at once the most urgent and most necessary for opinion's sake." *

The same language to the Government!

"I said to Mr. Corboli, that to-day there were only but a few days, perhaps a few hours, before the revolution might commence; that it was not longer a question of foreseeing it, but of governing it, of circumventing it, *of arresting it;* . . . . that it

* Mr. Rossi to Mr. Guizot, 18th December, 1846.

was absolutely necessary to do, without the least delay, two things: to realize the promises made, and to found a solid government; in other terms, appease opinions which were not yet perverted, and repress every temptation to disorder; to satisfy the moderate party and govern it." *

In exposing to Mr. Guizot the policy which he had followed, for Mr. Guizot had given him great latitude, and asked of him counsel rather than given it to him, Mr. Rossi said, in his letter of July 28th, 1847:

"1. Give in the Pontifical States a liberal and honorable satisfaction to the party of reform. 2. Enlighten and control the national party by making it understand that impatience might cause it to lose. This double labor appeared to me easy for the Pope, of whom only such reforms were expected as were moderate and henceforth practised in almost every European State, whether constitutional or not; agreeable to our policy, which desires reforms without disturbing the peace of the world, and just by leaving to the times its rights; honest and useful in itself and to Italy, which is not in a condition to attempt great and powerful adventures."

But this also was Mr. Guizot's policy.

"Mr. Rossi should carefully guard our position and carry boldly our flag; he should, nevertheless, not avoid acting occasionally with his colleagues of

*Mr. Rossi to Mr. Guizot, July 18, 1847.

the diplomatic corps. The foreign powers, even Austria, are reasonable. The exigency is unpleasant to them; they may recognize it at the latest possible moment, but finally they will accept it. Let us announce the exigencies when they appear; let us be their interpreters in Europe. It is our game. Let us not make others what we are; but let us not isolate ourselves. In concerted action it is we who shall prevail. . . . In case of material danger and of an appeal to foreign aid, let nothing be done without us. Let nothing be demanded from any person, without, at least at the same time, demanding it from us. We will not neglect our friends." *

And besides, in another private letter to Mr. Rossi, he added: "We must be careful in Italy not to found any hopes upon a European conflagration. This illusion has already lost, and may lose again, the Italian cause. Let each one attend to their own affairs — the Romans at Rome, the Tuscans in Tuscany, the Neapolitans at Naples, and success is then possible. Without respect to existing treaties there is no success possible. The triumph of partial reforms in each State will afterwards bring in the triumph of the national Italian cause. To aim at it to-day would be to aim at a revolution in Italy and to risk a general conflagration. . . . The French fleet remains at the door of the Mediterranean."

* Private instructions from Mr. Guizot to Mr. Rossi, July, 1847.

He wrote to the same effect to Mr. Bourgoing at Turin.

In the meanwhile, the Italian question had entered into a new phase. They did not preoccupy themselves about reforms; they discussed the national cause, and they discussed it with so much the more heart as Austria was about to take an aggressive attitude.

"I do not doubt the good intentions of the Holy Father," wrote Prince de Metternich to Count d'Appony, in August, 1847; " but will he be able to do what he wishes? The revolutionists and the ill-disposed are there to draw a fatal advantage from reforms good in themselves, and which Austria is, besides, disposed to approve, since she advised them herself in 1831. Would any one wish to lead the Pope further? Ought he to permit himself to be led? Can he do so? The position of chief of the Christian Communion leaves to him, as to every other chief of state, the right of doing everything temporal. That is more than doubtful. Let him not permit himself to be seduced by the doctrines of Gioberti and de Lamennais, who preach to him to lean upon the democratic party of Catholic ideas; that is a false and fatal force. If the Pope wishes to have recourse to it, he will expose Europe to the greatest danger that she has been exposed to since the fall of the French throne.

And, persuaded by these ideas, the Grand Chancellor was not content with occupying Ferrara and exercising his old influence upon the Italian Cabinets, but, by his secret agents, he endeavored to create embarrassments everywhere, to put on shackles, to counsel resistance to Princes, and to excite the most over-excited, as well as the most retrograde, men to disturbance, and to take on airs of formidable provocation.

Perhaps at London this attitude was not altogether unpleasant; because at London they wished to destroy, at any price, the understanding which appeared to be established between Venice and Paris, and particularly to create a new centre of power for England, after having lost by the Spanish marriages that of the Iberian Peninsula. But the double action of Austria and England frightened the Tuileries and its agents abroad.

"My inquietude," said the Duke de Broglie to Lord John Russell, " arises neither from Rome nor from Sardinia, nor even from Naples, where the general movement makes itself felt, but from the centre of Italy, where we see a multitude who cry out, who crowd the streets, and a government that yields, that humiliates itself; and, on the other side, the Austrian government, which is at the door, and they insult it, provoke it, and menace it. It has family rights and reversible interests, which may serve it for a pretext. There is the true danger. For what is to be done? Every Sovereign that might be shackled by a foreign Power in its meditated reforms, every people that marches in this harmonious way with its Sovereign, if it invokes our support, is sure to obtain it. But if it is a question of exercising or sustaining insensate populations in revolt against their princes, if it is a question of sustaining them in the enterprise, still more insensate, of attacking Austria upon her own territory, and to make a kingdom or a republic of Italy, they must not count upon us. Consequently, it is necessary to quiet their minds. Believe me, do not counsel the Italian people to any other thing, do not excite them to any other measure. The Italian people are but too much disposed to take songs, dances, and cries of joy for acts of patriotic heroism, and to say to us: 'Perform our business and compliment us!' If they go too far, you will not be able to do anything to assist them, and we, even when we shall desire it, we shall not arrive in time." *

But Mr. Rossi concealed nothing of the situation, which always became more serious and clearly marked out. At the same time, he performed his part, and made a pressure upon the government to dissipate the danger and to provide for the public exigencies.

"What the masses wish to-day," he wrote to Mr. Guizot, 7th September, 1847, " are reforms and a respect for independence. Without doubt, this second sentiment, which to-day is profound, developed, and

* Despatch of the Duke de Broglie to Mr. Guizot, of the 16th September, 1847.

general, is not favorable to Austria. Doubtless, it is foreseen that the reforms will successively contribute, little by little, to develop it more. What is to be done, unless we design to exterminate Italy, and make of it a land of slaves? We must resign ourselves to what a more or less distant future reveals is in her bosom; only we must be prepared for it. We ought not, however, to excite premature crises. But it is this which Austria appears to do by making herself conspicuous, in provoking the national sentiment by measures which irritate more than they terrify."

To which Mr. Guizot replied by a private letter of the 29th of September, with a new declaration of principles: "We are not at all stationary," he said, "and not at all revolutionary, no more for Rome than for France. We know that there are social requirements that must be satisfied, a progress which must be accomplished, and that the first interests of governments is to live in harmony and in a good understanding with their people and their times; that the first interest of a sensible government that desires to exist is to resist the revolutionary spirit. . . . We are at peace and in good relations with Austria, and we desire to remain so, because bad relations and war with Austria is general war and revolution in Europe. We know that the reforms necessary for the Italian States are not pleasing to Austria, no more than our revolution of July and our constitutional government pleased it;

but we also know that sensible governments do not regulate their conduct according to their tastes or their displeasures. . . . The Austrian Government is a sensible government. . . . But if the folly of the stationary party, or that of the revolutionary party, or of both together, meditate a foreign intervention, do not leave the Pope in any doubt that in such a case we will support him efficaciously, — him, his government, and his sovereignty, his independence, his dignity."

After what we have just said at length, with superabundance of official notes to fix very authentically the policy of each cabinet, and to destroy the prejudices, — that is to say, the extra-revolutionary policy of Lord Palmerston and that of the extra-revolutionary policy of Mr. Guizot, — we see that, willingly or unwillingly, no European Power placed fetters upon the so much desired reforms. If these reforms were retarded, if they were given too late, when the people, convinced of the want of power and of the bad faith of the Princes, aimed at a species of guarantee more efficacious and more normal, the fault was not with the people whom they have so much calumniated, but with the princes, who were then, who are to-day, and will be to-morrow, incorrigible and untrustworthy. The sinister attitude of Austria hereafter renders the national sentiment popular and ineffaceable; the equivocal and restive attitude of the princes makes them feel the need of a republic. All this was in the bosom of the nation as the spark is in the stone. Austria and the Kings were the steel which made it strike fire. And, curiously, then, as at Naples to-day, they wished to smother the national sentiment by the narcotic of reforms and constitutional liberty.

At first the Pope, and then Tuscany and Piedmont, made a few insufficient reparations; but they made them sensible that they had been wrested from them, and that they were far from meeting the requirements, the expectations, and hopes of the people, without reflecting that in politics, as in nature, abundance extinguishes desire. The foreign powers were satisfied, Austria irritated; Lord Palmerston perhaps did not professionally relish these half-measures, because Lord Palmerston, the most powerful political understanding in Europe, understood, that to arouse hunger is not to satisfy it, and that a people who have been made to have a glimpse of the liberty of the press, who have been made to inhale a breath of free discussion regarding its interests, will soon demand it: Why should I not have all these things fully, like America, England, Belgium, and Switzerland? Shall I be forever a minor? And it will agitate for the purpose of obtaining it.

The whole of Europe, then, the people and the diplomacy, had their eyes chiefly fixed on the Vicar of Christ, and they agitated, near to and around him, to raise him to the comprehension of the situation. For this squall there should have been a man at the helm of St. Peter's vessel, who possessed the soul of Julius II., and the vigorous political constitution of Alexander VI. There should have been an Italian Prince with a serene judgment, a calm will, but of brass, having an aim, loving his country, not fearing to risk all for the purpose of gaining all, knowing how to tack, how to await the providential hour, but forcing it with his hand to advance upon the dial, fearing nothing, believing in the people and in the right, profiting by the sympathies for the Italian cause, making headway against Austria stupefied herself, taking in tow the other Princes of Italy by a vigorous example of justice and of dignity, by giving liberty to his State. There would have been wanting a Pope, willing to change *the keys of St. Peter* into a *labarum* for Italy, and to place himself at the head of a crusade against the foreigner; he would have been necessary .... but alas! there was only Pius IX.

CHAPTER XXXI.

PIUS IX. AS HE IS.

THE prevailing trait in the character of Pius IX. is mildness. It is perceived in his countenance, in his smile, in the tone of his voice. Nevertheless, from the excessive mobility and sensibility of his nerves, he frequently suffers himself to become violent. This mildness is not then angelic, and is not wanting in malice. Pius IX. can hardly moderate his inclination for mockery. He is sullen, close, like all men who would be wicked, if they possessed the necessary force of character to be so, and could be so with impunity. The mildness of Pius IX. resembles those coverings which are put on old arm-chairs, to conceal stains and rents. This exterior mien is completed by aristocratic and even elegant manners, and by a certain taste which he has for the fine arts, or rather a certain weakness for everything that is beautiful, and elevates him above the crowd. He is indolent, idle, and somewhat changeable. "I am like a stone," he says; "I remain quiet or I fall." He foresees the evil, but from fear of encountering a worse, he permits it to take place and looks elsewhere. He is very skeptical as to the nature of human actions, and as to the morality of men. As a young man, he believed in the sovereign reality of pleasure; as an old man, he believes in it yet.

Pius IX. is as full of vanity as a poet, and as fond of dress as a woman. The Vicar of Christ is, besides, very womanish. He has their mobility, their exaltation, their freedom on intimacy, their little coquetries, their gossiping, talking by fits and starts, their neatness, their absolute need of luxury, of silk, of perfumes, of flowers, for the brilliant and costly, inconstancy in taste, a little given to gourmandizing, a propensity for pleasures, exquisite and lively sentiment but not profound, a loving nature like the wheedling of a cat, the countenance apparently cheerful, and that veil of concealed melancholy, without cause, vague, colored by the thousand dreams which envelop his aspirations, and the tendency to tears which terminates in smiles. On the days that Pius IX. plays his great part of Sovereign Pontiff, he is happy. His dresses exalt him more than his faith. He enjoys his laces, his embroideries, his jewelry,—for him, this Lieutenant of God, it is the entrance to a ball. He studies his draperies, his poses, and his smiles before the mirror; he grimaces; if he could he would paint; and he regrets the period when he was twenty years old!

Pius IX. is the *lorette* of the Papacy. His intelligence is neither elevated nor extensive, but it is quick. He invents nothing, but comprehends everything. He feels more than he thinks. He has memory and enthusiasm, ready words, a dramatic and impassioned delivery. He lives to converse, and when he finds himself on well-known ground, he converses well. He can neither be ranked among the theological nor among the political Popes. Personally, he might with justice be placed among the sluggards. Not that he has not a tendency to mix with politics and theology, but that he quickly becomes fatigued and starts back before the first obstacle. Little things terrify and arrest him. He would be delighted to perform great things, because he possesses boldness for the idea when he sees it clearly; but any man, even his valet-de-chambre, could inspire him with respect. And here is the reason why, detesting Cardinal Antonelli, speaking the greatest possible evil against him, secretly, counting upon his fingers the profits, the thefts, the villanies, the rudeness of this Cardinal, laughing at him immoderately with Cardinal Ferretti or with Cardinal Altieri, and understanding everything that is fatal in the system of this man, he keeps him as his Secretary of State.

With a soul harmonious and very impressionable, Pius IX. is accessible to every sentiment; but he is powerless in resisting any arguments. A logician easily overpowers him, and causes him to become dejected or abrupt. So that having been accustomed to mistrust himself, and from natural inclination, he has become indecisive or weak, when he is not angry.

Above all, women exercise a magnetic and irresistible power over him. The voice, the look of a woman plunges him into an extreme depression of the will. When young, his mistresses pushed him forward or held him back, retarded or promoted him, either openly or secretly. At a ripe age, the influence of women directed his conduct. As Pope, he still obeys this force. Two days ago, Dona Clara Colonna made a Liberal of him. Yesterday, the Countess de Spaur prostituted him to

Austria. To-morrow, a pretty Miss, becoming Catholic, will excite him against Lord Palmerston. After to-morrow, a Duchess of the noble Faubourg will make of him an apostle of Henry V. The Queen of Naples made him at Gaëta a child's nurse and an accomplice of King *Gibet*. Old and infirm, no longer able to love, he now invents the dogma of the Immaculate Conception. The Queen of Heaven is the Montespan of the gray-beard.

Behold, why in the life of Pius IX. there is nothing resolved upon; he had not even an aim in his career. His weakness, his irresolution, his excessive fear, which he endeavors to conceal by a theatrical exaltation of designs and impossible aspirations, his sudden fits, and his attacks of his feeling of authority, his poutings and his whims without reason, as well as his undignified familiarities, his sybaritism, and his thirst for martyrdom, his sultanic airs and his avarice, make him a despicable and despised being whom able men disdain, and whom good-natured people pity. Deprived of spontaneity, incapable of the initiative, Pius IX. is like a flint-stone, which it is necessary to strike to draw from it a spark.

The only active element of this uncultivated nature is faith.

Not that faith which proceeds from reason, and which has almost the authority of a principle, but that spontaneous faith engendered by sentiment, which the heart nourishes, and which, when it surrounds itself with senseless practices and remains sterile, is called superstition.

Pius IX. believes! he has taken in earnest his vicarship of God. Under the impulsion of this belief, he has caused all the great misfortunes of the Italy of the present, and committed many faults. For, not having sufficient lucidity, energy, or grasp of mind to perform great things, by the assistance of so great a power, he does not elevate himself to the stature of God, but shrinks God to the stature of a poor priest, and drags him into all the follies, passions, and interests of a caste which is confounded with humanity. Pius IX. has the faith of a woman, not that of a genius. But, having the instinct of the Papacy, without comprehending it, and the character of the Popes of the twelfth, thirteenth, and fourteenth centuries—not having the instinct of the temporal sovereignty of the Pope of the pontiffs of the fifteenth and sixteenth centuries, — he is a pitiable mixture of fancies and weakness, of bold aspirations and miserable results. And this is why one has seen and sees this shocking phenomenon, who, although existing, *as sovereign*, under the orders of an Austrian Corporal, under the ironical and dreaded protection of the son of Voltaire, and trembling under the deadly look of Cardinal Antonelli, — *as Pope*, he excommunicates peoples, kings and kingdoms, solicits the Concordats of the Middle Ages, proclaims new dogmas, and permits the King of the Two Sicilies, the posthumous Lothario of the cross-streets, to kiss his slipper and to follow in his train. We see Pius IX. *as sovereign* detesting Austria and France, who again aim to snatch from him his States and hold him in vassalage; and as Pope, prostituting to them the State, Italy, and the Church. Pius IX. entered upon the scene with the persuasion that he had a part to play, because Europe imposed one upon him, because Italy, misled by the insensate doctrines of the Neo-Guelfs, called to him, "Be Alexander III." When he attempts to choose, his instinct betrays him. He tacks for a moment, then he falls. The balloon has collapsed. The elbows of the priest immediately pierced the splendid mantle of the Italian Sovereign, with which they had ridiculously clothed him. Cowardly with the people, a hypocrite with the diplomates, deceitful with the Romans, a traitor towards Italy, devoted to Austria but not daring to avow it, a dancing-jack in the hands of the Sacred College, he lent himself to all the buffooneries that the People, the Romans, Italy, Austria, and the Sacred College demanded of him. The Vicar of Christ became a lay figure of the workshop, which any one could place in any position which he liked best. Pius IX. was the maid-of-all-work of the reaction; since then he has preserved these functions.

Here I stop. Mr. Edmond About has told the remainder, and it is impossible to tell it better and more truly. What precedes is the preface to the

Roman Question, which at this moment fixes the eyes of the world upon it, and warms the bowels of the Ultramontanes; but whatever they may do, whatever they may say, " Garibaldi has killed Pius IX."

Now, let us conclude.

CONCLUSION.

I.

FOR many centuries, Society has had three principles for its foundation, of which three dogmas have been made — Feudality, the Empire, and the Papacy. The origin of these principles was force; but in the historic evolution followed by humanity, under the impulsion of these three principles, the primitive force was masked, and they called it *God*. From thence, sprung divine right.

These three principles represented the organic facts of society — property, law, faith; and the whole together, the principle of authority. From thence, property, with the name of majorat (the right of succession to property according to age), of mortmain, of fief, of commandery, of benefice, which have become inviolable, transmissible but not alienable; laws and faith might become consubstantial for a man and for an institution — the Papacy and the Empire; both irresponsible and inviolable.

So long as property had force for the origin of its right, Feudality had also its reason for existing, its legitimacy, and its social mission; it settled property by changing the possession into a right. But so soon as the new era of society consecrated labor as being the right to property, Feudality not only had no further mission, but it became dangerous, and through that even, it fell.

So long as Feudality existed and acted, the Empire had equally its reason for existing and its mission. It represented universal right, absolute right, collective right, extra-human right opposed to the individual right of Feudality; it was justice, law, authority. The Empire gave a summary of the people. But when the latter felt sufficiently strong to take back its right, and to exercise it by itself, or to delegate, by a mandate, the regency to whomsoever it pleased,—when by the anointing of labor, recognized as the only right to property, the people understood that the right of authority, the laws, was equally in itself, and not out of itself, the Empire ceased to have a part to play in the evolution and development of society; it mouldered away, it vanished.

The Papacy has been an illusion so far as it has been an active and living principle of society, that is to say, up to the fifteenth or sixteenth century; since then it has been a cheat. The Papacy had for its mission to control, in the name of God, the absolute exercise of property, and of authority; it ought to represent the right of the people as opposed to Feudality, the control of the people as opposed to the Empire. The Papacy never executed this mission. It used Feudality as an instrument, and wrestled against the Empire in order to arrogate to itself its rights, in one word, for an entail, not for a claim of rights in favor of the people. In the sixteenth century the Empire subdued the spiritual Papacy, and the Pope became a monarch who found his support and his principle of existence in the Empire.

Monarchy had abolished Feudality. Richelieu struck down the last obstacles which counterbalanced the absolute authority of the monarch and created modern monarchy, — absolute monarchy, that of which Louis XIV. was the type.

The People, formulated in the Convention, smote the monarchy, and, incarnate in Napoleon, — the highest expression of human right, the rudest personification of the sovereign right of the people — smote the Empire at Presburg and the Papacy at Tolentino.

As a *right*, then, the Papacy exists no longer, no longer having any expression in the development of humanity, any civil mission in social life. Like Feudality, like the Holy Roman Empire, she exists no more.

The spiritual Papacy exists not otherwise but by a fiction — the identity of the Pope with God — the unity of the dogma in the world, the principle of authority emanating from God. Now all this seems here ridiculous, there illegal, and elsewhere criminal. In the new phase of society the individual is substituted for God.

In point of property, the right to it is labor, that is to say, in the individual. In point of sovereignty, the right to it is in the suffrage, that is to say, in the individual. In point of faith, the right to it is in free examination, that is to say, in the individual. Feudality exists no longer except as a hateful exception in some corner of Europe, under the protection of the Civil Code and of social order, and although entirely transformed, it is effaced every day. Absolute monarchy exists no longer but as a social menace, as a danger to public order, in a few countries of Europe, although profoundly changed as to its ancient irresponsibility. The half of Europe has ceased to be Catholic. The Catholic religion, as a State religion, is a form in some States, but rather a theoretical impertinence than a fact; since even at Rome they think themselves obliged to tolerate the Jews.

Historically, then, the spiritual Papacy is extinct. Charles V. killed it in the person of Clement VII., and Luther in the person of Leo X. *Theoretically*, it has disappeared, having no further mission to accomplish in the moral and material order of society, being even a fetter upon social development, an injury to progress, a rebellion against the organic laws of society. *In fact*, it no longer exists, because the Papacy may be a belief for a few individuals, but no longer a social dogma, since society is found united with so many beliefs, all equally protected by laws; since liberty of conscience is a right of man; since schism has ceased to be a crime punished by the code, and orthodoxy a social duty.

The *spiritual* Papacy is no longer believed to be either an institution or a dogma; it is the banner of a party—the party of the Old World. There are still some Catholics to-day, but there is scarcely any Catholicity. In order to preserve a few privileges of this Papacy, the Sovereign of Rome has been obliged to finish the Concordats; and the Catholic powers have had to submit these transactions for the approbation of the popular authority, to the legislation of the Chambers. The spiritual does not even perform its functions any longer as a hierarchy; the executive power of the States nominates the bishops, disposes of the benefices, authorizes the publication of the Papal decrees, and the Civil Code makes the observation of the sacraments an optional duty. One need not be married by the Church, need not confess, need not go to Mass, may die without the priest, and yet for this not be cast into the highway. The Pope henceforth speaks no longer *urbi et orbi*, but to a sect. His bulls are ordinances for a few, but they are no longer organic laws for the world, like those of the Popes anterior to the sixteenth century. The Pope is no longer a

Vicar of God, even for the Church, since he cannot decree his dogma without the sanction of a Council. And Pius IX. has made a 2d of December Catholic, by proclaiming almost by himself alone the dogma of the Immaculate Conception.

The Catholic Papacy remains, then, only a fiction, so much the more so as it would be an anachronism if it was again to exist. The Civil Code, the new constitution of the principle of monarchical authority, the moral sciences, physics, mathematics, social organization upon the basis of right, have given the death-stroke to this species of Papacy. The principle of authority to-day no longer comes from on high; it springs up from below. Conscience has replaced revelation and dogma. Justice has taken the place of grace; observation, that of faith. This has rendered the Catholic or spiritual Papacy impossible, and it exists no more.

Nevertheless, it is this Papacy which the Court of Rome, for ten years, has endeavored to galvanize, under the protection of the Holy Ghost of Paris and Vienna.

For four centuries the Pope has existed in reality but as an Italian Prince; as such he has been recognized since the sixteenth century; as such he has performed his functions; as such he performs them to-day. He is called *Pope*, and is a *priest* by state tradition, as the chief of the republic of Venice was called *Doge*, and was a patrician; as the chief of the Danubian Principalities is called *Hospodar*, and that of Russia *Czar*. The form does not alter the essence.

As Prince, the Pope could not then withdraw himself from any of the historical and social consequences of that institution, for he is no more than Louis XVI., than Charles X., than the Doge Marino, than Leopold II., and Francis Joseph. Napoleon never recognized him or treated him otherwise.

The Court of Rome, seeing the danger to the monarchical institution, feeling itself to be in hostility with the social organization of our times, invokes the principle of the irresponsibility of the Spiritual Papacy, and endeavors to disguise the *Sovereign of Rome* by the *Catholic Pope*. A faction in Europe, an accomplice of the same social incompatibility of the Papacy, seconds this proposition, and responds to the appeal of the Prince of Rome, as if it was the appeal of the Sovereign Pontiff and Vicar of Christ. But what, in the face of Europe, of Italy, and even of civilization and of the Church, is the situation of this Vicar of Christ?

II.

Catholicism — that is to say, the Pope — is no longer in Europe a principle of order.

In Europe he acts in the double character, and with the double influence, of Pope and King. As *Pope*, he gathers around him the Catholic faction, and holds in check established governments, or conspires against them. As *King*, he ranges upon his side the monarchical principle, and adds his weight to that of Princes, in order to crush out Democracy. He threatens the *Prince*, and raises up against him the Clergy. Against the People, he approves and blesses violent measures, perjuries, the massacre of citizens, the violation of laws, the organization of religious societies, the annihilation of university instruction, and intolerance under every form. In Europe, Catholicism, personified by the Pope, is a sect in a permanent state of conspiracy. In those places where it reigns, — in Italy, France, Spain, and Belgium, — it conspires against the people and against liberty: in those places where it is only solemnized, — in England, Prussia, Russia, and in Sweden, — it conspires against the established government, against the other religious sects; everywhere it dreads the sons of science and of liberty, and scatters darkness.

In England, the Roman Papacy is no longer feared as a danger, but they hurt themselves against it as against an impediment. England has curbed the Pope, but she has not decatholicized Ireland. Ireland has become powerless, but she still remains the misfortune of Old England. The Pope denationalizes Ireland: the virtual chief of this isle is the Pontiff — the true country of these islanders is Rome. All the ridiculous stories spread over the Continent against England are carried by Irish Catholics; for to lie, to calumniate, to assassinate your neighbor, to deny your country, for the cause of religion, enters among Catholics into the category of duties. One of the merits of St. Louis de Gonzague, which was spoken of in his act of canonization, was never having looked upon the form of his mother! When any one wishes to insult England, they cite her conduct towards Ireland and India. When they wish to cause her trouble and difficulties, they provoke insurrection among the Catholics and Sepoys. Ireland and India are the levers of foreign hatred to trouble England: France stirs up Ireland, Russia provokes India. The Pope puts Ireland in a permanent state of revolt. His Holiness does better still, — he breaks the homogeneity, the national compactness of England; for wherever the soul does not beat in unison, the forces of a nation are scattered. If the French should disembark to-morrow upon British soil, would the Catholics fight for the liberty of Old England?

The Pope usurps a part of the Queen's authority. He appoints her lieutenants in the United Kingdom; he lords it over their souls and lays down the nature of their right and duty. The Pope is not a Prince friendly to England; and, under all circumstances, he will be found on the side of the enemies of this nation. If to-morrow Napoleon wished to make a descent upon the United Kingdom, he would be preceded by bulls from the Pope, who would hurl them forth with joy.

Certainly, England has nothing to fear from the Pope, because England is armed for liberty; but it is not the less true that, if any danger whatsoever should one day menace this power, this danger would be aggravated by every means which the Court of Rome could make use of. And it is not less true that, as a temporal power, the Pope holds in check the English influence in Italy, whilst, as a spiritual power, she relaxes the liens of her national unity. In the great calamities of Great Britain, the Pope has always conspired for the lion's part. But the Pope has not changed his character. His forces are enfeebled; his authority is found damaged, but his interests remain the same. Ireland is the haircloth of England. The Irish band in Parliament will always have a vote against it matters not what ministry, that shall defend the cause of liberty and civilization, at home as well as abroad. Cardinal Antonelli and the King of Naples always find a Hennessy and O'Donoghue, a Bowyer, to justify their conduct and to canonize them.

The Pope does not treat Catholic France any better.

The old alliance which the Papacy contracted with the Bourbons has neither been broken nor altered an atom; it is this which has held and holds the Pope in a state of continued hostility against every government which has succeeded it in this country. There have been a few truces, but never a complete peace. The Papacy has made a civil dogma of legitimacy. Louis XVIII. himself had to submit to the demands of the Congregation. The complacencies, the weaknesses of Louis Philippe were of no use to him. To Gregory XVI. and to Cardinal Lambruschini the King was Henry V., and as such they received Count de Chambord at Rome in 1844. The Pope scoffed at and dishonored the republic; he conspired against it by favoring the election of Bonaparte, making no account of the promises which he had lavished on it for the purpose of causing his restoration to Rome, knowing, in brief, that he had the ill grace of having taken a part in this transaction which was more conformable to the nature of Austria. The Pope and his partisans were accessory to the 2d of December, and became themselves the support of the government which followed the *coup d'état*.

Then, so long as David was an instrument in the hands of Samuel, Samuel blessed, caressed, and conducted affairs after his own way. The congregation was reinstalled, the corporations augmented and enriched, the sect of St. Vincent de Paule entwined around, penetrated, and sucked the life out of France, public instruction changed its character, the commission for distributing books studied the Index, and the *Univers* inspired the *Moniteur*. The Papacy conspired against France and against every thing which was free and great remaining in that country. The councils of the French govern-

19

ment, the French army at Rome, did not inspire in him any gratitude; it was a tribute which they paid to him; it was the hackney which the Emperor presented to one who had prepared for him the Crown, and had fixed it firmly upon his head. The day upon which David wished to leave the altar, Samuel anathematized him; and the episcopacy now undermines the empire; and the Legitimists re-assemble around the general of the Immaculate Conception, who has five times, politically, changed sides.

Ultramontanism has its principal seat in France. Its European capital is found in that Thebaide which is called the Faubourg Saint Germain. Rome is almost a chapel of ease in comparison with the zeal which the sons of the Cross display at Paris. In France the Pope undermines the people as well as the government. It associates with the government for the purpose of robbing the people of their liberty; it raises a moral insurrection in one portion of the people and exercises such a pressure upon the government that it shackles its liberty of action and participates in its power. In France, now, all is done by the intermediation of the Society of St. Vincent de Paule; whoever is not affiliated with it will succeed in nothing. Napoleon III. flounders in the meshes of the net in which this Society has enveloped him. He is not free as is believed in Europe; the Society holds him everywhere. His life itself is in the hands of that dropsical old man that sits in Rome. He lives, literally, as King Charles Albert said of himself, " between the chocolate of the Jesuits and the bombs of Orsini's heirs."

The Papacy morally injures France, and every day empoisons its genius. The sons of Voltaire have their souls draped in the robe of St. Ignatius. The government of France falls back before the remonstrances of the French Episcopacy, who receive their orders from Rome. Napoleon III. does the dirty work or agrees with Veuillot.

France cannot call herself an independent power, she is bound by the Concordats. Bonaparte, who dares to tear up the treaty of Vienna, and to make a cartridge of the constitution of 1848, dares not infringe the treaties of his uncle with Pius VI. Of what is he afraid? The spiritual Papacy has no longer real progress, for her excommunications do not even amount to a fillip; the temporal Papacy breathes under the protection of its army; the Papacy wavers like a phantom;—of what then is he afraid?

The Papacy is a phantom; but it is, an underorder, a sect, a species of Freemasonry, to which all the débris of the Old World rally,—the aristocracy, decayed sovereigns, smitten privileges, all those who have a dread and horror of liberty, all those who live in ignorance, and a party of women. This hidden conspiracy against progress and civilization is grouped around the political altar of Rome, and gnaws at its base everything which is not her or of her. The Papacy is like the subterranean sewers of large cities: it carries all the filth, and where it is stopped and filters, it spreads infection and death. The Pope has always been the promoter of, or the accomplice in the disasters of France. Each time that France has wept or bled, the blow came from Rome, or on account of Rome. Mirabeau has said : " To have liberty, we must de-catholicize France." He should have said *the World*. But so long as there shall be a Pope, there will not be any liberty in France, there will be no independent French government. The Pope opposes it and his partisans second him.

Germany, although for a great part Protestant, does she withdraw herself from the influence of the Court of Rome? Alas, Germany has almost as much reason to complain as Italy of the action of the Sultan of the Vatican. The Papacy divides Germany, and fetters its union. Enter Northern and Southern Germany, Rome places herself like a quoin, which will hinder for a long time yet the formation of the nation. To form Germany, you must subjugate the Catholics and treat them as England treated them, for centuries, as enemies of the country. Germany is an *organized anarchy*, as Voltaire said, chiefly because Catholicism mingles itself everywhere — between State and State, between the people and the governments, between the native and the foreigner. The Pope imposes Concordats which embroil the peoples with the governments, as but lately at Baden; which puts the governments in danger, as Austria and Hungary. The Concordats violate the liberty of conscience, and outrage the equality of citizens before the laws. The Protestant in Hungary, the Jew everywhere in Germany, are outside of the common law, tolerated perhaps, and owing their legal existence to a special law, not to their being essentially the children of the same country.

In Prussia, the party of the *Kreuzzeitung* undermines the national homogeneity, the law of the country, and bars the way, as the limit of progress. The Chamber of Lords is the Joshua of Prussia, the duchy of Posen is their Ireland. The Archbishop of Cologne hardly recognizes the King and Parliament, and depends upon Rome. The Catholics make compromises with the State, as a Power with Power, their eyes turned towards Austria as the virtual representative of Germany. The Pope attracts towards Austria the Catholic States of the Confederation, and divides it into two groups, so that it will never be any other than a weak confederation.

The spirit of Germany bifurcates into two rays, eternally parallel, which will never form a bundle, and consequently no force. Germany has a double conscience, a double tendency, a double *criterion*, and her science justly wanders because she is con stituted one half of observation, intuition, and manifestation of conscience, one half of faith and revelation. One party of German thinkers, in meditating upon their works, are sensible of the Pope, who listens behind them. The synthesis of Germany is found broken also in spirit, and the Pope divides what nature has created one. Two groups, impossible to be brought together on account of religious rather than political opinions, divide Germany. Catholic Austria, having no autonomy of the soul, bound to the oracles, to the faith, to the orders of the Vatican, will never be as German as Prussia, which, notwithstanding her Poland and her *Kreuzzeitung*, still entirely belongs to herself as a State, and covers entirely with her hegemony the Protestant party of the nation.

Even in the Austrian sky, the Pope hovers like a storm. His Concordats compromise the Empire, breaking that famous *unity* of the programme Schwartzenberg-Bach, changing into rebels to the faith of the Crown, like the Hungarian Protestants, a part of the subjected nationalities, or rather into the slaves of a *Credo* which is not their own. Hereafter the Jesuit and the soldier will divide between them the soul of the Empire. The aristocracy has its eyes turned towards Rome, and receives from thence its word of command. Complicity with Rome leads Austria into an abyss from which she will never rise again. The Jesuit makes a monopoly of instruction, of the public benevolence, of a part of justice; the observance of the sacraments is a state duty. The non-Catholic worships are under the regulation of the police. The Pope reigns like an autocrat over Austria: he violates the equality of the citizens before the law, the liberty of conscience, the freedom of thought, the freedom of instruction, the Civil Code in the law of marriage and in that of succession; he imposes the maintenance of mortmains, the religious corporations, the inveigling of legacies from the dying, and all that sinister cortége of abuse, intolerance, and misfortune which Ultramontanism leads in its train.

A country of traditions, Germany still remembers her contests with the Papacy. She still believes that the Pope is a power, a force, a word; she still seriously takes him as a friend or enemy. In Germany they still discuss a bull, an encyclical,—even to-day, when bulls have taken possession of the stock-exchange—like the last of Pius IX., who, with texts of the Holy Fathers and the Holy Scriptures, treats about the rate of a loan, and the places for its subscription. The Papacy, an institution which lives equally upon tradition, has not forgotten her contests with Germany, the blows which she gave her, the blows which she received from her; and not a fibre of her old hatred is relaxed. The Papacy hates Germany; and whether she counsels or guides her, or whether she resists her, she is always the enemy of the old empire.

Ultramontanism keeps up the same separation in

the Helvetic Confederation. The Cantons of the Sonderbund are Swiss only in name, and, perhaps, republican by force. In Switzerland the Pope has done more yet: he has lighted up civil war, he has placed liberty in danger, and menaced the nation. The Catholic Cantons are a stain upon the Helvetic Union. In passing through them, the hand of Rome is felt there in the smallest details — in the bearing of the people, in culture, in the neatness of the inhabitants, in morality, in the appearance of the villages, in the degrees of instruction, in the social, hygienic, and economic condition of the people. One feels that Rome gleans in this country, that she gleans these men, gold, souls, genius, and that the wind from the Vatican dries up the sap of the mountain and of liberty. One might say that the Catholic cantons were Austrian débris, strayed into Switzerland. Need I recall the history of the Sonderbund, and the last exploits of Bishop Marullaz? If the Confederation exists, it is not to the credit of the Catholic cantons. If the Confederation has reformed its constitution, it has not been done with the consent of these cantons. In the simplification, in the strengthening of the federal lien, the Sonderbund saw a great mass of liberty, and the nucleus of a nation — the two things which Rome detests the more, being herself but a principle of authority and universality.

The Papacy is dangerous to Switzerland, — dangerous as a germ of civil war; dangerous as a permanent opposition, and even in the Federal Council; dangerous to liberty, on account of her reactionary teaching which is given in the Sonderbundist cantons; dangerous, in a word, because these cantons break the harmonizing and necessary concurrence of elements, which can alone form a political nation of a people belonging by race, language, and tendencies to three different countries. Rome breathes upon this attraction of diverse molecules and disperses them. She is the negative pole of the geographical nationality of Switzerland. Attacked in these mountains, the Papacy is stifled; not being able to fight, it conspires. Pius IX. is the retrograde Mazzini of Switzerland.

The Papacy plays an identical part in Spain and Belgium.

In the latter country the Pope represents a principle of reaction and discord; in Spain, he serves as a leaven for civil war, with respect to the dynasty; and as to the nation, he inspires and directs the conspiracy of the Court, of the Queen's husband, and of the *polacos* against the national institutions. For both countries the Pope is the cause of troubles, an element of discord, a menace. In Belgium, the Catholics hinder the development of the constitution; in Spain, they hold it in check. Here, it is the alienation of lands held in mortmain; there, it is freedom of instruction which serves it for a weapon for combat, and for demolition.

The Pope pushes the court of Belgium towards

Austria, and keeps the nation separated into two courts, one of them reversing on the morrow what the other has done the day before. The Pope renders Belgium an unnecessary State, useless to Germany, troublesome to France; a creation of political hatred for the latter, of religious hatred for the former. To corrupt, to divide, to obscure, to plot against liberty, this is the Pope's rôle in Belgium.

In Spain he plays the part of a seditious agent. The Cortes displease Queen Isabella and the Court, they displease the partisans of Montemolin. And behind these, the Pope counsels, stirs up, and hastens the temptation to revolution. If in Spain they are always on the watch for a *coup d'état*, it is the Pope who is the cause of it. The Pope nourishes the worship of the *rey neto*, and of the *auto da fé*, or if you like it better, of *the right divine* of the clergy and of the monarchy. The theory of the *despotismo illustrado*, of the *polacos*, is reduced to this: an irresponsible and absolute king, under the direction of an infallible Pope. After fifty years of labor, of revolutions, of combats, of every kind of effort, Spain has not yet been able to secularize itself. St. Ignatius is cut down, and St. Vincent de Paulo takes on a second growth more vigorous than his brother. The convent is abolished, and the monk conceals himself under the black robe of Donozo Cortes and his partisans. The Inquisition disappears, but the Holy Vehme of the Jesuits redoubles its energy and audacity over the consciences; and while the former burned individuals, the latter devours a nation. The churches are empty, but they remain standing, their mouth gaping to suck in a people, when Spain shall be populated. The convents are deserts, but they are ready to receive guests. The Catholic nest has not been deranged. If the bird has been a little frightened, it has flown off but for an instant; it can return; for nothing has been removed from its place. Have they been able to obtain the consent of the Pope to the disamortisement? Have they yet found in the Cortes enough Spaniards to dispense with this Roman *placet?*

An Italian people—that is to say, the enemy of the Pope — Piedmont, in ten years of liberty created a nation, made Italy, and sowed in it liberty: in fifty years of an intermittent liberty, it is true, but hardly now completely abolished, — Spain — a Catholic country — has ceased to be a nation and remains a geographical denomination. Does Europe know that Spain exists? Does it care? The Bourbons and the Popes have annihilated sixteen millions of Europeans. Spain exhausts herself in the work of Sisyphus. The Liberals by night and day push up the rock of civilization and of progress towards the summit of the mountain, but arrived there, the Pope pushes it back, and the rock falls into the abyss. And the labor of the Liberals recommences. The profound, absorbing sentiment of nationality — the antithesis of Papacy — has saved Italy. Spain can be only saved by another antithesis — Protestantism, or some other equivalent thing — the old Pelagianism.

Spain is to-day the natural country of the Papacy. Pius IX., as Isabella, is there also King: the Spaniards being grouped under two banners, the one of the Liberals — who are citizens before being Catholics — the other of the *moderados* or *polacos*, or Carlists, the color does not matter, who are Catholics before being citizens. For Spain, the Pope exists as a reality; yet more, as a principle; still more, as a human necessity. The Pope uses Spain as a witness of his rights, authority, and vitality.

At the council of Toledo, in 901, King Witiza declared the Spanish people and himself independent of the Holy Chair, and by a decree he prohibited all the inhabitants of Spain from testifying the least appearance of obedience to the Church of Rome. When Gregory VII. wrote to the Spanish nobles (Ep. VII. 1), that he prohibited them from fighting the Moors, if they did not consent to invest him with the conquered lands, as a fee of the Church, the Spanish nobles replied, that they would have delivered the Peninsula of Infidels, for its glory, its interests, and its utility, and that the Holy Father was a fool with his right to interdict the conquest and his pretension to be invested with the fruit. These are the ancestors.

The Spain of Isabella demands from the Pope permission to digest her laws, to dispose of her wealth, to regulate her ecclesiastical administration; she made for the Pope the famous expedition of Fiumicino in 1849, and would have obeyed the voice of St. Peter if Lamoricière had been willing to translate the Latin of that Apostle. It is true that the Holy Father has made a present to Spain of a carcass taken from the Catacombs, which they have baptized with the name of St. Felix. It appears that the Queen required a St. Felix.

If Spain lives like a nation in a state of decline, the Pope is the cause of her consumption.

Russia herself, although schismatic, is not protected from the action of the Papacy. We have seen it before, in the case of Poland. The Greek Pope certainly does not fear the Latin Pope, but he feels a profound disgust for him. The Pope rises in his face in Poland, not as a rival, but as a rebel. The Czar has broken, but has not destroyed him. But at each shiver of this beaten body, the master recalls the offence and the offender. The Pope makes himself small, very small in Poland. He humiliates himself, he performs every species of baseness and indignity which his brother of the Eastern rite imposes on him; but he has not abdicated, and he has not ceased to bite his heel under the mud into which the other has forced it. The Czar knows it, he feels it. This petty King of Rome is the *insect* of that great Autocrat who has his head in Europe and strikes China with one foot and India with the other. Dressed as a Pole, the priest who disowns, combats, and excommunicates the Italian nationality, proclaims and attests the Polish nationality; and thus masked, St. Thomas seeks chicane from St. Athanasius, and Escobar undermines Photius. Since nationality may be a weapon, the Court of Rome seizes upon it. *Adversus hostem æterna auctoritas esto!* That is to say, Every weapon is good for the purpose of killing your enemy.

In Russia, then, the Pope is factious, without being a reformist. In fact, the Catholics are the most bitter against the emancipation of the serfs. The Pope secretly undermines the great creation of Panslavism: the religious idea reveals the national idea. For, after all, the Poles, like the Russians, are slaves. But they are Catholics—which has lost Poland and weakened Russia. The Pope is the Luther for the Slavic race. Happily for this race, however, the Pope has not the power, nor the principles of the Luther of the Teutonic race; for while the latter acts as an active principle, as an element of life and liberty, the Pope is a negation, a bound, a tradition. In Russia the Pope is not a force, nor a dogma, nor a right, nor a peril: he is simply an incumbrance. The Greek Church has yet a future — the sap of the Slavic race. The Catholic Church is dying; for the peoples who had recognized it are repudiating it every day, and Italy, which she has for thirteen centuries endeavored to kill, will in the end kill her.

The Papacy, then, as I have said in the commencement, is not in Europe an element of order. Everywhere it fights against liberty; among some peoples it goes so far as to menace the Government. It divides nations among themselves, and within them, the elements of the same nation. Everywhere it conspires to retard the future, to overturn the present, and to bring back an impossible past. The Papacy plays in Europe the part of Monck of the Old World. The *Sovereign* of Rome galvanizes the *Pontiff*, and the *Pontiff* sustains the *Sovereign*. The spiritual power beats the big drum for the temporal power; and the latter, to the best of its ability, stirs up the other and arms it, and imbrues it in blood, as it is able. This horrible concubinage at this moment troubles Europe and alarms Italy.

III.

No, it does more than alarm: it kindles up there civil wars.

The Papacy has never been Italian, although for many centuries care has been taken to choose an Italian Pope, and although it figures in the *Gotha Almanac* among the Italian principalities. The Papacy has always been Spanish or Austrian. The Pope mixes often, perhaps always, in Italian affairs through foreign intervention: he has held in check Italian Princes by foreign intervention, and held the foreigner in check by creating rivals to him either without or in Italy itself. He knows that any preponderance whatever in the Peninsula, as well a foreigner like Napoleon, as an Italian Prince like Victor Emmanuel, was the abolition of the temporal Papacy. The Pope has held Austria in check by France, and France by England. It is the history of the Papacy since 1815. In the meantime, in the midst of this anarchy of influences, the Pope, in silence, has gnawed or devoured his State.

Piedmont has just interrupted this play of the Acrobat. By forming a focus of liberty, outside of the common mould of the other States of the Peninsula, Piedmont has embroiled the party, and has formed precisely that centre of propaganda for propagating principles so feared by Rome and by Vienna. At first the preponderance has been altogether moral; after the war and its annexations, it has become material. The Papacy has then found itself thrown out of the centre, and has lost a part of its States.

Not being Italian, having lost the foreign support, what could the Papacy do? Nothing but what it has done!—declare itself Catholic and call Catholics to its defence, to the rescue, to save for it its patrimony, and help to recover what it had lost.

The Catholics have not replied to this appeal; for, in truth, there is only but this handful of rabble in earnest from any country who go away from Rome to make a crusade under the orders of that Godfrey de Bouillon of the *table-d'hôte*, General

Lamoricière. The *denier of St. Peter* will not pay the expenses of that General and for Cardinal Antonelli's pot of wine. The fact is certainly not serious; but the principle is much too serious. The theory proclaimed by the Papacy is impious as well as impossible; it can be formulated thus:

"The temporal and spiritual Papacy are consubstantial. The Pope can be the chief of the Church only by being the sovereign of three millions of Italians. And these three millions of subjects, living upon a land geographically Italian, are not Italians; this land is not Italy: but men and land belong to the Catholic world, who have invested the Pope with it. These States are the free city of Frankfort of Christianity — but denationalized. Geography, language, race, instinct go for nothing; policy, Catholic reason overrides it and says: "Let that not be! These *Italians* are *all the world*, and belong to all the world, in the person of His Holiness."

This seems like the wandering of a lunatic's imagination; nevertheless, such is the principle which the Court of Rome has propagated, and which it endeavors at this moment to put in action. This Italian land, this Italian people, where the Papacy encamps, are a primary bed, a substruction upon which the Catholic world is convoked for the purpose of encompassing and propping up the Pope. The Roman States and their inhabitants are the theatre and the furniture upon which the court of Rome convokes foreign actors and spectators to play their piece.

This amputation of Italy, or, to speak better, this extirpation of one part of Italy from the body of the nation, would be a sacrilege, if it were possible. But as the Court of Rome sees that its labor has no chance of success, it threatens to apply to the whole State the treatment of Perouse, and to burn up the whole of Italy by civil war, and by an appeal to the superstition of the masses. Pius IX. has played the great game of excommunication; and this volcano has not even produced the flame of a match. The Catholic religion is dead, very dead, in Italy. The Pope now organizes an explosion by arms. This expectoration of a man in decline can have no other result than to conduct Victor Emmanuel more speedily to the Capitol.

If all that ought to pass between the Italians and the Pope, doubled by his General and even by the King of Naples, we should not have gone to the expense of a piece of paper to speak of it. If all that was but a fact, and not the incarnation of a principle, we should have passed it by. But the idea which moves us is that behind the Pope and his General there is Austria, that the Pope proclaims a principle which has all the appearance of a dogma — the denaturalization of Italy changed into the property of the Catholic world.

The alliance exists among the Pope, Austria, and Naples. The fundamental compact of this alliance is the destruction of Italian authority. Hapsburgs, Bourbons, and Popes are incompatible with Italy; they have never existed, could never exist together. It is necessary then that one or the other should no longer exist. The Pope formulates this negation of the country by breaking with his Keys of St. Peter the geographical and ethnographical existence of the nation; the two other princes throw their rights into the scale of partition. The Pope, consequently, is the most perfidious enemy of Italy. He there plays a double rôle of hatred: he contests the national right, and he calls in the foreigners to break up the formation of the nation. The Italian people, being the least Catholic of the people of Europe, the *Pope* cares but very little about parading his spiritual power. He hurls an excommunication in robe-de-chambre in order not to violate the precedents,—which are the only rights of the Court of Rome,—but he counts no more upon their effect than upon his sneezing for the purpose of overturning the Chamber of Deputies at Turin. On the contrary, he shows himself entirely and completely as *Prince*, with his apparatus of loans, of foreign enrolments, secret treaties, of public appeals to force, of armed struggles, extortion of taxes, by his administrative, coercive, and his exceptional and police laws.

Pius IX. has felt that the Pontificate was ended, or that it was useless, and he has cast it aside.

Europe has proved, by sending *personal* succors,

and not *State* and *national succors*, — by sending secretly such weak succors, so dishonorable, of such base alloy, — Europe, I say, has proved that she does not consider the spiritual policy inherent in the temporal, and that she sees in Pius IX. the Italian Prince and not the Head of the Church.

Let Pius IX. then undergo the fate of a Prince, as he exercises his functions and invokes his rights. In this case, if Pius IX. is only a Prince, why should he pretend that Europe should do more for him than she has done for Leopold II., for Francis V., and for the Duchess of Parma? Why should Italy tolerate the conspiracy which is hatched against her in the Pontifical States? Why should not Pius IX. undergo the fate of the Grand-Duke and Duchess, who certainly were less grievous and less culpable than he?

Here is the question.

In the real Roman Question the Pontiff is out of the case. Either he no longer exists, or he is not the same as the Sovereign of Rome. We live no longer in the time of religious wars. Liberty of conscience is one of the rights of man, — it is one of the bases of existing society, and a canon of international law. In virtue of what principle should there, then, be imposed upon the Italians a creed which they no longer believe, and, above all, a man in whom this symbol of faith is incarnated, which they repudiate and throw down?

That which is right in man — liberty of conscience — would it be a crime in a nation? The head of the Catholic Church has not the right to invoke the aid of Catholic countries for the purpose of sustaining him upon a throne which the nation demolishes. But the Pontiff appertains to the Catholic world: granted! Rome appertains to Italy. Let the Pope transport his seat to the place that any one desires, and let him quit a land that drives him out. The dogma and the theatre upon which this dogma is represented are not identical. The Pontiff can be a Pontiff at Rome as well as at New York, or at Noukaiva, or at Jerusalem. Rome can be neither France nor Austria. The power, then, which, like France now, would intervene for the purpose of supporting the head of the Church in a place which repels him as an evil, would violate the right of liberty of conscience which the Italians possess in the like manner as Englishmen and Russians, would violate the law of God, which is called Geography. Englishmen, once upon a time rejected the Pope, as the Italians reject him to-day: should the right of the Italians be less valid than that of Englishmen? Should Austria make war upon Italy if to-morrow this nation as a body should abjure their religion? Let the Pope be a dogma; if Italy abjured it, no power has the right to impose this belief upon the Italians.

No more interventions then, no further appeals to Catholicism, no further Catholic aid for the Pontiff. The Pontiff is out of the case in the true Roman Question. The Romans have as much right to drive away Pius IX. and Company, as to become Quakers, Mussulmans, or Brahmins.

Let, then, the Prince that France maintains at Rome remain; and in the true Roman Question, Pius IX. is but a Prince.

The question thus divided, we demand: Has the Pope failed in his duty? is he a possible Prince? have the Romans the right, as they understand it, to settle their controversies with him?

The excellent work of Mr. About, the facts which we have cited, the entire history of the Papacy, have proved what the government of the Popes is, what the Pope is. It is useless even for us to sum up. A priest-king is impossible; it is absurd, it is against nature, morals, law, civilization, progress, and society. If it has existed, if it still exists in Italy, it is because there are still Croats and Frenchmen to maintain it there by force. Shall it be said of a man thrown into a dungeon, that he is in a normal state because he lives there? Such, however, is the case of Italy in relation to the Papacy. The Papacy in Italy is a violence and a crime. In the other countries of Europe it attacks certain principles, certain parts of society; in Italy it attacks everything, it violates the whole spirit of the nation, and strangles all its manifestations.

Whatever he may do, the Italian encounters the Papacy; he is absorbed by it. Does he aspire to be an Italian? The Papacy calls upon Austria, or it matters not what foreigner, to sink Italy to the bottom. Does he desire to be a man? the Papacy takes from him liberty, dignity, the exercise of his faculties and rights, his thoughts, his conscience. As a citizen, the Papacy denies to the Italian a country, a vote, and the right to take a part in State affairs. The Papacy imposes upon the father of a family, a faith, sacraments, liturgy, and an obligatory orthodox instruction. As a thinker, if he escape censure, it holds up the Index and the Holy office to him. Let him do as he may, the wire net of the Papacy envelops the Italian. The Pope outrages man, corrupts woman, degrades the old, demoralizes and violates the mind of the child; a scandal, for the generation which passes away; a scourge, for that which is in action, a poison for that which is to come.

The Papacy proves itself to be incompatible with the nation, incompatible with the individual. In the face of the nation, it is cosmopolitan, and opposes to it Christianity; to individuals, it opposes the principle of authority — irresponsible and infallible authority — and forbids liberty under all its forms, in all its manifestations. The Catholic communion does violence to the individual; the Church denies the man.

In his character of Pontiff, the Pope stands in Italy as a negation; in his character of Prince, he stands as a reaction. As *Pontiff*, he says: There is no Italy! as *Prince*, he adds: There is no liberty!

Behold the formula of the Papacy in the Italian Peninsula!

We have hardly touched the political history of the last three Popes. It was useless to say more about them. The history of the Popes is the history of the Papacy; and from St. Peter to Pius IX. there is nothing more compact, nothing more uniform than this history. It is composed of a series of facts of the same value — I might say almost identical — of which this is the signification:

To exalt the institution by degrading the individual and annihilating the nation.

Thus the constant aim of every Pontiff has been this:

At the first period, by the war against the Empire, to prevent the *unity* of Italy. At the second period, by a constant appeal for foreign intervention, to hinder *independence*. At the third period,—after the Council of Trent, after the fall of the Republic of Florence, after the appearance of Protestantism in the world, — by its liturgy, by its alliance with Spain and Austria, by its complicity with the other Italian Princes, to prevent, by every means, the hatching and propagation of *liberty* and of *thought*.

Behold the wicked attempt of the Papacy against Italy!

In fact, take the biography, it matters not of what Pope, of the most stupid, the most adroit, the most holy, the greatest cheat, prince or monk, young or old, the life of this man will have had but this aim:

Without pointing out the speciality of each of them. Pius IX. does that which Gregory XVI. did; and if the last loved the bottle, the former loves the women and the trappings of the courtesan. Gregory XVI. did what Leo XII. had done — persecuted patriots, rendered the gibbet permanent, decreed judgments, administered badly, called in Austria; and, further, Leo persecuted infamous priests; Gregory made them Cardinals. Leo, an incredulous and diplomatic Pope, aimed at the reform of the Church; Gregory, a monk and Catholic, would have made a masked ball of it. In a reign of fourteen years, Pius IX. has run through every phase of the Papacy: he opposed himself to the war of independence in 1848, has persecuted the patriots from 1850 to 1860; and now he takes up arms against the unity of Italy.

How, then, could Italy love the Papacy?

Happily for Italy, the days of the Papacy are numbered. Lamoricière exhausts it; Garibaldi will kill it. A soldier made it; a soldier crushes it. This will be the signal of the final deliverance of Italy. This country has nothing to do with the Papacy. Let the European nation who believes it indispensable give it an asylum, and let God help it. Will Spain even dare to do it? Will Austria? Italy should belong to the Italians; this is the axiom which to-day governs politics. The Pope is not Italian. Is he Christian? I do not know. He has never, in any case, shown himself to be one.

In 1821, all the nations of Europe took up the business and cause of the Greeks, a Christian people who fought against the Turks; the Pope alone gave no signs of life. In 1830, Catholic Poland revolted against schismatic Russia. The Pope, upon the demand of Russia, excommunicated almost and calumniated the Poles. In 1858 the Roumanians rose in insurrection against the Porte; every power interposed in favor of the Roumanians except the Pope and Austria. Is the Pope a Christian?

In every case, I have said that he is not Italian; he is not even in his language. He writes in Latin, and speaks in his official discourses in Latin. But Italy has driven off the Duke of Modena, who was an Austrian Archduke, and Europe has said: It is all right! Italy has driven off the Grand-Duke of Tuscany, who marched with the baggage of the Emperor of Austria at Solferino; and Europe has said: It is all right! Italy has driven off the Duchess of Parma, who was a Bourbon, because she acted like an Austrian lieutenant; and Europe answered: It is right! Sicily, at this moment, drives away the Bourbons from Naples, and the two hemispheres shout out: Long live Garibaldi! Italy has already driven the Pope from the Romagna, and Europe has answered: So much the better for the Romagnians! And a handful of Ultramontanes, making common cause with Italy, comes to-day to say to Italy: No, the Pope is the Vicar of God; this poor man can only live comfortably at the Vatican, surrounded by his Nardoni, his Lamoricière, his Antonelli, being the master of three millions of subjects, not one less, Catholic by will or by force; pariahs, if you will, but by divine right; brutes, if you wish to call them so, but to the greater glory of God (*ad majoram Dei gloriam*); let nobody stir, or there are soon our Croats or Irishmen to fire grapeshot into the people and towns, women and children, to preserve the very Holy Father upon his throne and his altar.

If it was not frightful, it would be ridiculous. Nevertheless, the Ultramontanes say it and do it.

We shall do no outrage to the soldiers who have fought the Austrians in Varese, at Palestro, and at St. Martino, in believing that they could trouble themselves for a moment about the bands of the General of the holy-water sprinkler; but had there been but only one drop of blood shed, this old man, this priest, should he have provoked that assassination? Italy hates the Pope; the Romans, if they would let them alone, would hang him to the statue of the Immaculate Conception. Who is to blame? who? Italy is a young nation, full of sap and life, launched into progress, on the level with the times and civilization. The Pope is a corpse, lying on the Index, and galvanized by Austria. Can they remain together? Let the French take leave, and Europe will know the rest.

The Bible Society spreads every year millions of the Bible. It would be more useful to print a popular edition of the Index and throw it upon the world. The Index is the pillory of the Papacy, the condemnation to death of Roman Catholicism. This cemetery of intelligence accuses the Papacy more than all its crimes! the Index is the St. Bartholomew of the soul. The dogma of Rome is the antipodes of science, of civilization, of progress; it condemns physiology, philosophy, mathematics, comparative anatomy, astronomy, chemistry, physics, history, the moral sciences, political economy, socialism — the one the physiology, the other the pathology of society — in one word, the human mind. The Papacy, this Brinvilliers of civilization, can it remain in the midst of a people that spreads her wings toward the future; and, at the same time, be the czar of its soul and the sultan of its politics?

Behold the whole Roman Question!

We make no appeal to the passions: anger, insult, violence, injustice, perversity, are a Catholic avocation; we make an appeal to reason, and we say to it: Judge thou!

As to the Church we shall only say a word: She should desire the cessation of the Papacy and its replacement by the Council. Christianity might rejuvenate itself, and might still live by conciliating to itself science, progress, civilization, the age, and by putting an end to schism. If the Pope remains, the Christ disappears and the leprosy of indifference seizes upon souls. Without speaking of the violations of the canons which the Pope commits, that which remains hardly affects us. The question in regard to the Church may be thus laid down : More Pope or more Christ! We must choose.

The Papacy is, then, a calamity for Europe, for Italy, for the Church, for civilization. In order to conjure away this danger there is only one very trifling thing to do : oblige France to quit Rome ; oblige Austria not to interfere, and leave the Pope and the Italians face to face. That is the Roman Question, and that is how it will be solved. This solution is simple and definitive. If Europe does not take the initiative, Italy, when her hour shall have arrived, will take it.

London, May 24, 1860.

THE END.

www.ingramcontent.com/pod-product-compliance
Lightning Source LLC
Chambersburg PA
CBHW030018240426
43672CB00007B/996